A SAMARITAN STATE?

A
SAMARITAN
STATE?

External Aid in
Canada's Foreign Policy

KEITH SPICER

ᴏᴏᴏᴏᴏᴏᴏᴏᴏᴏᴏᴏᴏᴏᴏᴏᴏᴏᴏᴏᴏᴏᴏᴏᴏᴏᴏᴏᴏᴏᴏᴏᴏᴏ

University of Toronto Press

© UNIVERSITY OF TORONTO PRESS 1966
Printed in Canada
Reprinted in 2018
ISBN 978-1-4875-8548-8 (paper)

TO MY MOTHER AND FATHER

Foreword

It is a decade and a half since Canada was propelled by its own inclination and by international pressures into programmes of aid and assistance to developing countries (then identified less euphemistically as underdeveloped). As Dr. Spicer points out, we started with no very clear policy aim. President Truman had launched his "Point Four" concept, and the United Nations Charter seemed to oblige us in this direction. The feeling of obligation was strong, but if the policy was groping it is not surprising. The concept was new and even the largest countries were uncertain of their aims. For some time it was difficult to look clinically at the political economy of the question because the principle of international aid had to be fought for, and cynics were ready to exploit any criticism of the practice. On the other hand, advocates confused the issue with apocalyptic visions of a world transformed and demanded more and more money with fewer and fewer strings, regardless of the problems of spending it effectively.

Thanks to many scholars and experienced administrators, the approach to aid is now maturing rapidly. The idea that rich countries should help poor countries is still challenged but firmly established nevertheless. Those who believe passionately in the importance of international aid can be more ruthless in examining our experience, acknowledging failure and seeking sounder ground. It is the increasing sophistication of the argument in Canada which makes Dr. Spicer's study so very timely. He has compiled not only the first detailed record of our aid programme in the formative years but also produced an analysis which reflects his close examination of the subject both in Canada and abroad for the past six years. It is a scholarly work but not an exercise in abstraction. The history of Canadian aid is prefaced by a first chapter which poses the major issues of policy for Canadians and for all concerned in this revolutionary activity; this at least is essential reading.

Dr. Spicer is a lively and dedicated student, and it has been both pleasant and stimulating for the staff of the Canadian Institute of International Affairs to be associated with his research from the beginning and to help guide this important book to publication.

JOHN W. HOLMES
Director General
Canadian Institute of International Affairs

November 1, 1965

Across space, divergent traditions, with or without gratitude, and sometimes, so it seems, against our own self-interest, the imperative [of brotherhood] still operates. It demands of us that we put all our weight alongside these peoples straining, as they are, to break through the triple barriers of disease, poverty and ignorance to find a wider basis for dignity and self-realization.

DONALD K. FARIS, *To Plow With Hope*

. . . il serait, à mon sens, souhaitable que tout ce problème soit placé devant l'opinion publique dans les termes les plus réalistes. Dans plusieurs pays d'Occident, un mouvement d'opinion a pavé de bonnes intentions et d'humanitarisme ce qui n'était souvent que questions d'intérêts bien compris et de marchandage. Ces courants d'opinion ont eu sur la politique étrangère d'après-guerre une immense influence en même temps qu'ils se heurtaient à des échecs retentissants. Entre le casque colonial et le béret du boy-scout, il n'est pas impensable qu'il puisse exister d'autres couvre-chefs qui nous aillent mieux.

JACQUES PARIZEAU, in *L'Occident et le défi du Tiers-Monde*

Preface

For a time too embarrassingly long to mention, the manuscript of this book followed the course of perpetual revision. Perhaps, for a few weeks, a whole chapter may have kept its actuality. But always, inexorably, facts and opinions were overtaken by events: a new policy was proclaimed, a government overthrown, a federation dissolved, another formed, the volume of aid multiplied. As the machinery of publication ground toward its conclusion, the early effort to keep constantly up to date began more and more to resemble a treadmill. The only way to finish the job, to make the manuscript a book, it became clear, was to select a definite and irrevocable cut-off date after which new material would be ignored.

The date chosen was June 30, 1965. Since that time momentous happenings at home and abroad have made the temptation to tinker compelling. Yet for better or worse, and more through weariness than will-power, the cut-off date has been maintained. In fairness, therefore, both to officials whose work may be criticized and to readers who may be expecting a study of Canada's aid as of today, it must be made clear that the present tense in this book refers to the late spring of 1965. The only allusion to more recent phenomena is made in certain appended tables, released after mid-1965, which may interest a few readers as tools of further research.

Every book owes something to others. This one owes nearly everything to others. First, for information. Civil servants of three departments, External Affairs, Finance, and Trade and Commerce, have given me patient and sympathetic help. For the past two years especially, many friends (if I may thus compromise them) in the External Aid Office have extended me every assistance compatible with their official oaths. None of these friends has been more open in his thoughts and generous with his time than the Director General of the External Aid Office, Mr. Herbert O. Moran. Since our first meeting in Karachi in 1960, Mr.

Moran has been unfailingly helpful, always offering a stimulating blend of encouragement and candour. In addition to official sources, I am indebted to numerous private citizens and companies whose participation in the aid programme allowed them to add valuable independent observations.

Second, I owe heavy debts to several critics. Parts of the manuscript faced the scrutiny of that wise and warm-hearted gentleman who started our aid programme off with such verve and imagination, Mr. Nik Cavell. Mr. John W. Holmes, Director General of the Canadian Institute of International Affairs, read the entire text, and gave, together with sure counsel on style, penetrating and sensitive advice from an eminent experience of service to Canada. Others whose thoughtful reading caught many a gaffe in certain chapters included Mr. Mervyn L. Weiner of the World Bank, Dean J.-M. Quirion, o.m.i., Faculty of Arts, University of Ottawa, Professor André Patry, Faculty of Law, Laval University, and Professor D. R. Campbell, Department of Political Economy, University of Toronto. I thank Professor James Eayrs, my thesis supervisor, and his colleagues in the same department for helping an earlier version of this book to pass as a doctoral dissertation. Not the least useful of this help was Professor Nathan Keyfitz's timely loan, during a hectic time, of his secluded summer cottage. I am also grateful to the staff of the University of Toronto Press, particularly to Miss Francess G. Halpenny and Mr. R. I. K. Davidson, for the editorial guidance and general pre-natal care that a new author needs more than he at first realizes. Finally, I register deepest gratitude of all to my wife who, as well as supplying abundantly the usual feminine encouragements, offered common sense and literary taste all the more remarkable because she was tired of the subject and English is not her native tongue. As one normally says in such circumstances, and rightly so, none of the above can be blamed for the mistakes in fact and judgment that it is the reviewer's kindly duty to denounce.

I owe, finally, a very substantial debt to three institutions which have contributed financially to this book. The Canada Council supported early research, including a five-month tour in Asia, with two pre-doctoral fellowships. The Canadian Institute of International Affairs, under whose auspices the book was prepared, absorbed costs of revising the thesis. And the work was published with the help of a grant from the Social Science Research Council of Canada, using funds provided by the Canada Council.

K.S.

November 1965

Contents

PART ONE/Policy

PART ONE / Police

I. The Questionable Credo

Canada launched her development aid programme in 1950 with virtually no policy aim beyond a lively anti-Communist instinct and an exhilarating vision of a free, multi-racial Commonwealth. In the shaping of both these influences, the date and setting of the Colombo Conference were decisive. The colossal shadow of new-born People's China cast before delegates the appalling prospect that Mao Tse-tung's guerrilla triumphs might be retold against impoverished, inexperienced and dislocated administrations throughout Asia; and the unprecedented dialogue in an Oriental capital of white and coloured statesmen, united as equals in a Commonwealth welcoming the brotherly compatibility of monarchy and republic, moved ministers to glimpse a new mankind inspired by tolerance and solidarity. To this mingled threat and promise, Canada, like most of her Commonwealth colleagues, responded quickly and positively.

It became rapidly clear, however, that large-scale development aid was a far more complex challenge than originally grasped. As unsuspected political and economic interests came into play, and as the Canadian public sought questioningly to understand its government's action, foreign aid demanded policies of sharper and more persuasive definition. What was more difficult, it demanded policies flexible enough to accommodate all the shifting interests and emotions that might sooner or later find satisfying expression in overseas aid. Following a global pattern discerned by Eugene Black, aid policy grew empirically, as freshly valid justifications thrust forward new incentives for aid:

Recent history is full of instances where governments develop a rationale for what they are doing only after having done it for quite a while first. I suspect that this is the case with economic aid. The motives behind the West's economic aid programs have tended to metamorphose with the changing course of international politics, and this is hardly surprising in view of the novelty of the challenge with which the West is faced in the underdeveloped world.[1]

Nevertheless, through the evolution of Canadian policy since 1950, three broad motives for external aid have been constantly woven. As in most Western aid programmes, this trilogy of "aims" has viewed aid as a humanitarian, political and economic good.[2] "The Canadian Government," a UN committee was told in 1957 by the Minister of Citizenship and Immigration, Mrs. Ellen Fairclough, "has been motivated by moral, political and economic considerations"—which she identified as a "responsibility" to the "less fortunate," "the safeguarding of peace," and "world prosperity, including our own."[3] Dr. Sidney Smith, the Secretary of State for External Affairs, had himself a week before called Canada's aid grants "helping hands," that could both undermine "the seed-beds of unrest and . . . war" and, though it "worried" him "to speak in this vein," create "good customers and provide much opportunity for Canada."[4] Still more characteristic of the reasoning of ordinary Canadians, perhaps, was the homespun plea tendered the Commons on September 11, 1961, by the Hon. J. M. Macdonnell, for long Parliament's most eloquent advocate of aid:

There are, of course, three obvious arguments which we have heard again and again for aid to underdeveloped countries . . . First of all, there is the humanitarian argument. If these people were going to bed hungry just across the road from us we would not go to bed until we had done something about it. Second, there is the political argument which is that it is tremendously in our interests, indeed, it is vital to us, that these underdeveloped countries shall develop economically under free institutions and not under communist institutions. What we would feel like if we heard tomorrow morning that India had decided to proceed from now on under communist institutions I do not like to think. Then there is the third argument, which some people rather deprecate because it sounds as if we were doing it for our own interests. I have no objection to doing something in our interests as long as it is in the interests of other people too.[5]

[1]The Diplomacy of Economic Development (Cambridge, Mass., 1960), p. 54.
[2]See Georges Balandier, Les pays "sous-développés", aspects et perspectives, (Paris, 1959), pp. 142–5. Also Jean-Louis Gagnon, "La part du Canada dans les programmes internationaux," in Dialogue 1961, Canadian National Commission for UNESCO (Ottawa, 1961), p. 50.
[3]Canada, House of Commons Standing Committee on External Affairs, Minutes of Proceedings and Evidence (Ottawa, 1957), p. 85. Hereafter referred to as Standing Committee on External Affairs.
[4]Canada, House of Commons Debates, Nov. 26, 1957, p. 1516.
[5]Ibid., Sept. 11, 1961, p. 8197.

With varying emphasis to suit the current public mood, this traditional catalogue of apologies is recited annually in budget debates by all parties, almost as a ritual ceremony of purification. It has become a familiar and cherished litany, offered regularly to buttress the faith of believers, and to disarm, if possible, the latent or declared hostility of powerful adversaries. But like any liturgy, its constant formal re-enactment is an illusory substitute for analysis of underlying principles. If policy is to be more than slogans, each of Canada's alleged aims must be criticized and weighed against the sobering realities of Canadian government and power.

1. HUMANITARIANISM AS PRACTICAL POLITICS

Professor Benham perceptively observed that statesman of donor countries almost invariably place first in public defences of aid the moral obligation of rich to poor.[6] Most speeches on aid by Canadian leaders confirm this priority. In evaluating the role of humanitarianism in Canada's attitude toward aid, moreover, one is impressed at the outset by the strength of charitable sentiment in Canadian public opinion; yet further study indicates that charity can scarcely be a conscious aim of Canadian government policy.

First, what are the dimensions and quality of Canadian opinion on aid? If newspaper editorials, seminars, opinion surveys and voluntary group activity are pertinent standards, the Canadian people appear to support aid overwhelmingly, and largely for moral or idealistic reasons.[7] A small core of thinking citizens seem strongly attracted by the constructive nature of aid as the supposed basis for a deeper and peaceful unity of mankind; while the less reflective public, led more by emotion than calculation in their grasp of world affairs, probably find more excitement in a philanthropic crusade than in finely reasoned estimates of economic or political forces.

[6]For a sensible and closely reasoned discussion of motives for providing aid, see Frederic Benham, *Economic Aid to Underdeveloped Countries* (London, 1961), pp. 87–96.

[7]See Claude Lemelin and Jean-Claude Marion, *Le Canada français et le Tiers-Monde* (Ottawa, 1963). This 1962 survey of 550 French-speaking Quebec residents revealed that 82 per cent of respondents approved the principle of Canadian aid (p. 21); primary motives cited most often for supporting aid were: (a) "Christian charity" (21%); (b) "strengthening of peace" (15%); (c) "human solidarity" (12%); and (d) "anti-Communism" (8%) (pp. 74–5).

Many apologies for aid by private citizens convey unmistakable religious or spiritual overtones—doubtless, in part, an echo of Canada's century-old foreign missionary tradition.[8] Some of these declarations are even more meaningful because they are made by persons whose background might intimate a likely emphasis on political or material advantages of aid for Canada. A former Deputy Minister of Trade and Commerce, who for several years helped to guide Canadian aid policy (and who was later a senior executive in a large Canadian utilities firm with investments in Latin America), in 1961 publicly endorsed an approach to aid that was uncompromisingly moral. Rejecting possible commercial and security aims of aid policy as "nauseating," and calling for a "return to the simple principles of Christian charity," Mr. Mitchell Sharp insisted:

> There is one good and sufficient reason for international aid and that is that there are less fortunate people in the world who need our help. If they are grateful for our help so much the better. If by reason of the aid they receive they become bigger customers for Canadian goods and services, better still. If our aid helps them to achieve what Professor Rostow calls "take-off", to set their feet firmly on the road to higher standards of living without resort to Communist dictatorship, the benefits to us are beyond measure. But the inspiration for what we do must be essentially humanitarian and unselfish. If it is not, if the primary purpose of our aid is to help ourselves, rather than to help others, we shall probably receive in return what we deserve and a good deal less than we expect. Many of the troubles with which international aid is beset today may be laid to the fact that we of the free world are losing this humanitarian inspiration. We have got ourselves into an international rat race using aid in an effort to win friends, influence customers and outbid the Communists. Small wonder that some recipient countries seem to be taking us at our face value by playing off one side against the other.[9]

This resolutely anti-political definition of aid objectives took on still deeper relief, of course, when Mr. Sharp became Minister of Trade and Commerce after the April 1963 general election.

[8]See C. J. Woodsworth, *Canada and the Orient* (Toronto, 1941), pp. 252–71; also Lionel Groulx, *Le Canada français missionnaire* (Montreal, 1962).
[9]Mitchell Sharp, "Canada's Stake in International Programmes," in *Dialogue 1961*, p. 47. See also F. A. Brewin, "Canadian Economic Assistance to Underdeveloped Areas," *International Journal*, vol. 5, no. 4 (Winter, 1950–51), p. 314, and S. G. Triantis, "Foreign Aid—a New Canadian Experience," in *Texts of Addresses delivered at the 25th Annual Couchiching Conference* (Toronto, 1956), pp. 55–63. The emphasis on humanitarian aims was almost unanimous among speakers at the two national conferences on aid held in 1955 and 1956 by the United Nations Association in Canada; see *Conference on Canadian Aid to Underdeveloped Countries* (Toronto, 1955), and *Conferenece on Canada and International Development Programmes* (Toronto, 1956).

Philanthropy has been pivotal, moreover, in the striking proliferation of private Canadian groups promoting so-called "people-to-people" aid schemes—whether for sponsoring overseas students, selling Christmas cards, or exporting medical supplies, sewing machines or eager young volunteers. Adherents of such groups display a genuinely fervent idealism for what they see as a pressing human obligation, if not crusade. And the impressive moral and financial support given their enterprises by service clubs, churches, companies and individuals suggests that similar motives for aid are shared by a substantial segment of Canadian opinion.

But are they shared by a commanding majority of the electorate?[10] More than one observer has concluded that aid will be stridently opposed as long as anyone can fairly apply to a depressed region or group in Canada the slogan "charity begins at home." Grumblings against aid may be heard, for instance, from the unemployed (with doubtful logic, since almost all bilateral aid funds are spent in Canada); from business circles not enjoying a portion of aid contracts; from a few doctrinaire isolationists; from depressed Eastern rural areas; at least until the birth in 1961 of Canada's French African programme, from certain electioneering Quebec politicians[11]; from the less prosperous Maritime

[10]It seems not, according to recent studies. Results of the Lemelin-Marion survey differ interestingly, however, from those of a national poll conducted in 1963 by the Canadian Peace Research Institute. Both surveys asked voters' opinions on the volume of aid Canada should give compared to the current level (which was 8.5 million dollars lower during the CPRI survey):

	Lemelin-Marion (p. 62)	CPRI
More	18%	12%
Same	37	51
Less	17	23
No aid	9	3
No opinion	19	11

See "The Way to Peace: Views of 1,000 Canadians," *Globe and Mail*, Toronto, Nov. 15, 1963, p. 7. The CPRI study showed, nevertheless, that between 44 and 75 per cent of the Canadian "élite" (defined as business, labour and political leaders) supported aid increases.

An illuminating discussion of Canadian public opinion and external aid, with numerous examples, is found in James Eayrs, *Canada in World Affairs, October 1955 to June 1957*, (Toronto, 1959), pp. 201–11. Canadian aid policy as a whole is treated in pages 204 to 213 of the same book.

[11]During the 1956 Quebec provincial election campaign the *Union Nationale* used in a rural constituency the slogan: "Duplessis donne à Nicolet, Ottawa donne à Colombo." This motto was bitterly condemned as "lâche et mesquin"

provinces[12]; and even from Prairie farmers, when increases in foodstuff
aid are judged to threaten support prices for grain. (It is true that
development of a World Food Bank for more stable disposal of surplus
wheat—mainly at the expense of urban taxpayers—has revealed within
the Canadian Federation of Agriculture unsuspected resources of
idealism).[13]

Such resistance is sufficiently widespread and clamorous, especially
in time of economic recession, to cast serious doubt on the alleged
philanthropy of the Canadian people as a nation. As André Siegfried
said of the French Radical-Socialists, Canadians have, it seems, "le
cœur à gauche et le portefeuille à droite." For many, if not most, charity
is praiseworthy precisely as long as it does not diminish personal
prosperity.

Anti-aid pressures are persuasively countered, of course, by frequent
attempts to contrast degrees of poverty suffered in Canada and abroad.
Duties toward fellow Canadians and peoples overseas, it was argued
by Premier Roblin of Manitoba, are not competitive, but concurrent:

... I am reproached by some with the saying that "charity begins at home."
And, of course, that is profoundly true. I know that no one is satisfied with
the standard of technical education in Canada, that we must acknowledge
the unmet obligations to our own underdeveloped communities, particularly
among the Indians and Métis, and that we need to do 10 times—and in some
cases perhaps 110 times—more at home before we can be satisfied. But,
although charity begins at home, I think it is very important to understand
that it does not end there and that today, while home may be Winnipeg or
Manitoba or Canada, it goes beyond that, because in these days we know
for whom the bell tolls when we hear it ringing in Africa and in Asia.[14]

in an editorial by André Laurendeau in *Le Devoir* of Montreal on May 25, 1956.
The incident is referred to in Eayrs, *Canada in World Affairs*, p. 211. The same
warcry was used by certain backbench Liberal members during a debate six years
later in the federal House of Commons. See " 'Ottawa donne aux étrangers' :
retour d'un fameux slogan duplessiste," *La Presse*, Montreal, Jan. 31, 1962, p. 1.

[12]Some years ago, a cartoon in a Halifax newspaper denounced both the inadequacy of federal grants to the Maritimes and the anomaly of giving Canadian
assistance abroad while parts of Canada were still in need. Under a news caption
announcing "Soviet Offers Aid to Any in Want," the four Maritime premiers,
huddled in furtive conference, whispered, "Dare we?"

[13]See "Noble Motives: Farmers Agree Aid Necessary to Hungry Nations, but
Support Needed," in *Globe and Mail*, Toronto, Feb. 22, 1961, p. 11. See also the
CFA's *Presentation to the Prime Minister of Canada and Members of the Cabinet*,
Ottawa, Feb. 23, 1965, pp. 14–15.

[14]Duff Roblin, "Canada's Role," in D. L. B. Hamlin, ed., *Diplomacy in Evolution*, Proceedings of the 30th Annual Couchiching Conference (Toronto, 1961),
p. 116. Premier Roblin's government founded in 1961 the first provincial foreign
technical aid programme in Canada, by co-operating with the External Aid Office
in sending four Manitoba teachers to Ceylon.

Yet deep pockets of antagonism to aid remain. Scorning what they consider misplaced benevolence, dissident groups deny humanitarian motives through specious analogies with personal charity: recipients are ungrateful; they are unwilling to help themselves; external aid will destroy whatever incentive to improvement their poverty may now provide.[15]

Public pressure on Ottawa concerning aid is therefore diffuse, and in some ways conflicting. Countrywide emotional support for the principle of aid is tangible, but clouded by vigorous local objections to both the size and forms of Canada's contribution. How then and to what extent has a humanitarian impulse—as defined by public opinion—shaped the purpose of official Canadian aid policy?

Speeches of political leaders acknowledging the breadth and vitality of public support for aid often vaguely recall the people's emotional endorsement. Sidney Smith, the Secretary of State for External Affairs, assured the Seattle Colombo Plan Conference in 1958 of "the continued warm support which public opinion in Canada is giving to the policy of the Canadian Government to cooperate with the less developed countries. . . ."[16] And his successor, Mr. Howard Green, told the Commons in September, 1961, that the aid programme was "supported by Canadians from coast to coast. Since I have been Minister . . . I have heard very few complaints about Canada supplying aid."[17]

Many such declarations echo the appeals of popular moralists more distinctly. At a Malayan banquet in 1959, Prime Minister Diefenbaker affirmed that "each of us regards the other as his brother's keeper . . . the first responsibility of each of us is to assure . . . that men everywhere may have something of the better things of life."[18] Later that year, he reminded a Vancouver audience that "the good citizen and the good

[15]See Benham, *Economic Aid to Underdeveloped Countries*, pp. 96–7. See also the stimulating arguments of one of Canada's foremost aid theorists (and practicians), Dr. Nathan Keyfitz, "Foreign Aid Can Be Rational," *International Journal*, vol. 17, no. 3 (Summer, 1962), pp. 237–50.

[16]*The Colombo Plan for Cooperative Economic Development in South and Southeast Asia, Proceedings of the Meetings of the Consultative Committee* (Washington, 1958), p. 80.

[17]Canada, *House of Commons Debates*, Sept. 11, 1961, p. 8196. On the other hand, an executive assistant to the Hon. Paul Martin confided to a group of student overseas volunteers in August 1963 that the Minister, in his first four months in the East Block, had received less than thirty private letters proposing an increase in aid. At that time, employment was rising, and bilateral aid had already been cut by 8.5 million dollars the previous year.

[18]Canada, Department of External Affairs, Information Division, *Statements and Speeches*, no. 59/13, pp. 3 and 4, a series hereafter cited as *Statements and Speeches*.

nation must recognize his obligations to the broad community of man. . . .
While we have our duty to ourselves and our special relationship to our
families and our neighbours, more and more, we, as Canadians and as
citizens of the world, must seek to share the problems of every continent."[19] The Leader of the Opposition, Mr. Pearson, emphasized in
the September 1961 external affairs debate that "we help these countries
because it is a good thing for us to do, it is a good thing for the peace
of the world and because the world is one." Then, paraphrasing Lincoln,
he warned, "Indeed, the world cannot exist half poverty-stricken and
half an affluent society."[20] Finally, Mr. Paul Martin, later Secretary of
State for External Affairs, avowed that his colleagues' noble sentiments
were if not inspired, at least confirmed, by popular agitation: "It is not
without significance that one finds, apart from governments, writers,
students and zealous individuals reminding us that in this kind of world
we are indeed our brother's keeper. . . ."[21] Since 1958, in fact, every
party in the Commons has stressed its moral commitment to larger overseas aid.[22] Within the arena of parliamentary rhetoric, the humanitarian
justification of external aid long ago attained the status of a sacred cow.

[19]*Ibid.*, no. 59/103, p. 1.

[20]Canada, *House of Commons Debates*, Sept. 11, 1961, p. 8199. Mr. Pearson
also cautioned, however, against allowing "charity" to become patronizing, advice
vigorously supported by the following commentary in a Karachi newspaper, the
Dawn, on December 20, 1959: "From the earlier rather other-wordly approach
to the question of aid to backward regions as a task of humanitarian rescue, there
has been already a marked shift to a more practical outlook. . . . Both the aid-
receiving and the donor countries are progressively shedding their earlier illusions,
as a more realistic appraisal of the problems and possibilities is shaping out of
closer contact. . . . It is puerile to assume or expect that any sizeable aid can be
"disinterested", as the term is used in current jargon. . . . any sizeable aid can only
spring from a genuine interest in the aims of the undertaking. There is no reason
for either the donor or the recipient to be squeamish on this point. Nor indeed
should it be necessary to play down the sovereign reason ["mutual security"]
and sound practical objectives of the aid programme or lace it with the lingo
of fine sentiment."

[21]Canada, *House of Commons Debates*, Sept. 11, 1961, p. 8192.

[22]See the external affairs debate in the House of Commons on September 7, 8
and 11, 1961. Mr. Green states the Government position on September 11, 1961,
p. 8196. NDP policy, including a demand for a global Canadian aid level of 2
per cent of GNP, was outlined in *The Federal Program of the New Democratic
Party*, adopted at the August 1961 founding convention (p. 28): "The New
Democratic Party believes it is morally necessary to use Canada's agricultural
and industrial potential to capacity in order to relieve famine and aid economic
development in other parts of the world." Mr. Réal Caouette, still speaking as
Deputy National Leader of the Social Credit Party, expressed a similar moralistic
view in a transposed paraphrase of Goering's celebrated "guns or butter" option:
"Nous, du Crédit social, sommes officiellement opposés aux armes nucléaires.
. . . Nous sommes en faveur du pain et du beurre, en faveur de ceux qui ont faim
sur la terre." (Canada, *House of Commons Debates*, Jan. 25, 1963, p. 3140).

But politicians, like their constituents, seem unable to translate the imperatives of conscience into practical approval of great increases in aid. For while popular benevolence may broadly support some increase, it imposes rigorous bounds which statesmen ignore at their peril. Cautioned the Chairman of the Standing Committee on External Affairs in 1961: "Canadians are generous. They approach external aid as a Christian problem but they are also beginning to ask, what have we to show for our external aid dollar? They do not believe in a Colombo Plan that extends into perpetuity."[23] Mr. Green himself, while confessing as Minister that he would "like to get more money for the External Aid Office," summarized the Government's impotence in the candid reminder, "but you know where the money comes from and we can only get so much."[24] Later, the Opposition Leader, Mr. Pearson, stated the Minister's dilemma more precisely, by underlining the inescapable link between policies of foreign and domestic welfare:

I must say that I have some sympathy for the Minister in his desire to discharge his obligations . . . in respect of international economic assistance. I know that he will get more trouble from the Department of Finance and the Minister of Finance than he will from the opposition in this regard because, however idealistic a view we take about our obligations in this matter . . . , we come up against the exigencies of domestic affairs and the desire of the Minister of Finance to balance his budget. As a result, these considerations of domestic policies . . . perhaps have an effect on what we can do in the field of international economic assistance. There is always a relationship between what can be done in Canada for people who need help and what can be done for people in Pakistan who need help.[25]

What then, on balance, is the real influence of humanitarianism in Canadian policy? Philanthropy is plainly no more than a fickle and confused policy stimulant, derived exclusively from the personal conscience. It is not an objective of government. Love for mankind is a virtue of the human heart, an emotion which can stir only individuals— never bureaucracies or institutions. Governments exist only to promote the public good; and, as a result, they must act purely in the selfish interest of the state they serve. Altruism as foreign policy is a misnomer, even if sometimes the fruits of policy are incidentally beneficial to foreigners. To talk of humanitarian "aims" in Canadian foreign policy is, in fact, to confuse policy with the ethics of individuals moulding it, to mix government objectives with personal motives. The satisfaction of charitable aims can be tasted only by human beings, for it is in their

[23]Canada, *House of Commons Debates*, Sept. 7, 1961, p. 8094.
[24]*Ibid.*, Sept. 11, 1961, p. 8196.
[25]*Ibid.*, p. 8198.

hearts that such feelings are born and only there that pity can find its catharsis. Government policy implies conscious choice among real alternatives; for the true philanthropist, there is no alternative to love.

But if humanitarianism must be rejected as an official objective of Canadian policy, it can be a useful tactical support for policy conceived in more rational terms. Realistic politicians know that flattering appeals to generous instincts are a tested device for rallying popular acceptance of aid—as indeed of almost anything else. And diplomats argue, though less cogently, that professed disinterestedness is a practical way of reassuring recipients that aid will not compromise political independence. Yet even these laudable functions do not raise charity to a purpose of government.

Given the selfish nature of government, it is plausible to seek the true objectives of aid policy in Canada's real or imagined national advantage, in the alleged political and economic benefits which a euphemistic age calls "enlightened self-interest." In principle, such aims are appropriate to state policy; but viewed against the harsh limits of actual Canadian resources, most of them prove disappointing, and some melt into tawdry, though harmless, clichés.

2. POLITICAL AIMS

Popular resistance to using aid as a vehicle of "neo-colonialism" or purely negative anti-communism has tended, in Canada, to deny the propriety of any political aims for aid at all. Add to this sensitiveness the distaste many citizens feel for politics itself; add the intolerance some aid supporters display toward any selfish motive whatever; and discussion of political aims becomes slightly indecent. For a very large number of Canadians, external aid is an end in itself; it is an ethereal and disinterested goal to be pursued between peoples, a human debt to be paid, with little or no reference to the interstate framework within which it must work.

Yet can it be doubted that external aid, like professional diplomacy, trade, and military preparedness, is by nature and patronage inescapably an instrument of foreign policy? As an expression of our government's will overseas—a will that must be coherent to be effective—how can the objectives of aid be divorced from the aims of Canada's world policy as a whole? The true vocation of aid as a technique of diplomacy has been recognized institutionally by inclusion since 1950 of aid appropriations in the estimates of the Department of External Affairs; by attribution in 1960 of exclusive responsibility for aid administration to the Secretary of State for External Affairs; and by the perpetual chairmanship of interdepartmental committees on Canadian aid by a high-ranking Foreign Service Officer.[26] Much of Canada's aid administration in Ottawa, and most of it abroad, has been carried out by career diplomatists. In practice as well as in theory, Canadian external aid is under the intimate direction of professional foreign policy makers and executants.

But even while accepting general political control of aid, some extreme humanitarians refuse to envisage the inevitable corollary of subordinating aid to diplomacy: aid, as a potential factor of political change abroad, is intrinsically political in character. "Foreign aid is inseparable from the problem of power; and where there is power, politics is the governing factor, not an incidental factor which can be dispensed with."[27] Is it possible to have "policy without politics," to use aid for seeking shifts in the world distribution of power without making political choices?

Misapprehension on this score appears to grow from the failure of public opinion to recognize that political implications of aid can be almost endlessly diverse. In particular, misunderstanding arises from popular confusion of political aims with political conditions or "strings" which, being ill-defined, are all the more easily imagined to be invariably

[26]Ministerial responsibility for aid was until September 1960 somewhat unclear, since most of the administrative machinery for aid was controlled by the Minister of Trade and Commerce, while formal responsibility for the aid vote remained with the Secretary of State for External Affairs. See Chapter 4 on the early years of Canadian aid administration.

[27]George Liska, *The New Statecraft* (Chicago, 1960), p. 15. Liska develops impressively the political theory of foreign aid. Note that the American government has never been as squeamish as Ottawa in admitting the selfish purpose of aid: "The sole test of [foreign aid] is the national interest of the United States. [Foreign aid] is not something to be done, as a Government enterprise, for its own sake or for the sake of others. The United States Government is not a charitable institution, nor is it an appropriate outlet for the charitable spirit of the American people." 84th Congress, 2nd session, *Report of the Senate Committee on Foreign Relations: Technical Assistance and Related Programs* (Washington, 1956), pp. 4–5.

General Lucius Clay, Chairman of the President's private Committee to Strengthen the Security of the Free World (a title in itself typical of the realistic US attitude to aid), likewise told the US Senate Committee on Foreign Relations on July 11, 1963: "I think the validity of the argument for foreign aid is whether it is in our own national interests and in the interests which we espouse in the free world." 88th Congress, 1st session, *Hearings before the Committee on Foreign Relations*, US Senate (Washington, 1963), p. 649 (hereafter cited as *1963 US Senate Hearings*). An attempt to base aid allocation on scientific, rather than political, criteria is described in Charles Wolf, Jr., *Foreign Aid: Theory and Practice in Southern Asia* (Princeton, 1960), pp. 355–82.

harmful to recipient countries. Sensing the dangers of this confusion, Mr. Pearson stressed in 1956 the unavoidable political significance of aid and the need to distinguish different qualities of political objectives:

> There is another gap in policy which is hurting the West; that is the separation between economic and technical aid to underdeveloped countries and political objectives; or, maybe I should put it this way: we are suffering from efforts to close that gap in the wrong way by associating aid with the acceptance on the part of the receiving countries of "cold war" political and strategic objectives. I think myself . . . that the purpose of foreign aid is as important as the aid itself. Aid of this kind, economic assistance of any kind on an international scale, is, I admit, bound to be a political act of some kind. The question is: what kind?[28]

Assuming Canadian aid policy to be consonant with, indeed circumscribed by, Canadian foreign policy, one should properly seek its objectives within the major aims of Canada's diplomacy. In their simplest terms and in the measure they may apply to external aid, these aims can be identified as: (a) preservation of world peace (without which no other policy is conceivable); and (b) reasonably successful prosecution of the Cold War.[29] In many ways, these aims are closely related; but by treating them separately one can better weigh the various political arguments advanced in favour of aid, and possibly form a more realistic expectation for aid policy.

a. Preservation of peace

Desire for peace is undoubtedly the deepest diplomatic aspiration of Canadians, as of all peoples not prisoners to some temporary hysteria. Sizable public opposition to NORAD and even to NATO, agonized reticence of political parties to approve nuclear arms for Canadian forces, and stubborn perseverance of Canadian governments in apparently insoluble disarmament negotiations, all testify to a profound and anguished concern for peace. In external aid policy, as in other aspects of foreign policy, this hope—if not all the conclusions drawn from it by some extremists—is clearly the dominant popular pressure felt by Ottawa. For reasons of both its own electoral and Canada's physical survival, the Canadian government has made the preservation of peace its foremost and fundamental foreign policy objective.

[28]*Standing Committee on External Affairs*, 1956, p. 14.
[29]These two major political aims are also noted in United States Government publications on foreign aid. See *U.S. Foreign Aid* (Washington, 1959), p. 4; also President Johnson's Message to Congress on January 14, 1965: "If freedom is to prevail, we must look beyond—to the long-range needs of the developing nations. . . . Foreign assistance programs . . . help build stable nations in a stable world."

But what concerns us here is the widespread belief that external aid is almost axiomatically a contribution to world peace, and therefore a sound instrument of Canadian foreign policy. This notion, held by much of the public and constantly offered by Canadian officials to justify aid, springs from a postulate which critical analysis shows to be partly challengeable.

The postulate claims that external aid strengthens peace because, by stimulating economic development, it brings to recipients political stability and a pacific, "satisfied" approach to international problems. Nations whose internal political stability is bolstered by foreign aid are supposed a far less tempting prey for outside aggressors who might otherwise profit from an intended victim's intestine unrest; and at the same time, countries thus assisted are thought less likely to initiate international violence. If, through aid, the more flagrant inequalities between rich and poor nations are diminished, latent aggressiveness of the underprivileged will be smothered in the satisfaction of conquering domestic economic enemies inherited from nature and a wicked colonialism. Contented countries, it is believed, do not start wars. External aid can therefore remove a major source of world tension and sublimate the so-called "revolution of rising expectations" into the eminently peaceful task of economic construction. In the light of both these hopes, external aid would indeed seem an unusually positive and practical device for securing world peace.[30]

Not surprisingly, a common appendix to this argument is a comparison of the peace-keeping merits of aid and military expenditures. Such juxtapositions occur most often when Defence Department purchases leave in doubt the military value of new equipment: the cancellation of the Arrow supersonic interceptor in February 1959 (followed in less than six months by purchase of a probably inferior American replacement), the prolonged nuclear decapitation of a fickle Bomarc anti-aircraft missile, and the interminable development of the Army's

[30]The credibility of this proposition is enhanced by the support of many leading aid theorists. See, for instance, M. F. Millikan and W. W. Rostow, *A Proposal: Key to an Effective Foreign Policy* (New York, 1957), p. 21; and Barbara Ward, *The Rich Nations and the Poor Nations* (Toronto, 1961), pp. 20 and 92.

In Canada, belief in aid as a political stabilizer was affirmed in warnings to Parliament by the Indian and Pakistani prime ministers as early as 1949. See Brewin, "Canadian Economic Assistance to Under-developed Areas," p. 305. For representative Canadian approval of the aid-stability axiom, see Gagnon, "La part du Canada dans les programmes internationaux," p. 50; "We Can Afford Generosity," an editorial in the *Star Weekly*, Toronto, Oct. 21, 1961, p. 39; and Jean-Marc Léger, "L'écart tend à s'accroître entre les pays nantis et les pays pauvres," *Le Devoir*, Montreal, March 8, 1962, p. 6.

Bobcat personnel carrier led many Canadians to question searchingly
the usefulness of a large military budget. Would not a reduction in arms
spending allow a diversion of resources to aid that could stabilize world
security far more effectively? Does not a rational defence policy demand
a ceaseless measuring of available funds against just such constructive
alternatives?[31]

While rarely attempting to explain in concrete terms exactly how and
where such a re-allocation of resources could strengthen Canadian defences, numerous Canadian statesmen have endorsed the principle of this
budgetary diversion. In so doing, of course, they accept the assumption
that aid exerts a stabilizing political influence. But they also recognize
the appeal of diversion for a Canadian public already deeply sceptical
of the security assured by Canada's present defence expenditures. "I
think," said Mr. Pearson as Leader of the Opposition:

. . . we can still do a great deal more and I think we should do more, because
after all $40 million, $50 million or $100 million which is wisely spent in
international economic assistance in the right places at this time might do
more to increase stability and security in the world than spending $100
million or $150 million on some forms of arms defence.

Therefore without criticizing the minister or the government in what has
been done I express the hope—and I feel quite strongly about this—that
perhaps we can do more in the future than we have in the past in making
this contribution, not so much to assist other countries but to assist ourselves;
to assist security and stability in the world.[32]

[31]This argument does not, of course, take into account either the diversity of
current military threats to peace or the relatively small portion of Canada's military budget devoted to equipment purchases. (See "Army Budget Said Suffering
From Pay Raise," *Globe and Mail*, Jan. 20, 1962, p. 3). Since the great bulk of
Canadian military expenditures supports a fixed overhead of salaries, pensions,
maintenance of buildings, etc., any substantial savings made on present expenditures without reducing our armed forces' already thin ranks could be realized only
by purchasing less new equipment—a saving which would soon render the whole
military establishment technologically obsolete. The allocation for new equipment
in the main 1965–66 budget estimates was only $247,242,000 in a total military
outlay of $1,550,000,000. See also the thoughtful proposals of Professor Alastair
M. Taylor, *For Canada—Both Swords and Ploughshares* (Toronto, 1963).
[32]Canada, *House of Commons Debates*, Sept. 11, 1961, p. 8200. Likewise the
Hon. Paul Martin, as Secretary of State for External Affairs, met the diversion
argument in a sympathetic, if non-committal, manner on July 25, 1963, before
the Commons Special Committee on Defence: "None of us . . . is pleased with the
fact that we are spending more money on defence than we are in assisting underdeveloped countries. Indeed the whole effort in the disarmament debate . . . is
designed—and certainly this is the policy of Canada—to try to bring about, within
conditions of security, a reduction in the conventional and nuclear arms to a
point where we might hope to transfer expenditures into other areas. . . .
Undoubtedly a way to promote peace in the world, among other ways, is to
provide for an improvement in the standard of life of peoples in the world who

This view of aid as an instrument of specifically Canadian defence was at no time challenged by the government during the debate. Indeed, in this and other debates, such reasoning was regarded by government and opposition alike as a truth perhaps hard to define in practice, but self-evident and irreproachable in theory.

If the pursuit of international stability may be taken, then, as a permanent basis of Canadian aid policy, its underlying assumption is worth questioning. What evidence from Canadian experience can be marshalled to support or disprove the aid-stability relationship? What theoretical weaknesses can be discerned in the postulate?

The results of Canadian aid as a factor of stability within a recipient country have been mixed, though conspicuous attempts have been made to use aid in this way. Among visibly successful examples are assistance given in settling thousands of refugees in North-West Pakistan and hundreds of landless farmers in Ceylon; and the Warsak Dam, which for five years offered employment to some ten thousand troublesome Pathan tribesmen, of whom several hundred received skilled training of value on other power or irrigation projects. It is true that the Pakistan government's inability to find new work for these men could prove the apparent pacification illusory; but at least a temporary calm was established in the strategic Khyber area, and this, during a period of strained Afghan-Pakistani relations, was of crucial importance to President Ayub and his predecessors.

On the other hand, Canada's stabilizing policy was scarcely vindicated by the dissolution of the West Indies Federation, to which country Canada had given two large passenger ships with the avowed aim of strengthening inter-island political and economic cohesion. Of course, the break-up of this embryonic state was no proof that the ships did not *tend* to unite the islands; after some years of service the vessels might well have contributed modestly to the Federation's unity. But in the short run, they were powerless against incomparably deeper centrifugal forces,[33] and so did not accomplish the immediate aim of stabilization. In the same way, external aid to Indonesia—aid on a massive scale and from every major source, including Canada—has left that country

do not enjoy our economic advantage." (Canada, House of Commons, Special Committee on Defence, *Minutes of Proceedings and Evidence* (Ottawa, 1963), p. 246. It remains to be proven that public opinion would in fact allow savings from arms reduction to be spent on aid: the 1963 CPRI survey shows aid as a "poor fifth choice" of Canadians for use of such savings, well after a tax cut and increased health and education benefits in Canada itself.

[33]For a perceptive *post mortem* on the Federation, with an assessment of these dissolving factors, see Elisabeth Wallace, "The West Indies Federation: Decline and Fall," *International Journal*, vol. 17, no. 3 (Summer, 1962), pp. 269–88.

among the least orderly and most aggressive of all Asia. At any rate, neither alleged "successes" nor "failures" could conceivably be attributed to Canadian aid alone: a reliable assessment of Canada's impact would have to weigh not only the influence of other domestic forces in recipient countries, but the availability and quality of alternative foreign aid.

Other Canadian projects have tried to exert a stabilizing effect in an international context. These schemes have sought to narrow political differences between two or more recipients, by inducing them to co-operate in regional projects of mutual benefit. A clause in the Canada-India Reactor agreement, for instance, opened the facilities of this vast atomic research installation near Bombay to scientists of other nations in the Colombo Plan area, including Pakistan. The Mekong River Project, for which Canada completed extensive aerial surveys in 1961, aimed, by assembling riparian nations in a great co-operative plan for the economic profit of all, to attenuate many ancient and recent enmities separating the Vietnamese, Laotians, Cambodians and Thais. Likewise, in announcing Canada's financial contribution to the Indus Waters settlement between India and Pakistan, Mr. Howard Green made clear that it was ". . . in Canada's interest to help in the solution of a problem which has stood in the way of better relations between two of our Commonwealth partners in Asia."[34]

But however politically constructive these projects may be in principle, have they led to a decisive or even noticeable effect on regional stability? Since outside training began in 1958, not a single Pakistani researcher has accepted India's standing invitation to work on the Canada-India Reactor; the Mekong Project has not prevented endemic suspicion and even armed subversion from poisoning relations among the Indochinese states and Thailand; and the Indus settlement can scarcely be said to have diminished Indo-Pakistani distrust for more than a brief and uneasy interlude. Naturally it is extravagant to expect every project of this kind to produce immediate and fundamental changes in state policies; yet it is a measure of the limits of aid as a stabilizer that probable diplomatic benefits of the above, much-publicized projects have invariably been outweighed by essentially non-economic factors.

A corollary of attempts at positive stabilization through aid is avoidance of aid transfers likely to increase international tension. Projects or goods of potential military significance are, if requested under economic development programmes, normally rejected outright by Canada. Preliminary soundings by Pakistan in 1960 and 1962 for a possible Colombo Plan gift of Canadair CL-44 transport aircraft, for example, were quickly discouraged for this reason—though

[34]*Statements and Speeches*, no. 59/23, p. 7.

it is true the proposal was also opposed on economic and technical grounds. Acquisition of such equipment by Pakistan could only be sub-sidized—as were a number of De Havilland Caribou transports bought by India in 1963—through export credit. For less persuasive security reasons, Canada in 1963 rejected an Indian request under the Colombo Plan for khaki knitting wool, granting it later under a special military aid scheme. This Canadian military aid to meet the Chinese emergency, though given outside regular economic aid programmes, itself incited Pakistan to make "strong representations" to Canada.[35]

This distinction between economic and military aid has not always been applied with equal sensitivity. Three Canadian Otter aircraft—obviously ideal for jungle warfare and subversion—were given to Indonesia in 1959–60 to strengthen domestic air services. The planes were immediately incorporated into the Indonesian Air Force because of an alleged lack of pilots for the civilian airline, *Garuda*. And in January 1965, British authorities informed Ottawa that Indonesia was using these aircraft in subversive attacks against Canada's Commonwealth partner, Malaysia.

A potentially more worrisome case is that of the Canada-India Reactor. In the 1956 Intergovernmental Agreement for the CIR, New Delhi undertook to ensure that the reactor and its end-products would be "employed for peaceful purposes only." Yet India has consistently refused formal inspection of the CIR itself, either by Canada or the International Atomic Energy Agency (IAEA), on the ground that in-spection of plant would be discriminatory unless extended to all countries engaged in nuclear research. India does, it is true, allow Canada to carry out an audit of Canadian-supplied fuel elements. But these 200 NRX-type fuel rods are now greatly outnumbered by Indian-made rods, with the result that verification of Canadian elements stored, burnt-up or under irradiation offers no assurance at all that Indian rods are not being dissolved, after partial burn-up, to produce military-grade plu-tonium. Certainly India's opening in 1964 of a chemical separation plant (for removing plutonium from irradiated fuel) will furnish the Trombay scientists with the most important ingredient for building an atomic bomb, even though the plant is ostensibly designed to make India self-sufficient in fuel for eventual enriched uranium reactors.

Canada accepts as entirely trustworthy repeated declarations by India's present leaders and scientists that India has no interest in military

[35]See "Ask Canada to Stop Aid for India," *Globe and Mail*, Oct. 3, 1963, p. 33. One wonders in which category, economic or military, the Canadian government's reported 1000-year supply of long underwear would fall, if requested for Himalayan winter warfare. Presumably colour, rather than strategic value, would decide.

applications of atomic energy.[36] Needless to say, Pakistan does not; and this alone is enough to view the CIR as a doubtful factor of international stability. But more important, who can be sure that pressure on Mrs. Gandhi or some successor to change India's position on atomic weapons will not become overwhelming? If Chinese incursions continue, if some form of Western-Soviet "umbrella" is not devised to reassure India against Peking's bomb, if the Kashmir crisis erupts again, if extreme nationalists take power, may not India at some future time feel a lesser obligation to respect the CIR agreement?[37] In such a context, refusal to supply khaki knitting wool as economic aid seems a less apposite exercise of Canada's pacific scruples.

A second rule for avoiding conflict abroad prohibits Canadian aid to territories of disputed sovereignty. No Canadian aid has ever been given explicitly, for instance, to Jammu or Kashmir: Canada wishes, said the Colombo Plan Administrator in 1954, to "keep clear of all trouble" in that area.[38] But even a donor's abstention may cause resentment in India and Pakistan, by implying non-recognition of sovereignty claimed by each; aid thus becomes a factor both of regional tension and of inescapable embarrassment to Canada. In sum, active and passive Canadian policies to manipulate aid as a stabilizing influence have shown results only moderately gratifying, and generally inconclusive.

A fairly convincing case can be made, moreover, to challenge the general theory that aid produces stability. Does not Indonesia prove

[36]See "India Capable but Unwilling to Build Bomb," *Globe and Mail*, Nov. 5, 1960, p. 2. Dr. Homi J. Bhabha, Director of India's atomic research programme, is quoted as saying, "India has the knowledge and facilities to produce such a weapon, but finds it much more worthwhile to concentrate all its efforts on power reactors." The "facilities" referred to by Dr. Bhabha can only be the Canada-India Reactor, since India has no other equipment able to supply significant amounts of fissile materials for nuclear weapons. In the agreement of December 16, 1963, establishing Canada's export credit aid to India's Rajasthan nuclear power station, Canada improved her means for measuring India's trustworthiness by specific, though reciprocal safeguards. Dr. Bhabha died in early 1966.

[37]See "India Enters Atom Bomb Race," *Globe and Mail*, Nov. 4, 1960, p. 3. Mr. William Stevenson reported here that Indian Food Minister S. K. Patil advocated construction of the bomb (in the reporter's words) "not for any war purpose but to arouse popular enthusiasm and inspire the people with confidence." See also an article entitled "India and the Bomb," in the *Economist*, London, Dec. 12, 1964:

"If the Indians want to go nuclear on their own account, they are able to do so. They estimate they could set off an atomic explosion within eighteen months of the word go, and they already have enough plutonium. Their Canadian research reactor can produce enough for one or perhaps two explosions a year. . . . A government that believed national survival depended on misusing [the CIR and a future American reactor] for warlike purposes would hardly feel bound by earlier pledges—which have, in fact, been given—not to." (p. 1221).

[38]*Standing Committee on External Affairs*, 1954, p. 224.

that too-easy availability of foreign aid from competing donors allows recipients to extort economic support for military adventure? Did not pre-war Japan show that excessively rapid development can lead to inflated national pride, sometimes bordering on militant chauvinism and emboldened territorial ambitions? If aid stimulates progress in one social sector—say, education—before the recipient's economy can exploit this progress, will not such imbalance result in dangerous frustrations and unrest? North Africa and South India bear witness. Each of these questions admits of conflicting answers, but the doubt remains: there is no universal and provable relation between external aid and political stability. While it seems logical that economic aid should lead to greater satisfaction of needs and a corresponding reduction in social and international tensions, it can be argued just as plausibly that aid, to be effective at all, must be injected into a stable, orderly and efficient administration.[39] One can even deny the ideal of balanced growth, by maintaining that unbalanced progress—presumably a cause of political unrest—is the very dynamic of development.[40] The theoretical relationship between aid and stability is therefore so complex and controversial that it is tempting to discount its basis altogether.

What, in these conditions, is a realistic hope for Canadian policy? It is plainly impossible to imagine a concentration and composition of Canada's present aid that could exert more than an absurdly marginal influence in maintaining world or regional security. Even if some reliable link were established between aid in general and political stability, Canadian aid is far too small (and would still be, if quadrupled from the 1965 level) to have any appreciable effect upon the broad evolution of international affairs toward war or peace.

Nevertheless, Canadian aid has occasionally proved a useful temporary relief to local tensions and a symbol of Canada's *concern* for stability and peaceful change. Both of these roles are worth playing, if only because they demonstrate an attachment to values of human solidarity and tolerance which we hope will be shared by our beneficiaries. Within the limits of these more humble but meaningful possibilities, the

[39]See Brewin, "Canadian Economic Assistance to Under-developed Areas," p. 306. For a unique scientific attempt to explore the relationship between economic change and political behaviour, see Wolf, *Foreign Aid*, pp. 303–10 and pp. 333–51. Related themes are treated in Nathan Keyfitz, "The Interlocking of Social and Economic Factors in Asian Development," *Canadian Journal of Economics and Political Science*, vol. 25, no. 1 (February, 1959), pp. 34–46.

[40]See Albert O. Hirschman, *The Strategy of Economic Development* (New Haven, 1958). Professor Hirschman tries to combine the "pressure-inducing" and "pressure-relieving" functions of external aid in a single definition: "It is the role of foreign capital to enable and to embolden a country to set out on the path of unbalanced growth" (p. 205).

pacific aspiration of Canadian aid policy seems both justified and attainable. Any more ambitious prediction does not spring from a reasonable estimate of either Canada's resources or the true gravity of world problems.

b. Aid as a weapon in the Cold War

Discussions of Canadian aid policy increasingly tend to deny, or dismiss as secondary, the aim of Free World security. A powerful—and in its own way intolerant— body of opinion rejects as unworthy almost the recognition that aid has Cold War implications. To a marked degree, this delicacy has coloured even the speeches of politicians, who prize above many qualities that of realism.

There are, of course, sound political reasons for underplaying motives of East-West antagonism, especially when donor statesmen are within electronic earshot of recipient governments. But such refinements of expression are mistaken by some Canadians for evidence that Canada's aid is somehow uniquely untainted by ideological calculation. No judgment could be more misinformed or illusory. "In order to test our real motives," as Mr. Pearson refreshingly suggested in 1955,

> we should ask ourselves from time to time whether we would be doing what we are if the political and military menace of Soviet and Chinese communism did not exist. It sometimes seems to me that we in the West come near to owing at least one debt of gratitude to the international communists—and we have precious little else to thank them for over the past few years—for helping to keep us up to the mark in these matters. It is a sorry commentary on the postwar period that without them and the threat which they represent we might not so readily have done what we should have been doing anyway.[41]

This commendable frankness by Canada's chief delegate at the 1950 Colombo Conference was imitated in 1960 by the Quebec economist Jacques Parizeau, who added a note of still greater precision:

> ... l'aide actuelle ne serait qu'en partie disponible si des motifs de politique internationale n'incitaient les gouvernements à distribuer ce que, par humanitarisme, ils hésiteraient à fournir. L'aide extérieure aux pays sous-développés s'inscrit, en effet, dans un contexte politique et n'est complètement intelligible que si on en fait le prolongement de la lutte entre les grandes puissances. On peut regretter qu'il en soit ainsi, mais on peut difficilement se le cacher.[42]

---

[41]*Conference on Canadian Aid to Underdeveloped Countries*, p. 4.
[42]*L'Occident et le défi du Tiers-Monde* (Montréal, 1960), p. 44.

But circuitous demonstrations are not necessary to test the prominence of anti-communism in Canadian aid policy; statements by Canadian leaders in the formative years of the aid programme proclaim this with perfect clarity. "Communist expansionism," Mr. Pearson warned the House of Commons just after the Colombo Conference,

may now spill over into South-East Asia as well as into the Middle East. . . . It seemed to all of us at the conference that if the tide of totalitarian expansionism should flow over this general area, not only will the new nations lose the national independence which they have secured so recently, but the forces of the Free World will have been driven off all but a relatively small bit of the great Eurasian land mass. In such circumstances it would not be easy to contemplate with equanimity the future of the rest of the world.

. . . we agreed that the forces of totalitarian expansionism could not be stopped in South Asia and South-East Asia by military force alone. . . .

. . . If South-East Asia and South Asia are not to be conquered by communism, we of the free democratic world . . . must demonstrate that it is we and not the Russians who stand for national liberation and economic and social progress.[43]

And Mr. Diefenbaker, speaking on January 9, 1950, over the CBC, argued that "50 million dollars a year . . . would be cheap insurance for Canada, for the opinion of Asiatic representatives [at Colombo] was that this plan, if launched in time, would do much to halt communism in Asia."[44]

In subsequent years, the theme of fighting communism through aid was repeatedly advanced both by political leaders and the Canadian Colombo Plan Administrator. Some, like the future Finance Minister Mr. Donald Fleming in 1956, while hoping "that our principal reason and motive [for aid] is humanitarian," sensed with apologetic realism that "nevertheless we have to bear in mind the strategic nature of [Asia] and the fact that Russia has its eyes on it as well."[45] Others, like the Administrator (who presumably echoed the policies of his political masters), insisted more bluntly that Canada had to help the Asians "if we want to keep them in the free world. . . . if we seek, whilst there is yet time, to lay plans for a free world that will attract and not repel our free brothers in Asia, we can become so strong that the communist world will not dare to attack us."[46]

After about 1957, direct official references to Cold War objectives became rarer. Perhaps this change in tone owed something to the new

[43]Canada, *House of Commons Debates*, Feb. 22, 1950, p. 131.
[44]Canada, Department of External Affairs, Information Division, Reference Paper no. 60, *Canada and Technical Assistance*, 1950, p. 9.
[45]*Standing Committee on External Affairs*, 1956, p. 137.
[46]*Statements and Speeches*, no. 52/52, pp. 5 and 11.

Conservative ministry's sharper emotional emphasis on Commonwealth brotherhood, and to unease before the flamboyant, messianic anti-communism of US aid programmes. Whatever its source, the shift in language can hardly be taken to mirror a fundamental *détente* in Canadian relations with the Sino-Soviet bloc. Canada's global foreign policy was still to oppose communism, even if this opposition expressed itself more flexibly; and, as Mr. Martin reminded the House on November 14, 1963, aid is "an integral part of our foreign policy."[47] It follows easily that anti-communism remained—as it remains today—a cardinal, if not indispensable, objective of Canada's aid policy.

Yet objectives are not justified merely by their active pursuit. While plausible during the panic of 1950, the anti-communist aid thesis was never thought through rationally in the light of either feasible alternatives or even of its own demonstrable results. Brief analysis discerns three major assumptions in the thesis, each of which, however, is substantially challengeable: (i) aid promotes liberal democracy; (ii) aid gives donors significant control over recipients' foreign policies; and (iii) aid creates goodwill likely to dispose recipients favourably toward donors' external policies.

(i) *External aid and liberal democracy.* This relation envisages a strategic function for aid, as a long-term agent for the protection and advancement of pluralistic societies. By implication, it foresees the frustration of communist doctrine and interests as forces competitive with the West in developing nations. Such an association of aid with more or less specific political behaviour obviously rests on still another assumption, whose validity has already been shown severely limited: that of aid as a factor of economic and political stability. But before pursuing the argument itself, it is worth recalling the central place held by the "aid-liberty" postulate in official Canadian thinking.

Inspired partly by the fallacious, if irresistible, analogy of a spectacularly successful Marshall Plan, most Western governments in 1950 viewed aid as a natural rampart of liberal democratic institutions. The Colombo Conference report itself declared economic improvement in Asian nations "necessary to strengthen their free institutions," and stressed that "nothing could do more" than their progress "to strengthen the cause of freedom."[48] Canadian officials found no quarrel with this reasoning and indeed exploited it fervently. "We feel that if you help these people to help themselves and to raise their standard of living,"

[47]Canada, *House of Commons Debates*, Nov. 14, 1963, p. 4718.
[48]*The Colombo Plan for Co-operative Economic Development in South and South-East Asia* (London, 1950), p. 1.

Mr. Pearson assured the Standing Committee in 1955, "that in itself is a good way of stopping communism."[49] The Administrator, for his part, swayed an eager conference of UN enthusiasts a year later with a variation joining ancient Chinese philosophy with a homely Salvation Army type of formula for political proselytism: ". . . it is human freedom which will be at stake [in the "race" between India and China] . . . first must come enough food. As Confucius once said, 'An empty stomach does not dwell on high principles.' "[50] Less vividly, though perhaps no less wisely, the Deputy Director General of External Aid promised a similar group in 1963 that "through our aid programs we can show the less-developed countries that our way of life, with its freedom for the individual, is a better way of life than that achievable through totalitarian rule."[51] The premise is then clearly part of Canada's policy; but its foundations cannot withstand intact the assaults of either theory or experience.

The theory linking externally aided economic growth to stable democratic government is questionable on several counts. First, even expressed by its most lucid exponents, this doctrine lacks precise definitions of terms and goals: Professors Millikan and Rostow recognize a long-term anti-communist mission for aid, but manage to define their ideal only as the achievement of "societies with a successful record of solving their problems without resort to coercion or violence."[52] It is extremely unlikely, however, that a single definition of "coercion" could satisfy equally a North American liberal, an Iranian conservative, an African neo-Gaullist, an Indian socialist, a Brazilian *latifundista*, and an Indonesian "guided democrat." Nor is it more certain that such a disparate group could share a common definition of "violence." Argument in these conditions is idle because of fundamental ambiguity in major premises.

But a clearer definition of terms, if at least allowing debate, scarcely promises a more meaningful conclusion. Those who do bother to define "liberty" other than by slogans or paraphrases demanding still further definition almost invariably have in mind some form of Western constitution—whose paper existence all too often suffices to soothe their democratic yearnings. This school habitually identifies liberty with the

[49]*Standing Committee on External Affairs*, 1956, p. 28.

[50]*Conference on Canadian Aid to Underdeveloped Countries*, p. 13.

[51]P. M. Towe, "Outline of Canadian External Aid," mimeographed speech delivered on August 20, 1963, before a joint conference of the Edmonton Branch of the United Nations Association in Canada and the Canadian Institute of International Affairs (External Aid Office, Ottawa), pp. 9 and 10.

[52]M. F. Millikan and W. W. Rostow, *Foreign Aid Program: Compilation of Studies and Surveys*, US Senate, 85th Congress, 1st session (Washington, 1958), p. 20. Quoted in Liska, *The New Statecraft*, p. 16.

proliferation of parliaments, prime ministers, presidents, parties, bills of
rights, free elections and—where at all possible— stock exchanges, a
lively if not irresponsible press, and earnest wig-wearing judges. But
political concepts, like truth and beauty, are relative to times and
cultures. Did not Montesquieu speak of a "certain peuple d'Orient, pour
qui la liberté consistait en le droit de porter une barbe longue"? Is it
realistic to expect a Westminster-style parliament to function in true
liberal democratic spirit when imposed upon a tribal- or caste-dominated
society? None of this is quibbling, if one desires argument both limpid
and fruitful.

Semantic problems can be overcome, however, if advocates of the
liberating mission of aid will admit that their basic concern is not really
the positive advancement of freedom, but anti-communism. It is true
that even "communism" is open to widely divergent definitions; but there
is still a reasonably clear Rubicon beyond which a régime has unmistakably rejected liberal democratic values to join officially the "socialist
camp" of "international communists." And is not this formal adhesion
to the cause of a strategic enemy, after all, the only deeply disquieting
feature of "communism"?

This clarification allows us to test the reasoning itself. To begin, we
are asked, at least by implication, to assume that poverty alone is the
underlying cause of communism. But such an assertion hardly conforms
to historical experience. Has not communism generally failed to capture
the minds of exactly those people—the backward peasants, the totally
ignorant and oppressed—who are crushed by unmitigated hopelessness
and misery? Has not communist leadership nearly always burgeoned
from an urban proletariat or from frustrated, idealistic bourgeois intel-
lectuals who have themselves tasted a few crumbs of economic justice,
and thus glimpsed an attainable utopia? India's communists are not
found in the appalling squalor of hinterland villages, but in the relatively
well-paying factories of Calcutta, on the docks of Bombay, in the civil
service and in universities. Of course, poverty offers fertile terrain for
communist exploitation; and the more satisfied people there are, the
more difficult it is for communist agitators to carve out an audience from
existing evils. But always the inspiration, direction and fanaticism come
from a small group whose economic and social circumstances have at
some time been comfortably above the local average. These leaders have
known—if only briefly and imperfectly—a better economic justice and,
in their own context, a better liberty. They have, as a result, hope for
improvement and confidence that progress is possible; because of this,
they despair of a political and economic system that seems incapable of
sharing, much less implementing, their vision. It is this indignation

against entrenched inequality—and not their personal poverty—that feeds their frustration.

To pursue the argument, it is logical to ask whether economic progress (and one of its supposed stimulants, external aid) is not potentially a cause of, rather than a prophylactic against, communism. One can argue cogently that external aid, by injecting hope of progress into a country, actually stokes the very discontent it plans to stifle. Demonstrations of "international solidarity" through aid inevitably make more cruelly obvious the contrast between donors' wealth and recipients' indigence. The conditioned optimism and dynamism of donors are meant to be, and often are, contagious; but resulting expectation by recipients is far less bearable than previous ignorance and inertia because means to realize quickly the expectation are not at hand. Foreign aid awakens appetites it can probably never assuage; it is less a vehicle of tranquillity than of unrest. The most generous aid can be little more than an economic *apéritif*, exciting ever greater claims on domestic and foreign budgets. Within the recipient country, aid can stir increasingly bitter competition for development funds and more acute outrage at fiscal injustice; abroad, it can trigger a gathering momentum of demands for always larger aid, through the calculated pressure of planned deficits and more or less crude devices of Cold War blackmail. Both in internal and foreign policies of recipients, radical extremism may therefore be encouraged by external aid. From intensified dissatisfaction at home and the more apparent niggardliness of donors overseas, the communist agitator can derive only comfort and strength. Is not this result even more probable from Canadian aid which, in relation to needs, can never be more than infinitesimal?

Furthermore, the basic economic goal of external aid itself may multiply possible disruptive consequences of aid. Most economists—both liberal and Marxist—stress that the development "sound barrier" can be permanently crossed only through industrialization. This technique is usually considered indispensable for all economies but the smallest, or the poorest in natural resources. Industrialization, none the less, can promote "communism" in at least two ways. First, it tends to create a cohesive, eventually class-conscious urban proletariat, which is classic raw material for communist indoctrination. It has been asked, for instance, whether the uprooted and proletarianized Pathan tribesmen at Warsak will not now be far more open to communist promptings than when they were content to practise the disorganized, traditional joys of freebooting marauders on the Khyber Pass.[53] Second, artificially accelerated development of one sector in a primitive economy may

[53]Eayrs, *Canada in World Affairs*, p. 209.

easily provoke the jealousy of other, less progressive, social groups. Advancement—however beneficial in itself—of one group inevitably underlines the relative stagnation of other communities; and the laggards' resentment can lead to class rivalries facilitating, even in non-industrial areas, communist agitation. The feeling of peasants that foreign aid is nearly all going to cities (usefully or otherwise) is probably one reason for the success of anti-Western campaigns by communists in rural Indochina.

Still another way external aid can foster discontent exploitable by extremists of the left is by inducing unco-ordinated development of opportunities for education and employment. Of what use to liberal democracy are technical schools and universities if most of their graduates languish in bitter idleness plotting revolt? Even mass literacy campaigns are risky in the short run if the only inexpensive literature available is communist propaganda. Was it not relatively well-educated Kerala, with a literacy rate 25 per cent above the Indian average, that brought to power the first communist government freely elected anywhere in a fair contest?

Finally, it can be argued that aid incubates communism because it panders to recipients' nationalism against manifest economic common sense. Professor Milton Friedman insists that aid will "almost surely retard economic development and promote the triumph of Communism" because recipients will blackmail donors into giving them "modern monuments" (such as steel mills, where not warranted) as useless as the pyramids and far more costly.[54] Further, when recipient governments constantly pour aid into prestige-bearing state enterprises of every kind, increasingly centralized development programmes may throttle private initiative and lead quickly to communist-type economic and political systems.

These, then, are some of the arguments advanced to prove or deny the effectiveness of aid as a long-term strategic weapon against communism. The indications of both theory and practice are deeply conflicting; yet this confusion can at least help to place the central assertion in more balanced perspective.

First, Canadians should recognize that there is at present no proven relation between external aid and the flowering of liberal democracy. Sanguine predictions by Canadian leaders about the rescue of "liberty" overseas through Canada's aid are not only without systematic founda-

[54]Milton Friedman, "Foreign Economic Aid: Means and Objectives," *Yale Review*, vol. 47, no. 4 (June, 1958). Quoted in Benham, *Economic Aid to Underdeveloped Countries*, p. 98.

tion in fact; they are an extraordinary overstatement of Canada's real world role and power. To misrepresent in this way the true proportions and consequences of Canada's assistance is explainable only by the need to rally domestic opinion, or by refusal to rethink easy, predigested truths. The shibboleth based on a largely irrelevant Marshall Plan experience has long been laid to rest by qualified observers abroad, including Eugene Black:

It is not that there is any certain and established relationship between economic progress and the values of freedom and tolerance. There is no such relationship; economic development is a fickle process; it destroys old habits and attitudes toward life even as it creates the wherewithal for a better material life; it creates human desires often much faster than it provides the means for their gratification; its one continual and overriding requirement is change; by itself it leads nowhere in particular and may lead anywhere in general.[55]

But even more significantly, early optimism about the politically purifying grace of aid has been resoundingly disavowed in studies sponsored by the world's largest donor, the United States government. "It is not clear today," said an independent Congressional report in 1959,

. . . what the relationship is between the U.S. foreign aid program and the democratic development of the Asian and African countries. This is so because we still do not understand fully the nature of economic development and its impact upon the total life of an Asian or African nation; we do not understand the relationship between economic development and the national policy of the receiving country. The confusion of judgments among the economists shows we do not understand even what are the requirements for economic development in the non-Western world. Until we know the answers to some of these problems it would seem impossible to make easy and simple assumptions about a straight line between poverty and communism or between economic development and democracy.[56]

Still more affirmatively, General Lucius Clay, testifying before a US Senate committee on July 11, 1963, as chairman of a special Presidential committee on aid, refused to "accept the premise . . . that all countries will go statist and communistic if we don't provide them aid. I do think there are certain countries where political and economic stability is so lacking that a little aid may turn the balance in our favor. But I don't think that aid in itself is a conclusive factor in determining whether a country goes toward freedom or communism."[57]

[55]*The Diplomacy of Economic Development*, p. 19. See also Liska, *The New Statecraft*, p. 17; and Benham, *Economic Aid to Underdeveloped Countries*, pp. 88–92.
[56]*U.S. Foreign Aid*, pp. 85–6.
[57]*1963 US Senate Hearings*, p. 649. The witness ended his comment by suggesting that the premise was indeed based less on government conviction than on

If such prudence is thought necessary by the United States after giving almost forty billion dollars in development aid, how vastly more humble should be Canada's pretension of saving democracy after dispensing about one billion dollars! What measurable effect upon democratic institutions, for instance, could Canada's record allocation of $58,500,000 in grants and loans to India in 1964–65 exert within a yearly Indian development budget of some five billion dollars? While immense outlays of American aid might expect (according to the 1959 US study) to be "extremely important in certain selected situations,"[58] it is difficult to imagine a similar result from Canadian aid unless it should be multiplied many times and lavished on a single small country —both of which changes are profoundly unlikely.

Probably all that can be salvaged from the doctrine linking aid to liberal democracy is a judgment that, in the absence of a proven relation between economic progress and specific political behaviour, the unknown political risk of *not* helping less developed nations may possibly outweigh the futility or perils of aiding them. Moreover, while we have no assurance that aid in itself will guarantee democracy abroad, it is clear that part of a durable liberal democratic order must be economic development at a rate approaching reasonable local expectation. In this light, total inaction is not a realistic alternative to large-scale aid. Aid must be seen as a groping, but tangible, aspiration to promote viable indigenous democracies; for better or worse, it is the only practical influence on political institutions in developing countries—apart, where allowed, from buying the press—which is directly open to Western governments.

Yet whatever the role of aid in general, Canada's assistance can never serve world freedom decisively, for the means she is able and willing to offer are globally insignificant. As an instrument of long-term political change, Canadian aid must be viewed as essentially symbolic. It is not a reliable vehicle for projecting Western ideals abroad; it is, rather, a comforting expression of Canada's own wish to remain free in a dangerous, uncertain world.

(ii) *External aid and diplomatic pressure.* Another popular view maintains that aid can be used as a tactical weapon against communism, to exact specific pro-Western behaviour in recipients' diplomacy. This theory insists that aid can and should be given with "strings" attached, strings that the donor can pull to divert recipients' policies into channels

domestic political expediency: "I don't think there is much validity to the argument. . . . It has always been an easy one to make, one at times that has been very acceptable to the general public."

[58]*U.S. Foreign Aid*, p. 86.

parallel to its own. Expressed crudely, such a view hopes that aid will allow the "purchase" and subsequent intimidation of allies. These goals may be achieved "positively," it is thought, by demanding performance of a political bargain before aid is granted; or "negatively," by threatening, on default of agreed concessions, withdrawal of current aid. In neither case does Canada's potential seem impressive.

It is noteworthy that the principle of such conditions—if not their discreet application—has been denounced consistently by Canadian leaders as both immoral and (what is more damning) unworkable. It is "important," warned Mr. Pearson in a speech at Princeton University in 1955, "to guard against any false idea that we can purchase or should try to purchase allies. . . . The East will not become a mercenary in our ranks. It would be deplorable if Asians believed that Westerners had insulted their dignity, or misread their integrity, by entertaining such notions."[59] And the following year, before the Standing Committee on External Affairs, the Minister reaffirmed: ". . . I do not think we should tie up our assistance to promises of that kind, that they [Asian recipients] should join any anti-communist alliance. I hope we will continue in that way."[60] Similarly, Prime Minister Diefenbaker, during his 1958 Commonwealth tour, assured his Asian hosts that "Canada seeks to help without taking political advantage and without attaching strings to tie the hands of the nations involved. It's just as simple as that. What advantage is there to us, I ask anyone here?"[61] Possibly

[59]Quoted by Mr. Pearson in *Conference on Canadian Aid to Underdeveloped Countries*, p. 4. Canada's frequent public assurances that no "strings" are attached to her aid have found a wide echo in the private and official attitudes of recipients of Canadian assistance. A brochure issued by the Pakistan government for the opening of the Canadian power project at Shadiwal in 1961 stated: "In these days of international power politics, when every economic aid proposal is examined for the strings attached to it, it is well known that the aid from Canada, whether under the Colombo Plan or outside it, is motivated by nothing else but a desire to help a sister country of the Commonwealth to raise the level of its people through schemes for social and economic advancement." (Quoted in *Financial Post*, Toronto, Jan. 6, 1962, p. 7).

[60]*Standing Committee on External Affairs*, 1956, p. 28.

[61]*Statements and Speeches*, no. 59/12, p. 3. The same view has been expressed in numerous statements by members of all major Canadian parties. See *Standing Committee on External Affairs*, 1956, pp. 15–16, 137, and 152. Mr. Diefenbaker is quoted in the *Ceylon Daily News* of November 27, 1958, as saying, "Whatever kind of co-operation we extend, we are anxious to offer without in any way implying or having in mind the imposition of any new patterns of life in this country." The Director General of External Aid has also denied that Canada attaches commercial "strings" to her assistance: "There are no strings attached to Canadian aid. This has been made evident in many respects. There was a question in Pakistan during my period there of adding a third kiln to the Maple Leaf cement plant which Canada had previously donated. . . . An inquiry was

some members of the assembled Ceylonese Houses of Parliament, recalling earlier anti-communist rationalizations of aid in Canada, were privately tempted to take up Mr. Diefenbaker's rhetorical question; but the
assurance itself of "unconditional" aid was doubtless most acceptable.

It is wrong, however, to conclude that no political restrictions at all
guide allocation of Canadian aid. Its past distribution shows plainly
that Canada has practised, albeit with less candour, a policy close to that
announced in October 1961 by President Kennedy: "We should give
particular attention to the needs of those countries which share our view
of the world crisis."[62] More precisely, Canada's aid is refused to countries directly and systematically hostile to Canadian policy: Indonesia,
Ghana and Guinea, while at times virulently hostile to close friends of
Canada, and at least on good terms with the Soviet Union, are eligible
for limited Canadian aid; North Korea, in principle, is not. Canada's
true policy is therefore reflected in a more balanced view offered by
Mr. Pearson as Leader of the Opposition in September 1961:

> I do not believe we can keep Cold War considerations entirely out of
> economic assistance. I do not believe we could be expected, in Canada any
> more than in any other country, to give assistance to countries if that assist-
> ance is likely to be used against us politically. However, we cannot expect
> to get any results from economic assistance which is given to countries
> because we hope that by giving that assistance they will line up with us in
> the Cold War.[63]

How usefully can Canada make felt these "Cold War considerations"
upon recipients' foreign policies? Obviously, the relatively tiny sums
dispensed by Canada are unlikely to seduce recipients into accepting
substantial sacrifices of liberty. However concentrated, Canadian aid
could give annually but a few cents per head of population to any one
nation; and no country aware of going international prices for diplomatic
friendships is apt to sell its soul so cheaply. As a technique of international bribery on behalf of Western policy, Canadian aid at its 1965–
66 level is slender bait indeed.

Its potential for persuasion through threat of withdrawal is, if
anything, still smaller. To be effective, this threat must be believable;
and to be believable, it must clearly carry less painful sanctions for the

---

made of us about the country to which Pakistan might give the contract for this
extension, and we were asked whether there was a Canadian preference. The
answer given to the Pakistanis was that it was their factory; . . . We said: 'you
now own it, so operate it.' Similarly I have heard no suggestion in the recipient
countries of any strings being attached to Canadian aid." (*Standing Committee
on External Affairs*, 1961, p. 156).

[62]*New York Times*, Oct. 12, 1961, p. 20.

[63]Canada, *House of Commons Debates*, Sept. 11, 1961, p. 8199.

donor than for the ostensibly punished recipient. But in the Cold War context, withdrawal of aid implies for the recipient only a possible delay in its programme of development; while for the disenchanted donor, it usually means abortion of any dialogue at all with the former recipient, and this to the advantage of a delighted Cold War adversary. The latter can then enjoy unrivalled intimacy with the recipient and, to doubly ensure its ascendancy, can offer to replace the aid withdrawn by its competitor. After Mr. Dulles decided in 1956 to punish Egypt for resisting his "view of the world crisis," President Nasser got his Aswan High Dam from the USSR, and American influence in Cairo waned for several years. Again, in November 1963, suspension of US assistance to Somalia, far from achieving its aim of discouraging Sino-Soviet aid, immediately spurred communist deliveries,[64] while at the same moment, the role of US financial manoeuvres in undermining the Diem régime in Vietnam so dismayed Prince Norodom Sihanouk that he expelled the entire US aid mission from Cambodia himself, in terms poignantly unflattering. In all three cases, a strategic point fell at least temporarily to communist aid policy because recipients could not ultimately be shaken by Western withdrawal.

This lesson has not escaped Canadian policy-makers, whose smaller resources make such frustration even more certain. Nor is Ottawa unconscious of the disastrous diplomatic stigma attached to aid used for attempted blackmail. Certainly an awareness of these dangers motivated rejection of an appeal in the Standing Committee on External Affairs in 1953 to stop Canadian aid to Ceylon on the grounds that Colombo was shipping rubber to the People's Republic of China during the Korean War.[65] Likewise, following a bitter attack by Mr. Krishna Menon on Canada's disarmament proposals in November 1960, some members of the Canadian government contemplated "retaliation" through refusing support for a new Indian dam then under consideration. Fortunately, far-sighted counsel prevailed; and, though the dam proposal was abandoned by Canada for technical reasons, no reduction in volume of aid to India took place. Again, in December 1961, private demands were raised to impose aid "sanctions" upon India following New Delhi's military action against Canada's NATO ally in Goa.[66] The suggestion was of course ignored by Ottawa, for its implementation could only have had appalling results for Canadian policy and no effect at all upon

[64]A good case-study of this exercise in diplomatic "one-up-manship" is made by William Stevenson, "A New Tough Look at Foreign Aid by the West and the Russians," *Globe and Mail*, Nov. 19, 1963, p. 7.

[65]*Standing Committee on External Affairs*, 1953, pp. 126–8.

[66]See "Ethnic Groups Urge P.M. Halt Aid to U.N., Goa", *Globe and Mail*, Toronto, Dec. 20, 1961, p. 8.

Portuguese security. It is true that Canada made diplomatic representations in New Delhi just before the attack, to urge Indian restraint. But it is a measure of Canadian impotence to control a recipient's policies (as it was, in similar circumstances, of British and American weakness) that the threat of a curtailment in aid could not even be implied in this intervention.

Still more disappointing is the inability of aid to keep friends it is thought to have purchased. Once more, the complex relations of Cold War diplomacy—further confused by rivalries between recipients—make such political investments exceedingly hazardous. The intrinsic tendency of aid to induce not lasting alliance, but neutralism, is sensitively decribed by Professor Nathan Keyfitz:

... in the first instance a donor is inclined to help his friends in recognition of past and future diplomatic, if not military, support. Then he reflects that from the viewpoint of extending his influence the money would be better spent on those countries that are wavering between him and his enemy, even including some rather close to the enemy. This is perfectly sound if the donor can conceal his policy. But in the next round his friends become aware of what he is doing, and drawing the practical conclusion that the way to get more help is to waver, they adopt a degree of independence in foreign affairs which, in any case, fits better with their sense of national sovereignty. Over the dozen years of the Cold War, neutralism has become steadily more acceptable.[67]

Among the many examples of this evolution, Pakistan is the most spectacular. For years the United States and Britain were criticized by their SEATO ally for massive economic aid to neutralist India; when these countries, with Australia and Canada, began in 1963 to give special military aid to India against the Chinese Himalayan emergency, Rawalpindi's complaints turned to outrage, and even to deliberate flirtation with SEATO's major enemy, China. Canada's name in Pakistan, stated succinctly by an Ottawa journalist visiting Warsak in November 1963, was now "mud."[68]

External aid—and for better reason, Canadian aid—is therefore of the most dubious value for exerting tactical pressures in the Cold War. The very fact that there is a Cold War—and so at least two alternative sources of aid—weakens drastically the political impact of subventions by either antagonist. Far from being an effective Cold War weapon in

[67]Keyfitz, "Foreign Aid Can Be Rational," p. 238.
[68]Charles Lynch, "India: Good Progress in First Decade, but Development Program Drags," *Ottawa Citizen*, Nov. 20, 1963, p. 7. For a detailed analysis of Pakistan's *liaison dangereuse* with Peking, see Joe Rogaly, "L'Aide de l'Occident à l'Inde incite le Pakistan à nouer avec la Chine une liaison peu rentable," *Le Monde diplomatique*, Oct. 1963, p. 5.

the hands of donors, aid is in fact an instrument of bribery and threat in the hands of recipients: for these are able, like a coy maiden between rival suitors, to use the gifts of each to control the policies of both. Experienced recipients have sensed, through the sure instinct of self-interest, that their benefactors have a tiger by the tail, that donors are morally and diplomatically indentured to those they help. The more clearly Canadian policy-makers recognize that they are riding a tiger and not a Trojan Horse, the more appropriate to the real world their calculations and expectations will be.

(iii) *External aid and international goodwill*. It is widely believed that external aid earns for donors the "goodwill" and sympathetic understanding of recipients. Westerners—unlike many non-European peoples—instinctively expect gifts to invite gratitude; and gratitude can fairly be imagined a basis for friendship, itself a useful, though not essential, foundation of political solidarity. "There is no doubt in my mind," Canada's Colombo Plan Administrator assured a national conference on aid in 1955, "but that our aid programmes are promoting better understanding, and increasing the contacts and thereby the friendship between East and West."[69]

Similar views are accepted by most Canadian politicians as a key element of aid policy. During the external affairs debate of September 1961, a CCF spokesman affirmed that "this type of assistance and a programme of co-operation builds goodwill within and without the Commonwealth and is the sort of sound foundation to lay for the building of peace in the future."[70] In the same debate, the Secretary of State for External Affairs, Mr. Howard Green, suggested that "Canadian aid has been quite a lot more effective in gaining friends for Canada abroad than has been the case with aid from some of the other nations which are now being a little critical of us" [for not giving enough]. He then added, with engaging rustic frankness: "The more money we can get [for the External Aid Office], the better, because it makes our position much easier. We are able to make bigger fellows of ourselves and win more friends for Canada."[71] To "win more friends for Canada" may reasonably be taken as partly synonymous with creating sympathy for Canada's policies in the East-West struggle: presumably, countries on cordial terms with Canada are more willing to appreciate Canadian attitudes than are nations outside Canada's sphere of aid and supposed influence.

[69]*Conference on Canadian Aid to Underdeveloped Countries*, p. 13.
[70]Canada, *House of Commons Debates*, Sept. 11, 1961, p. 8200.
[71]*Ibid.*, p. 8196.

Doubtless there is persuasive evidence that goodwill can result from certain types of aid. The undeniable warmth of Canadian-Pakistani relations (at least before Canada's 1963 military aid to India) grew visibly from Canadian schemes such as Warsak, Shadiwal and Goalpara; valuable personal friendships have flourished between Canadian and local technicians at dams in India, on an aerial survey in Nigeria, and on construction sites in the West Indies; and gratitude of nearby residents, returned trainees, and government officials has often been expressed with authentic sincerity. "Any Canadians who have been abroad and seen for themselves," the Deputy Director General of External Aid promised a Banff meeting in August 1963, "cannot help but be impressed by the warmth of affection for Canada shown by the local peoples. And these feelings have their effect at the governmental level. Canada generally enjoys excellent and close relations with those countries where our aid programs are in operation."[72] Almost any country giving aid can cite parallel experience: Americans from aid to Indian village development; British and Australians from vast training programmes; Russians from such fine economic infrastructure projects as a sports stadium for Jakarta and a paved thoroughfare for the camel-filled metropolis of Kabul.

But such happy results are far from universal. Almost all aid programmes have at some time sown damaging ill-will and misunderstanding. Resentful ingratitude of some recipients toward the United States marred later years of the Marshall Plan, as it did, sooner or later, programmes in Laos, Vietnam and Cambodia. Communist donors too have made enemies: Arab students withdrew from Soviet universities in 1959, and African students left Bulgaria in 1963, amid angry charges of "brainwashing" and racial discrimination; Moscow was disgraced by sending hardened cement to Burma, winterized tractors to equatorial Africa, and a beet-sugar factory to Indonesia for milling cane-sugar; and Peking, whose deliveries have failed notoriously to keep pace with promises, has earned, in Ceylon and elsewhere, a name for bombast and hypocrisy. Frustrated recipients seldom feel it is better to have hoped and lost than never to have hoped at all.

Canada, for her part, reaped at least the private sarcasm of Indian and Pakistani officials between 1957 and 1962 for insisting that a large part of her capital allocations be spent on Canadian wheat, instead of on basic development aid; acrid administrative arguments—usually born in ambiguous or incomplete project agreements—have occasionally clouded on-site co-operation abroad; foolish or irresponsible behaviour

[72]Towe, "Outline of Canadian External Aid," p. 12.

by a small number of Canadian advisers, and hostile or tactless receptions for trainees in Canada have both left a harmful residue of indignation among recipients.

Most of these misfortunes can be traced to the nature of aid itself. Succour, however badly needed, tends to foster resentment in its beneficiaries. Especially in some Asian civilizations, a gift to an indigent underlines an inequality of condition between giver and receiver; and when elements of racial diversity and a different rhythm and level of life heighten this disparity, recipients' humiliation can become intolerable. Real or imagined insults to race and culture can then shock national pride into attitudes of dangerously inflammable hostility. Often suspicions of Cold War motives offer recipients a protective salve of cynicism for wounded national honour; but soon suspicion may turn to morbid distrust of all who come bearing gifts: *timeo Danaos*. . . . In either case, the relationship between benefactor and beneficiary begets an atmosphere singularly inhospitable to goodwill.

Another reason for conflict flows from the necessary intimacy of aid contractors. It is often thought that the close co-operation demanded by joint planning, administration and execution of international aid ensures a cordiality based on prolonged personal acquaintance. But mutual knowledge should not be confused with mutual understanding. If for some, proximity helps to overcome inherited bias, for others, it confirms old prejudices and forges new ones. Familiarity breeds contempt, as well as tolerance, depending on unpredictable factors like individual personalities and the success of attempts to harmonize at every stage the interests of contracting parties.

Yet another danger resides in the volume and complexity of contemporary aid. As programmes grow and diversify, so do opportunities for strife. Common confrontation of development problems by giver and receiver in no way guarantees a common view of proper solutions. Considerations of national—or racial—prestige can aggravate honest technical disagreements, replacing them with sterile contests of pride. Even off the job, or away from studies, foreign visitors propelled by aid programmes into an alien *milieu* can encounter or provoke disputes of lasting harm to friendly international relations.[73]

[73]At least one distinguished observer has suggested that a central reason for the generally uneventful collaboration of Soviet and Afro-Asian technicians is the lodging of most Russian overseas advisers in compounds, apart from local populations. Joseph S. Berliner, *Soviet Economic Aid* (London, 1960), p. 54. The "boondock" school, led by Burdick and Lederer (authors of *The Ugly American*), has, of course, denounced compounds for Western technicians as discriminatory ghettos.

Finally, misunderstanding can arise from the apparent permanence of continuing bilateral programmes. If, for any reason, a donor wishes to terminate its aid, a definite cooling, if not strain, is likely to fall upon a relationship grown too accustomed to a stable basis of economic assistance. Likewise, a reduction of aid, even to meet a budgetary emergency or normal demands from new recipients, can cause donors embarrassment. This problem will become increasingly acute for Canada, as fresh claims are forced upon its programme by new potential recipients in the Commonwealth, French Africa and Latin America; the only escape from the dilemma—if "escape" is the word—is through a costly increase in aid.

While these psychological pitfalls show the uncertainty of gaining goodwill from aid, they do not by any means disprove the postulate relating aid to friendship. It may even be assumed, in order to pursue the argument, that on balance, the goodwill earned by aid usually out-weighs the bad. One can then ask the conclusive question as to whether friendship and understanding, thus cultivated, can be exploited to mobilize sympathy for Western Cold War policies.

A first observation must be that factors influencing foreign policy are so complex and intermingled that it is impossible to attribute any single act of a recipient to aid that Canada or some other nation has given it. Considerations of interest, prestige, conviction, balance of power, pro-cedure and lobbying all disguise the path joining aid to the recipient's diplomacy. Occasional harmony of donor and recipient policies is excep-tional, and usually fortuitous. There is no impressive evidence to show that changes in recipients' policies—beyond the purely verbal—result from goodwill generated by Canada's aid programme. Similarly, United Nations debates indicate that American and British aid has not changed fundamental voting habits of Afro-Asian members. While French aid seems to have helped soften criticism of France's Algerian and nuclear policies by many French-speaking African states, cultural and political factors also influenced their attitude. And the examples of Iraq and Guinea suggest that even Soviet aid enslaves its recipients less than is frequently feared.

Any conclusion to these arguments must obviously be conditional. Certain types of aid, if executed competently, administered artfully, and offered tactfully, can indeed create goodwill. And goodwill is one impor-tant element, among others, in disposing a foreign government to heed a donor's diplomatic promptings. Any final judgment of the premise, however, must recognize that the fickle support of an emotional recipient public opinion is a meagre hope upon which to base Canadian foreign policy. Pursuit of goodwill through aid is itself fraught with risks of effects antithetical to goodwill; and such sympathy, even if deserved, is too volatile to survive stresses imposed by far more decisive forces of international politics.

c. Canadian aid and the Western Alliance

An accessory political aim holds that a high volume of Canadian aid is needed to encourage other Western nations to give generously. Not only, it is argued, can a larger Canadian programme offer an inspiring example; it can strengthen the hand of pro-aid circles in countries with resources vastly greater than Canada's. By "paying her dues" in Western aid clubs, Canada can stimulate the entire world flow of aid greatly beyond the level of her own, globally small, contribution.

Doubtless, other more immediate factors weigh in government budgetary decisions: fiscal deficits, national economic health, balance of payments problems, and domestic opinion. But the argument of emulation is commended by serious and widespread evidence. Legislatures and private reports in other donor countries constantly refer to aid efforts of allies, with opposing aims of raising or diminishing their own nation's sacrifice. "We are convinced," said General Clay's remarkable report to President Kennedy in March 1963,

that the burden of sustaining foreign assistance to the less-developed countries is falling unfairly upon the US and that the industrialized countries can and should do more than they are now doing. . . . Among our specific aims should be for . . . Canada to raise the volume of aid [most donors received a like admonition]. . . . Other developed countries cannot, in a realistic world, be expected to assume their proper proportions of the assistance effort so long as we are apparently willing to bear more than our fair share.[74]

The implied threat of a reduction in American aid was indeed carried out by President Kennedy in his message to Congress nine days later— partly as a tactical measure to ease passage of the foreign aid bill, but also as a warning to other Western donors that their contributions

[74]Lucius B. Clay, *Report to President Kennedy by the Committee to Strengthen the Security of the Free World* (Washington, 1963), p. 14. See also *1963 US Senate Hearings*, pp. 75 (David E. Bell, Administrator, Agency for International Development), 212, 489–90, 667 (Senator Wayne Morse), 226 (Secretary of State Dean Rusk), and 652 (General Clay).

The most penetrating international studies comparing aid are the annual Reviews by the OECD, Paris, entitled *Development Assistance Efforts and Policies*. The UN publishes a less critical but more complete world survey of aid (usually every two years) entitled *International Economic Assistance to the Less Developed Countries*.

ultimately fixed the ceiling of American aid. Years before, moreover, Congress enacted statutory restrictions holding American UN grants to a maximum of 40 per cent of any UN programme. Presumably, then, increases in Canada's aid would hearten the US—and other donor governments—at least to maintain, and perhaps to enlarge, their present assistance.

That such a relation between national levels of aid exists is confirmed by attempts of the Development Assistance Committee (DAC) of the Organization for Economic Co-operation and Development (OECD) to compare publicly and privately national contributions. DAC's confidential efforts to raise national levels of aid are noted for their persistence and frankness, both of which qualities have been used amply to coax improvements in Canada's volume of aid.[75]

But still more effective in developing international and domestic pressure upon defaulting donor governments are DAC's annual statistics. These figures, published with an eye to underlining both inequalities in effort and the deeper solidarity of purpose uniting OECD nations, are themselves reliable; always they clearly distinguish disparate aid components, and warn scrupulously against misinterpretation. Unfortunately, their over-simplification by private media and partisan groups has so deformed their sense that they now more often mislead than inform. The most flagrant distortion of relative contributions results from using DAC's net aid totals, without reference to their highly varied content, to arrive at alleged "comparative" percentages of each donor's gross national product. According to these private calculations, broadcast uncritically in newspapers, speeches and Parliamentary debates, Canada appears almost the most niggardly of all DAC members.

Regrettably, this simple and specious standard ignores completely the terms and quality of national contributions. Canada's aid, until 1964, was essentially in outright grants, carefully invested in basic economic development; while aid from other donors was often applied far less strictly to development, and given on terms less magnanimous: loans at market rates, export credit financing, private investment, and even war reparations.[76] Nor do such comparisons recognize that many

[75]See Chapter 2 for a review of multilateral co-ordinating machinery.
[76]Canada also began direct long-term financing of exports in 1960 (see Chapter 8). The expression "market rates" is itself imprecise, for it admits a number of variables such as grace periods, maturity and currency of repayment that can make a loan of nominally high interest equivalent or superior in "softness" to a loan with an interest rate nominally lower. The informal jargon of international aid meetings often combines all a donor's types of aid in the expression "mix" which, by comparison with other donors' "mixes," may be either "hard" or "soft."

TABLE 1.1

"Aid" by DAC Countries in Terms of Percentage of
GNP (1961)

Country	Percentage
Belgium	.86
Canada	.19
Denmark	.12
France	1.70
Germany	.83
Italy	.21
Japan	.48
Netherlands	.62
Norway	.21
Portugal	1.24
UK	.66
USA	.73
Total DAC	.75

SOURCE: Canada, *House of Commons Debates,*
Oct. 14, 1963, p. 3517. In 1962, Canada's
percentage fell to .16 following emergency austerity measures. In 1964, it was
roughly .39.

donors—Germany and Japan, for instance—whose records appear
better than Canada's, began serious aid activities eight or ten years after
Canada. Lacking a reasonable common definition of aid and historical
perspective, the GNP criterion based on a hodge-podge of net aid totals
is, to say the least, an inadequate measure of generosity.

This in no way suggests that Canada shares an equitable portion of
the Western aid burden; it does show a need to clarify terms of comparison. The central pitfall is the word "aid" itself which, by analogy
with personal relationships, implies not only benefit to the recipient but

---

The OECD-DAC *Development Assistance Efforts and Policies: 1963 Review*
says the following about the word "aid" (p. 21):

"No fully satisfactory definition has ever been given to this term. Normally it
is used in this Report to denote only the flow of government grants and official
lending exceeding 5 years and contributions to multilateral agencies from official
sources. These flows all represent resources or purchasing power made available
by the donor countries to less-developed countries, though they may differ widely
in the terms and conditions under which they are provided. While it may be
debatable whether such funds should all equally be called aid, there is hardly
any doubt that they would not have been available to the recipients through
normal commercial channels on the same terms and conditions and for the same
purposes."

See Appendices C and D below for a detailed analysis of DAC aid totals.

a degree of sacrifice by the donor. In reality, most of what passes for aid under present international definitions brings some return to donors, particularly outside North America. A first clarification demands therefore that the ambiguous general use of the word "aid" be dropped in favour of a descriptive phrase like "capital flow" or, as DAC puts it more precisely, the "flow of official long-term financial resources." "Aid" could remain as a popular shorthand for the general notion of assistance; but in its technical sense, it might more aptly be limited to covering grants and what DAC calls "grant-like loans." Second, a valid comparison of the usefulness of national programmes should study not merely the financial volume of aid, but its contribution to self-sustaining economic growth. Such a review would be complex and controversial; but it could also be honest and realistic, which current comparisons are not.

However imperfect the means of measurement, comparisons of aid efforts among allies are in principle desirable and potentially fruitful. Development aid has been since 1960 officially a joint enterprise of the richer Western nations, who promised in the OECD Convention to "co-operate in assisting to the best of their ability" the developing countries. As a collective task, aid must be a conscientious preoccupation of every DAC member valuing Western political and economic solidarity. In the same way that defence efforts of smaller NATO countries are significant not so much militarily as in symbolizing a will to shoulder a due part of a common responsibility, so can substantial aid levels be defended as one of the suitable ways of strengthening Western unity. While not a sufficient reason for aid itself, this purpose easily justifies maintaining an equitably large programme judged useful on other grounds. To the extent that Canada's aid reaches and surpasses an objectively fair level in relation to the common Western effort, it will doubtless tend to raise upwards the giving of Canada's allies. And, what is still more likely, its stagnation will quickly urge others to imitate Canada's own reluctance to give.

3. ECONOMIC AIMS

As in most contributing countries, claims are heard in Canada that aid brings economic benefits to donors. These claims, which have at least tacit support in Ottawa, can be reduced to two central arguments, both debatable: (a) aid is a useful short-term stimulus to Canada's economy; (b) aid leads, in the long run, to increases in Canadian trade. In discussing each theme, estimated benefits from aid must naturally be measured against the cost of aid to Canada. This comprises loss in giving goods and services free or on privileged terms rather than selling them at market prices; slightly increased inflation and balance of payments problems; and profit sacrificed by not allocating aid funds to some other investment assuring a still higher return.[77]

a. Aid as a short-term stimulus to Canada's economy
Probably between 90 and 95 per cent of all Canadian bilateral aid funds are spent initially in Canada. The Canadian government, especially when aid is attacked in periods of serious unemployment, understandably stresses that aid is really direct investment in Canada's economy, an injection of capital creating or saving jobs for Canadians. Canada's aid is not represented by "barrels of dollars shipped abroad," reminded the Hon. J. M. Macdonnell in September 1961, but by "Canadian goods and services."[78] "Our aid programs," agreed the Secretary of State for External Affairs on November 14, 1963, "provide a stimulus to the domestic economy and contribute to a betterment of employment conditions, since the main part of our aid funds is spent in Canada to purchase Canadian goods and services. . . ."[79] As an answer to demands for welfare benefits in Canada instead of "charity" abroad, this rejoinder is simple, positive, and seemingly irreproachable.

But aid has severe limitations as a Canadian economic catalyst, notably in fighting short-term recession. First, the very smallness of Canadian aid denies it an ambitious role in stimulating economic activity: Canadian aid of all types in 1964–65 formed about two-fifths of one per cent of Canada's gross national product. True, aid purchases were concentrated in a few industries which, on occasion, may have been visibly helped. But such a tiny outlay—however strategically placed—was unlikely to assert a tangible influence on general Canadian employment, prices or consumption. And benefit even to selected industries was with few exceptions sporadic, or too widely dispersed to offer a reliable and substantial livelihood.[80]

Next, even if established that aid has assisted intermittently certain Canadian industries, these might well have profited at least as much

[77]Many of the arguments here are based on a succinct and persuasive analysis by G. L. Reuber: "Why Canadian Foreign Aid?" *International Journal*, vol. 14, no. 1 (Winter, 1958–1959), pp. 13–16. For a general work on aid and trade, see Gerald M. Meier, *International Trade and Development* (New York, 1963).
[78]Canada, *House of Commons Debates*, Sept. 11, 1961, p. 8197.
[79]*Ibid.*, Nov. 14, 1963, p. 4718.
[80]No truly scientific study has yet been made of the actual effects of Canada's aid on her economy as a whole. All past attempts at general conclusions have been either impressionistic or based on unrepresentative case-studies, sometimes

from some other allocation of resources: say, to domestic development or research, low-cost loans or new tax incentives.

There are also drawbacks in using aid as a counter-cyclical measure. To begin, aid purchases would have to be synchronized with periods of sluggishness or unsold surpluses in the Canadian economy. This would be extremely difficult, for the health of each industry varies constantly with sometimes rapid fluctuations in demand and, in the case of agriculture, with the success of crops: aluminum and wheat are eloquent examples. Unless economic sectors involved in aid were watched painstakingly, miscalculations in timing aid expenditures could cause intensified inflation. This would be all the more likely since aid appropriations are increasingly committed at fixed levels for three or more years: for political as well as technical reasons, spending of appropriations cannot easily be modified to accommodate short-run fluctuations in the Canadian economy. But even if proven that certain industries were enabled through aid contracts to survive a temporary crisis, some might object that, compared to fiscal or monetary action, this assistance was not fairly distributed throughout the economy as a whole.

Synchronization is further complicated by intergovernmental negotiation. Since Canadian aid is normally given only upon specific request from recipients, the latter's precise requirements would have to coincide with goods or services which Canada, at any given moment, might wish to supply. Most recipients try to follow carefully-built long-term development plans, the progress of whose various segments relies partly upon reasonable harmonization of interlocking project schedules. Canada cannot impose shipments of aid—however desirable in the long run—at times convenient only to herself. Waste, resentment, and disruption of vital plans result inexorably from substitution of the donor's expediency for the recipient's interest. The possibility that

---

arbitrarily projected. For instance, the Director General, in a speech to the Canadian Export Association in Toronto on April 29, 1964, suggested that Canada's aid programme had created perhaps 6000 man-years of work for Canadians during the preceding year because it had been "estimated that each $1 million of foreign aid represents 120 man-years of work in Canada." Such a projection, which takes no account of the great differences in job-creating potential of different forms of aid (e.g., equipment and foodstuffs), must be considered no more than a hopeful guess. (American economists produced an equally challengeable estimate in "Impact of Foreign Aid on the US Economy," in *U.S. Foreign Aid*, pp. 92–3). In the same speech, the Director General mentioned one large project completed in 1965 (obviously the Kundah Power Project) which had given rise to 300 prime supplier contracts. He added that during the previous fiscal year "about 750 different Canadian manufacturers and suppliers participated in the Canadian grant aid programs." These results, while impressive, fall far short of the dimension needed to prove that aid is a powerful stimulus to Canada's economy.

immediate requirements of donor and recipient might coincide is lessened still more by the slowness and technical difficulty of negotiations between governments thousands of miles apart.

What can be concluded from this discussion? First, Canada's aid, to the degree it is spent at home, is at least not a significant loss to the Canadian economy. Second, it can be of only casual help to depressed areas in Canada when, occasionally, products of these areas happen to meet recipients' urgent needs.[81] Third, representation of this modest and transitory advantage as proof that aid is an effective weapon against general unemployment in Canada is unjustified, indeed fallacious. The proper place of the whole argument is that of a measured and moderate reply to criticism that aid is a drain on Canadian resources aggravating Canada's existing economic problems.

b. Long-term effects of aid on Canadian exports
Another common assumption is that aid will lead over a period of years to direct and indirect expansion of Canadian exports.

(i) *Aid as a direct stimulus to Canadian exports.* Canadian aid shipments (themselves exports, though subsidized) exert, it is argued, a "pump-priming" action in favour of Canadian commercial exports. Aid is thought to open up markets by making known Canadian goods and services, and to hold them by establishing Canadian standards and a need for Canadian spare parts. Some even maintain that a foothold or quota in certain competitive markets can be secured by obliging recipients to accept a portion of annual aid allocations in surplus foodstuffs.

Similar beliefs are widely accepted both in private and official justifications for Canadian aid. Not unnaturally, business journals (with at least the approval of Ottawa informants) have led private opinion in supporting such views.[82] In government statements, direct promotion of

---

[81]The likelihood that present industries of depressed areas in Canada would be stimulated by even greatly increased Canadian foreign aid seems remote. From a selection of depressed areas, it is apparent that industries with a labour surplus are not those whose goods or services are often, if ever, demanded in the aid programme: automobiles, metal-working, construction, service, transportation, clerical work, lumbering, coal, textiles, fishing, food and tobacco. See Stanislaw Judek, "Canada's Persistent Unemployment Problem: Labour Surplus Market Areas," a study appended to the *Proceedings of the Special Committee of the Senate on Manpower and Unemployment*, no. 7, Feb. 2, 1961 (Ottawa, 1961), p. 571.

[82]See "How Aid under Colombo Plan Is Helping Canadian Firms," *Financial Post*, Toronto, Jan. 16, 1954, p. 3; "More Business Ahead under Colombo Plan," *ibid.*, Dec. 18, 1954, p. 3; "Canada and the Colombo Plan: Our Investment Is Paying Off," *ibid.*, March 9, 1957, p. 27; W. T. S. Pogson, "Foreign Aid: Key to Future Trade," *Saturday Night* (Jan. 6, 1962), vol. 77, no. 1, pp. 14–15.

Canadian exports has often been suggested as a by-product of aid, though active pursuit of this aim has been viewed with varying favour.[83] Not all these statements, it is true, make extravagant claims for export benefits likely to flow from aid; but as expressions of a government desire to emphasize Canada's economic interest in aid, they sometimes encourage less cautious hopes in private aid apologists. At least three major uncertainties must be noted in a balanced assessment of these hopes.

First, would aid-generated exports be sold commercially even without the stimulus aid is imagined to offer? Surely the testing question is "are they competitive in price (including terms of credit), quality, delivery date and maintenance with similar products of other nations?" It is improbable that a lasting flow of exports can be assured unless the answer for most of these factors is affirmative. If a product cannot be sold in open world competition, it is illusory to expect a gift of that product to persuade a recipient to buy it subsequently. A product superior in every way to its rivals will sell itself; if uncompetitive, it will not. Certainly aid can make known a superior product which, on its own merits, may later be bought commercially. Among such examples are Canada's $35,000,000 sale to India in November 1963 of a nuclear power station for Rajasthan, as well as sales in 1964 of conventional generating equipment worth about $25,000,000 for two new Indian hydro-electric projects; earlier sales of several Beaver aircraft and nylon fishing line to Pakistan; and additional aerial surveys in Nigeria. From numerous other gifts, such as locomotives and telecommunication equipment in Ceylon and the Canada-India Reactor, occasional purchases of Canadian spare parts may be expected. But continued sales will succeed or fail strictly on the attractiveness of the product itself. Direct help to Canadian exports by aid is therefore essentially limited to advertising through samples.

A second limitation is the risk of actually endangering future exports through awkward attempts to secure "footholds" in competitive markets. By obliging South Asian recipients to pay scarce foreign exchange for shipping charges on unwanted surplus wheat, Canada for some years not only stirred resentment, but reduced the foreign buying power of

[83]See remarks by chief aid officials in *Standing Committee on External Affairs*, 1959, p. 125 (the ETAB Director here calls aid-generated export orders "probably incidental to what we are trying to do"); *ibid.*, 1956, p. 136 (the Colombo Plan Administrator describes how foreign trainees were deliberately dispersed throughout Canada to help Canadian businessmen learn of export opportunities); see also *Foreign Trade*, Ottawa, Oct. 19, 1963, for several articles on aid and exports.

potential commercial customers. Further, if surplus disposal were carried too far in "tie-in" or "loss-leader" deals, Canada would be less well placed to protest against similar practices by the United States, whose unrestricted disposal activities could lead to calamitous losses for Canada in traditional and potential markets.[84]

Finally, it is well to remember that Canadian trade is not composed only of Canadian exports. Canada must import from her customers to help them finance imports from Canada. Of course, in a world of increasingly diversified multilateral trade, it is neither necessary nor desirable that each bilateral relationship be artificially balanced. Still, there is a general need, implicit in the slogan "trade is aid," to increase Western imports from developing countries—both to help the vendors' industry and to allow them to purchase foreign equipment and materials required for their development. As this argument is endorsed more widely (since the 1964 UN Conference on Trade and Development it commands almost universal lip-service), new Canadian trade may lead to reductions in Canada's tariffs which—though possibly beneficial in the long run to our economy as a whole—could entail considerable short-run hardship to sectors directly attacked by increased imports.

Thus aid's vocation as a direct stimulus to trade in Canada's advantage is extremely modest. Aid can protect Canadian exports from the rigours of international competition only momentarily; and its use for export promotion is so circumscribed by dangers and doubts that no substantial policy can rest upon this postulate.

(ii) *Aid and a rising level of world trade*. The second argument holds that Canada's aid will benefit her exports indirectly, by leading to greater world trade in which Canada will enjoy a perceptible share. This reasoning is also broadly supported by both independent observers and official spokesmen. "As these [recipient] people become more efficient," predicted the Colombo Plan Administrator in 1956, "their needs increase . . . so will their ability to buy. We are, I think, creating a market for ourselves in this area."[85] Later, at the Seattle Colombo Plan Conference in 1958, Dr. Sidney Smith took up the theory in a wider framework, assuring that "as . . . our joint programs bear fruit, . . . the

[84]"US Wheat Hits Canada 'Alarmingly,'" *Financial Post*, Toronto, Dec. 15, 1956, p. 8; "Can We Really Blast US Wheat Deal with India?" *ibid.*, Sept. 20, 1958, p. 26; "US-India Wheat Deal Hits Canada," *ibid.*, May 7, 1960, p. 26.

[85]*Standing Committee on External Affairs*, 1956, p. 206. Cf. C. V. Narasimhan, "The Indian Approach to External Assistance," in *Conference on Canada and International Development Programmes*, p. 22; and Paul G. Hoffman, *One Hundred Countries, One and One Quarter Billion People: How To Speed Their Economic Growth and Ours—in the 1960's* (Washington, 1960), pp. 53 and 56.

demand generated by increases in national wealth in [Asia] will certainly provide a significant stimulus to world trade. In this, all countries, developed and less developed alike, may expect to participate and from it they may all expect to benefit."[86]

This theory invites several qualifications. First, one can imagine that aid, far from creating freer trade of benefit to all, may well impede it. Professor Myrdal insists it is "natural that in all underdeveloped countries industrialization should take the path of attempting to reach increased self-sufficiency in an increasing number of production lines."[87] Still more bluntly, Professor Liska affirms that aid "may also help to overindustrialize the world and to generate trends toward cut-throat competition or self-sufficiency—toward anarchy or autarky."[88] Can Canada create customers without building up rivals?

Again one must view as an important cost of aid the difference in "time, risk and uncertainty" between alleged gains from aid and those from competing investments.[89] Benefits to Canada from aid through increased world trade are usually estimated to occur only after five or ten years, if not much later. However, allocation of aid funds to domestic Canadian development would probably bring returns far more quickly, and certainly with less risk. It can even be argued that, in the long run, investment of dollars in Canada rather than abroad as aid may be in the best interests of less-developed countries as well. If investment opportunities in Canada offer a higher return than those in India, will not investment in Canada form new capital able to develop still more quickly both Canada and India?[90]

Further, even if Canadian aid were shown to increase recipients' buying power, nothing ensures this power would be used to purchase Canadian goods. If Canada's aid did stimulate capital formation later directed to imports, recipients would doubtless continue to buy from nations offering comparative cost advantages. Once more, the only reasonable guarantee of successful export promotion is in offering Canadian products in every way competitive.

Finally, the very potential of Canadian aid for stirring world trade

[86]*The Colombo Plan for Cooperative Economic Development in South and Southeast Asia, Proceedings of the Meetings of the Consultative Committee*, p. 78.

[87]Gunnar Myrdal, *An International Economy* (London, 1956), p. 280. See also the novel proposals of the Belgian Minister of Foreign Trade for assisting industrial exports of developing countries: "Le Plan Brasseur," *L'Echo de la Bourse*, Brussels, Sept. 24, 1963, p. 1.

[88]Liska, *The New Statecraft*, p. 15.

[89]Reuber, "Why Canadian Foreign Aid?", p. 13.

[90]Triantis, "Foreign Aid—a New Canadian Experience," p. 59. Eayrs notes this argument in *Canada in World Affairs*, p. 206.

invites scepticism. At its 1965–66 level of about $200,000,000, Canadian assistance is almost invisible within the annual total of some six or seven billion dollars of Western aid. Even concentrated, as it is, in a few countries, Canadian aid is clearly marginal in raising the trading capacity of any one of its recipients.[91] It is futile, therefore, to estimate what part of any general increase in world trade might be attributable to Canadian aid—and impossible to guess what share of such an increase would be enjoyed by Canada. Only if Canadian aid were multiplied many times could any appreciable effect upon world trade be even imagined.

The suggestion that aid will bring lasting increases in demand for a broad range of Canadian products is then, at best, hazardous. Yet Canada may still benefit in ways that are important, though now difficult to measure. Assuming Canadian aid is in theory a modest step toward faster world economic growth, and that recipients' industrialization will not push them to unreasonable autarky, the growing prosperity of less developed nations could lead to wider adoption of the principle of comparative advantage in trade between industrialized and developing countries. As a result, certain highly competitive Canadian specialities might find larger markets.[92] A condition of this would certainly be lower Canadian tariffs to allow increased imports of labour-intensive goods from developing nations. Through proper adjustment, Canada might gain in two ways: by cheap imports of goods formerly produced in Canada at higher prices; and by larger markets for a small range of Canadian specialized services and capital-intensive manufactured products. Moreover, growth of heavy industry in some underdeveloped countries (such as India) might strengthen demand for certain Canadian industrial raw materials.

[91]The record of Indo-Canadian trade since 1948—three years before the first Colombo Plan aid shipments—is highly instructive. Indian exports to Canada over fifteen years rose from 33.4 million dollars in 1948 to only 43.5 million dollars in 1962, after dropping to 29.4 million in 1960. During the same time, Canadian exports to India actually fell from 33.7 million to 29.6 million—hardly spectacular proof of the "pump-priming" virtues of aid in a country having received by far the largest single share of Canada's assistance. (An exceptional rise to 79.1 million dollars in 1958 is explained by special Canadian food aid given to meet a temporary Indian famine; nearly 40 million dollars of this total was in wheat, largely in grants, partly on credit). These results are even less impressive when it is recalled that after 1954 Canada's export figures included aid financed from an annual Canadian allocation to India of some 12 to 25 million dollars. See N. V. Raghuram, "Aid and Trade: A Case-Study Referring to India and Canada," unpublished essay (University of Ottawa, 1962), pp. 2–3.
[92]See C. P. Kindleberger, *Economic Development* (New York, 1958), pp. 238–9.

Still, such large-scale developments could scarcely be laid to the sole influence of a relatively tiny Canadian aid programme. Aid can dramatize Canada's wish for rising world trade, and perhaps encourage larger countries to promote freer specialized trade. But all the above benefits might easily occur without any Canadian aid at all. This basic difficulty of gauging the precise effects of Canadian aid on a vastly intricate world economy requires, therefore, abandonment of the final postulate as little more than a genial hope. The entire argument can stand only if framed in qualifications depriving it of nearly all cogency—or if buttressed by a gigantic increase in Canada's aid at present inconceivable.

4. POLICY OR PROPAGANDA?

The crucial problem of this whole discussion has been that of separating policy from slogans. The aims of any foreign policy are usually complex, and frequently confused with motives underlying them. But external aid has become such a glamorous enterprise, and its purposes so enmeshed in attractive, but irrelevant, myths and wishful thinking, that attempts to identify valid policy aims are not only painful, but often unwelcome.

Yet candid effort to clarify attainable objectives is acutely needed. Without reasonably definite aims, aid is certain to be increasingly questioned by a Canadian public rightly wishing both a sense of direction and some measurable evidence that its investment in aid is sound. Even more, rigorous and periodic re-assessment of supposed aims is required to avoid disappointments, bitter to donor and recipients, because of false expectations.

Realistic policy must constantly weigh advantages and costs of alternative courses of action. If to govern is to choose, intelligent choice is possible only when all pertinent facts are known and faced frankly. It is true that in foreign policy there are so many mobile, exotic and imponderable elements that alternatives are not always clear. Most policy discussion therefore relies on a degree of subjective interpretation; still, if policy is to have any meaning at all, the effort to "illuminate choices" must be disciplined, honest and unflagging.

There is no point in reviving arguments already stated for and against the assorted themes imagined to guide Canadian aid policy. A broad conclusion on aid purposes cannot judge specific objectives, for their validity usually turns on quickly shifting conditions. All that can be usefully attempted is a brief estimate of the proper place of aid in

Canadian foreign policy, based on a general impression of the above debate.

Aid seems a justifiable activity of Canadian foreign policy for two reasons, one negative and one positive. These reasons invoke no noble sentiments and make no spectacular claims of benefit to Canada; they may, however, provide our aid-giving with a rationale that is both stable and utilitarian.

The negative reason supposes that aid-giving is a necessary lesser evil. This theory promises Canada no substantial advantage from aid whatever; for it recognizes starkly that aid-giving produces no certain or measurable results. Yet in recognizing that such results are unsure, it admits that some of the benefits aid is alleged to confer upon donors *may* indeed accrue to them—in other words that it may be still more unprofitable not to give aid than to give it. This view, stated bluntly, sees aid as a kind of insurance policy, a premium paid against the risks—also unmeasured, but potentially disastrous—of withholding aid. Can Canada afford, for instance, to take the chance that, by refusing to grant aid while nearly all other rich nations do give it, she will incur the poor countries' lasting resentment? Resentment between nations, unlike goodwill, tends to endure. Is not such animosity likely indeed to harden if Canada's ideological enemies are allowed a clear field in aid and, perhaps to some extent through it, in opportunities for propaganda? Participation in international development may not guarantee Canada any tangible, verifiable protection against the dangers of a revolutionary world society; but her total abstention from development is certain to prevent her from even appreciating many of these dangers. On balance, then, giving aid seems less likely to threaten Canadian interests than withholding it.

The second reason restates the same idea positively. If we agree that absence from the work of development would be punished by ignorance, we accept almost axiomatically that presence, participation, should in some degree lead to understanding: to understanding of the developing nations' real needs, hopes, fears, prejudices, interests and expectations; to understanding of their mentality, their culture, their society, their government; to understanding, in sum, of their peoples—at every level of life, humble and exalted, to which the day-to-day operations of aid assure a donor access. For aid is the ideal door to dialogue with the peoples of developing nations; it offers a natural, believable excuse to study them at close hand; it provides, through shared experience in their most fundamental long-range preoccupation, concrete and varied opportunities to assess their motivations. Donors may not always be perceptive enough to translate such opportunities into better policies for dealing with these nations; but through aid, the opportunities for basing new policies on sounder premises, on premises derived from accurate knowledge, undeniably exist.

The kind of understanding aid can engender has nothing to do with sympathy or goodwill. It implies no more than comprehension. But comprehension, even imperfect and groping, is the first stage of realistic policy-making. Today this relation means simply that Canada cannot function effectively as a so-called "middle power" with a diplomatic culture rooted in a pre-1945 world dominated by the white race. It means that many of Canada's most fruitful independent initiatives— especially those designed to keep the peace in the "Third World"— depend on a deep and sure grasp of realities outside the Atlantic community.

In the broad perspective of mankind's history, such a grasp will undoubtedly stand out as the apanage of those Western nations which faced this age frankly and met its challenges with the weapons of their time. Indeed, if we are clever enough to exploit its potential gift of knowledge, our commitment to world development may even, in the long run, help Canada, in liaison with the entire Western family, to shape the current global revolution roughly according to Canadian interests. "If the West," reflected Eugene Black,

is to exert a continuing and constructive influence on the historic trans-formation going on in the underdeveloped world, it must make a multi-plicity of contacts with its leaders and its people; it must seek working partnerships capable of functioning in spite of the passions which bedevil normal diplomatic and economic relations. Such a course is the realistic course; for only with time and through working side by side at tasks of mutual concern can the West make good the promise of economic benefits, tolerant political relations, and human betterment. And economic develop-ment provides the best tasks, perhaps the only really important ones, through which such contacts can be made and maintained.[93]

These contacts cannot be made and maintained if one partner, the donor, obscures its only certainly attainable goal, self-education, with rationalized sentimentality and half-baked political and economic Machiavellism. The education in world politics that aid can confer is needed by few countries more than by Canada. It can be used to serve world peace, perhaps, by no country better than by Canada. Yet neither Canada's need nor her peaceful calling can be fulfilled unless Canadians base their aid's objectives on reason instead of reverie. Unless, in a word, they consider aid merely as part of the price of meaningful parti-cipation in the twentieth century.

[93]Black, *The Diplomacy of Economic Development*, pp. 19–20.

II. The Framework of Allocation

Whatever the theoretical aims of policy, their successful pursuit demands practical options and workable methods. Beyond often unreal if refreshing debates on lofty principles, sound aid policy emerges from wise choices of recipients and from skilful negotiation. It is here, in the specific allocation of resources, that statesmen grapple with the deeper challenges of aid as an instrument of power; and here, as a result, that the political fabric of aid takes on its peculiar relief.

Governments are never free to act on philosophy alone, in abstraction from the strains of an actual conjuncture. Always their mastery of events hinges on realistic assessments of pertinent forces in a precise environment. Like all aspects of foreign policy, aid allocation must respond not only to pressures of international diplomacy, but to the hopes, fears and prejudices of domestic politics. All these forces fashion the historical and cultural preferences fixing the destination of Canada's aid; and, though diplomatic factors dominate, all weigh heavily on the key issues of planning, initiative, and co-operation among donors.

1. HISTORICAL-CULTURAL PREFERENCES

Every bilateral aid programme, however large, is politically selective in its distribution. Choice of recipients may rest on many factors, all more or less related to maximizing the donor's influence. In Canada's policy this goal has suggested concentration on three areas: the Commonwealth, the French-speaking world and, more recently, Latin America. Each area reflects a popular Canadian outlook, and each presents advantages and objections rooted in international politics.

a. The Commonwealth priority

Since 1950, some 90 per cent of Canadian bilateral aid has gone to Commonwealth countries. All Canadian parties have supported this emphasis, which is constantly defined in ministerial statements as deliberate and radical. "We in Canada are Commonwealth-minded," the Minister of Finance, Mr. Donald Fleming, informed a Ceylonese audience in October 1958; ". . . we as a Government have expressed our feeling towards the Commonwealth in the way in which we have diverted the Colombo Plan contributions. . . . Canada has always directed an overwhelming proportion of her Colombo Plan contribution to the Commonwealth countries. . . . The Canadian Government intends to follow this pattern."[1] Likewise Mr. Diefenbaker, as Leader of the Opposition, insisted in the Commons on November 14, 1963, that in allocation of the Liberal ministry's just-announced aid increase "first consideration should be given to the Commonwealth countries."[2] The Minister himself, Mr. Martin, had immediately before stressed the "long and historic association" which justified raising aid to Commonwealth nations in the Caribbean; and a fortnight later, while reviewing the same region, he added with eager redundance that "nurturing of one of our other cornerstones of foreign policy, the Commonwealth, is a basic feature of our external policies."[3]

This striking priority rests on several well-known reasons. First, history is thought to have joined Canada and her Commonwealth sisters in similar political traditions—though it must be said the analogy has become somewhat threadbare in the face, for instance, of Ghanaian experiments in autocracy. This sense of historical community is bolstered by a well-tested system of intimate diplomatic consultation, and by an ancient if crumbling edifice of trading preferences.[4]

Out of this tradition, however diversely adapted, has grown a second, sentimental motive. "Canada naturally has a family concern for those countries achieving independence within the Commonwealth," explained Mr. Diefenbaker to the UN General Assembly in September 1960.[5] This emotional, quasi-mystical feeling of Commonwealth kinship, while rarely shared (though often exploited) by member nations of non-British stock,

[1]*Ceylon Daily News*, Colombo, Oct. 28, 1958.
[2]*Debates*, p. 4719.
[3]*Ibid.*, Nov. 28, 1963, p. 5199.
[4]See Alexander Brady, "The Modern Commonwealth," *Canadian Journal of Economics and Political Science*, vol. 26, no. 1 (Feb., 1960), pp. 62–73.
[5]*Statements and Speeches*, no. 60/32, p. 8.

brings many English Canadians, at least, to feel that Commonwealth aid is a unique fraternal obligation.

The bias is supported by objective calculation as well. British colonialism, whatever its evils, has usually left former dependencies with reasonably organized, competent, and by local standards honest, administrations. Only such governments, of course, can absorb substantial capital aid usefully. "India, Pakistan and Ceylon," the Colombo Plan Administrator pointed out in 1955, ". . . have planning boards and five-year plans. . . . Still more backward countries . . . have not as yet been able to evolve realistic plans. . . . We shall not give them any capital assistance until they have plans into which we can fit that assistance."[6]

Further, the Commonwealth emphasis is defended because it concentrates the "impact" of Canada's aid. "We must not dissipate our resources," warned a former Assistant Under-Secretary of State for External Affairs, Mr. John W. Holmes, in 1961, ". . . [we] are obliged to concentrate our efforts so that we can achieve results in chosen places rather than disperse them ineffectually in the vain hope of multiplying the number of our friends. . . . We have fixed our attention on specific Commonwealth countries and thereby made some impression on their economies. . . . If we must choose, there is good reason for choosing areas to which we have a prior commitment for political and historical reasons."[7]

These arguments have led Canada to direct her grants of capital aid (comprising 88 per cent of the 1964–65 bilateral grant programme) almost exclusively to Commonwealth nations.[8] This policy is clear in Colombo Plan contributions, and between 1958 and 1960 it was fundamental in creating new programmes restricted to the Commonwealth: the Commonwealth Caribbean Assistance Program, and the Special Commonwealth Africa Aid Program (SCAAP).

[6]*Standing Committee on External Affairs*, 1955, pp. 700–1.

[7]"Weekend Review," CBC radio, Toronto, June 4, 1961. This view was endorsed emphatically by the Director General of External Aid before the Standing Committee on External Affairs on December 12, 1963: "I agree entirely with you about spreading aid too thinly. . . . That way you have no impact. . . . We should try to strengthen the programme in the areas in which we are now working."

[8]Only Burma and Indonesia among non-Commonwealth countries have received significant capital grants. Non-Commonwealth countries do not appear vexed or bitter about this bias, as some would fear. An interview with senior Burmese aid officials in May 1960 indicated that Canadian policy was well understood: the emphasis was not viewed as economic blackmail or a political condition of increased aid to Burma, but simply as the expression of a "positive love" for the Commonwealth.

A similar but less exclusive emphasis applies to technical assistance. Again, distinct programmes have tried since 1958–59 to meet specifically Commonwealth needs: the Commonwealth Technical Assistance Program (covering countries omitted from earlier area schemes) and the Commonwealth Scholarship and Fellowship Plan—as well as the Caribbean Program and SCAAP, which include both capital and technical aid. In the Colombo Plan, however, which now groups a majority of non-Commonwealth members, technical assistance is limited by no discernible political discrimination; always it is given essentially on each request's technical merit and feasibility.

This Commonwealth priority will certainly continue to guide Canadian aid allocation. It is only sensible to strengthen acquired positions and old relationships before scattering a meagre aid budget still more thinly into the bottomless ocean of world development needs. Nevertheless, pressing domestic and international forces urge Canada's bolder entry into other areas having traditional claims on Canadian interests, if claims of a different quality. While obstacles to such expansion are more stubborn than imagined by many of its partisans, the cases for aid to French-speaking states and to Latin America deserve fresh and realistic review.

b. Quebec and "le monde francophone"

Following closely the post-1960 wave of nationalism in French Canada have surged demands for aid to French-speaking states comparable in volume and type to that accorded the Commonwealth. "Le Commonwealth n'est pas toute l'humanité," complained André Laurendeau in 1960, ". . . il existe des pays sous-développés où la langue de communication est le français. Des échanges avec le Canada leur seraient également utiles. . . . Il y a là une question d'égalité et de justice."[9] "Pourquoi serait-il impossible," despaired his colleague Jean-Marc Léger later that year, "que le gouvernement central décide une fois pour toutes de tenir compte de la situation particulière résultant pour le Canada de sa bi-ethnicité? Et, chaque fois où dans le cadre du Commonwealth un programme quelconque d'assistance est institué, d'y joindre un programme analogue en faveur des nombreux Etats de langue française?"[10]

---

[9]"Le Commonwealth n'est pas toute l'humanité," *Le Devoir*, Montreal, Jan. 16, 1960, p. 4.

[10]"Nouveau programme d'aide à l'Afrique britannique," *ibid.*, Sept. 24, 1960, p. 4. Three years later Léger, one of the most persistent and eloquent advocates of French-language aid, had decided that within the present Canadian constitution the Commonwealth aid bias "ne changera certainement pas beaucoup," and that

Clearly, if Canadian foreign policy is conceived as necessarily reflecting the "two-nation" theory of Confederation, Canada's assistance has not "fairly" projected Quebec's aspirations. In a 1963–64 bilateral grant budget of about $50,000,000, only $300,000 were allocated specifically to aid in French-speaking African states, primarily for education. (This scheme, announced in April 1961, was created as an obvious and proportionate counterpart to the newly-established one million-dollar Commonwealth Scholarship and Fellowship Plan.) Even a thirteen-fold increase to four million dollars in 1964–65 left Canada's yearly allocation to the eighty million people of these twenty-one French-speaking African states less than double the Canadian aid given that year to the four million people of the Commonwealth Caribbean. And during the first fourteen years of the Colombo Plan, until March 31, 1965, French-speaking Indochina received Canadian assistance totalling only 3.8 million dollars—while Ceylon alone, though with a four-year headstart, received over 25 million dollars. Within the logic of the Quebec nationalist's bicultural view of foreign policy, these figures indicate an arbitrary and unjust discrimination.

What advantages and problems might result from further large increases in Canada's "French aid"? In principle, increases would strengthen Canada's national unity by satisfying a natural and legitimate wish of the French-Canadian élite. For if sentiment and common traditions are valid reasons for helping Commonwealth countries, they must also be for aiding French-speaking ones. "Le Canadien français . . . est d'une certaine manière plus près du Malgache, du Tunisien ou du Sénégalais qui a étudié dans des institutions françaises," insisted Gérard Filion in 1960, ". . . Il existe entre eux une communauté de pensée, une discipline intellectuelle, une affinité de goûts."[11] Jean-Marc Léger, in a

---

contrary hopes were "illusions" ("Le Canada et l'aide au tiers-monde," *ibid.*, Nov. 16, 1963, p. 4). Not even the promise, two days earlier, by the Secretary of State for External Affairs, of "a larger and more effective program for Africa, including the French-speaking states," offered apparent redemption for Canada's English-dominated diplomacy (Canada, *House of Commons Debates*, Nov. 28, 1963, p. 4718).

[11]"Un Plan Colombo pour les pays de culture française," *Le Devoir*, June 18, 1960, p. 4. The shallow penetration of the French language in African societies suggests, however, that arguments of cultural affinity between Quebec and Africa may be somewhat overstated. An article entitled "L'Avenir du français en Afrique noire" in the *Sélection hebdomadaire du "Monde,"* Paris, April 1–7, 1965, and based on a paper by the chief of cultural and technical co-operation of the French Ministry of Co-operation, estimates that in ex-French Africa "le taux global de francophonie" is about 10 per cent. "Autrement dit, sur quarante millions d'habitants, quatre millions environ parlent français. Et encore . . . Un à deux pour cent parlent couramment notre langue et un à deux pour cent sans doute

series of articles entitled "Le Québec dans le monde francophone," called in July 1963 for "une politique de présence à la francophonie," including, among other measures, a distinct French-Canadian aid programme. Only such a programme, he implied on January 27, 1965, would aptly express Quebec's "solidarité culturelle" with French-speaking African brothers.[12]

Indeed, would not Canada's diplomatic advantage be served by a substantial and well-executed aid programme in French-speaking Africa? Without expecting to change recipients' policies, could not Ottawa hope through wider co-operation with these states better to understand their political evolution? Can Canadian policy afford to show only scant interest in countries having such a large numerical influence on UN debates and, in many cases, an instability likely to engage Canada increasingly in collective efforts to preserve peace?

Yet an expanded French programme must face several obstacles which suggest that natural sympathy be tempered with caution. First, relatively primitive administrations in former French and Belgian colonies leave some doubt that important increases in Canadian aid could be usefully absorbed. Although such allegations are difficult to document and easy to contradict, many observers returning from French-speaking territories emphasize that virtues of efficiency, public service and integrity are often less cherished than in neighbouring states formerly under British control.[18] It is a fact that neither France nor Belgium—in spite of sometimes excellent performances in classical education and social services—gave serious attention to training African civil servants in

---

pensent en français" (p. 11). It is true that the "taux global d'anglophonie" in the developing Commonwealth is probably no higher; yet Commonwealth claims of cultural affinity, as distinct from similarity of institutions and ideals, are perhaps less categorical.

[12]Léger saw no hope, however, that Ottawa would agree to let Quebec run the "francophone" programme, adding in his 1963 article that "il est humiliant, néfaste et à la longue intolérable de devoir passer par Ottawa pour nos relations avec le monde de langue française." ("Une grande politique de relations avec le monde francophone est l'une des conditions de notre émancipation," *Le Devoir*, July 26, 1963, pp. 1 and 10). Léger's demands do not coincide with the results of the 1962 Lemelin-Marion study of popular Quebec opinion (*Le Canada français et le Tiers-Monde*, Ottawa, 1963): in this poll only 14 per cent of those questioned thought Canada had excessively favoured English-speaking countries in its aid, and 71 per cent had no opinion at all; only 26 per cent thought that Quebec should have its own foreign aid programme, while 55 per cent opposed such an initiative and 19 per cent had no opinion (see pp. 79 and 63). As on many subjects, popular Quebec views on aid may now have grown somewhat more nationalistic. See also "La coopération internationale, tâche délicate et nécessaire," *Le Devoir*, Jan. 27, 1965.

[18]See René Dumont, *L'Afrique noire est mal partie* (Paris, 1962), pp. 63–71.

self-government until a few years (or months) before their colonies reached independence in 1959–61. Experience of French-Canadian aid administrators, both public and private, confirms that these new governments are not always reliable enough to exploit, or even formulate realistic requests for, straightforward technical assistance. The record of governments in former French Indochina is scarcely brighter, disorder there having been further spread by colonial and civil wars.

Part of the absorption problem is by many accounts the unfriendly reception given French-Canadian teachers and advisers abroad by expatriate metropolitan French technicians. Some twelve thousand European Frenchmen held more or less influential civil service posts in sub-Saharan Africa in 1963, and were reputed almost unanimously by informed French-Canadian sources to consider Africa as a kind of private preserve. "Il ne faudrait pas sous-estimer," wrote Professor André Patry, "la méfiance parfois rencontrée par les Canadiens français de la part des colons ou experts français déjà établis en Afrique et qui sont portés à considérer ce territoire comme une chasse gardée."[14] Other qualified observers have privately described their welcome by expatriate French as varying from "cool" to "hostile." This psychological obstacle owes something, it seems, to the difficulty of recognizing Canadian university degrees in countries geared entirely to France's education system. According to Professor Robert Cornevin, a French former administrator in Africa, "ce problème domine l'envoi des professeurs canadiens pour l'enseignement public."[15] French-Canadian diplomas, granted by religious institutions and, in French eyes, of inferior quality, are difficult to incorporate into African systems based on secularism and rigorous European standards.

Another difficulty is the need for strengthened Canadian field administration, a need made more urgent by the weakness of indigenous governments and the profusion of tiny separate French African states. To the cost of larger aid must then be added that of establishing new resident missions staffed by trained French-speaking Canadian administrators— a perennially unmet challenge of both the External Aid Office and the Department of External Affairs.[16]

[14]Letter to the writer, Nov. 23, 1963.
[15]"Que peut faire le Canada français pour l'Afrique francophone?" *Le Devoir*, Montreal, May 27, 1961. An EAO officer reported in April 1965 that the diploma problem was being made less acute by recent efforts of the Association des universités partiellement ou entièrement de langue française (AUPELF).
[16]Patry stresses, in speaking of African aid, "le peu d'expérience que possède dans ce domaine l'expert ou le technicien canadien-français envoyé en Afrique, ainsi [que les] problèmes que soulève son adaptation." Quebec's historic activity

But by far the greatest restriction arises from Quebec's own weakness in technical resources. Since 1960 the Quebec government has encouraged a massive programme of technical and scientific education, and it is to be hoped this welcome reform will in several years allow French Canada to play a role in overseas aid in the measure of her ambitions. Until recently, however, the great majority of French-Canadian students entered liberal rather than technical professions. "Les Canadiens français [représentent] 30 p. 100 environ de la population canadienne," lamented a Quebec science writer in May 1965, ". . . Pourtant, nous produisons moins de 8 p. 100 des scientifiques canadiens." According to the ACFAS (Association canadienne-française pour l'avancement des sciences), he went on, "le Canada français constitue un groupe scientifiquement sous-développé."[17] Still more disquietingly, a high official of the Quebec government explained in 1961 that the province was unable to supply large numbers of ordinary academic teachers for overseas service, because "nous en manquons nous-mêmes, surtout à l'échelon secondaire."[18] Even an optimistic observer like Jean-Marc Léger considered in October 1963 that Quebec's human and material aid resources were "modiques," that "dans l'état actuel des choses, le Canada français ne peut apporter qu'une modeste contribution à l'effort international d'assistance au tiers-monde."[19]

In these conditions, any significant increase in Canada's "French" aid must obviously be based on careful study of both Quebec's real resources and the absorptive capacity of likely recipients. Impetuous increases for domestic political reasons alone would be ill advised; but clearly there is scope for expansion in the light of what can be usefully invested. A realistic French programme might be conceived in two stages.

---

in private missionary aid trained few Canadian experts or administrators in these countries, because France for many years excluded foreign missionaries from her African possessions. L. Groulx, *Le Canada français missionnaire* (Montreal, 1962), pp. 263–322. In the spring of 1965, Canada had only one embassy situated in a French-speaking African state, namely Cameroun.

[17]Jean-Claude Paquet, "Attention! Le Québec ne produit pas assez de savants," *Le Magazine Maclean*, mai 1965, vol. 5, no. 5, p. 70. See also chaps. VII–XII inclusive in a study by a group of Laval University professors entitled, *Cri d'alarme . . . la civilisation scientifique et les Canadiens français* (Quebec, 1963); André Laurendeau, "Les Sciences chez nous," *Le Devoir*, Montreal, Aug. 29, 1963, p. 5; and Jules LeBlanc, "Sciences: réviser programmes et horaires," *Le Devoir*, Dec. 16, 1964, p. 23.

[18]Charles Bilodeau, quoted in "Québec ne peut fournir les professeurs demandés en Afrique et en Asie," *La Presse*, Montreal, April 6, 1961, p. 44.

[19]"L'Aide à l'étranger: la compétence prime nettement les bons sentiments," *Le Devoir*, Oct. 28, 1963, p. 4.

For a period of five to ten years, while awaiting the fruits of Quebec's technological revolution and possible improvement of French African and Indochinese administrations, Canadian aid might be highly concentrated both geographically and functionally. Three or four countries promising reasonably efficient use of aid would be selected, and an adequately staffed permanent mission established in each; then technical assistance, resource surveys and other pre-investment pilot projects would be offered in a few fields of maximum impact: say, education, economic planning, and public administration. This specialization is already broadly apparent in Canada's emphasis on educational aid to Africa, and could be developed with little disruption of current procedures.

After the preliminary period, which would vary with each recipient's growing ability to exploit aid, much more ambitious capital aid would be possible in power development, industry and equipment. With several years of French African experience, a larger Canadian technical élite, more mature recipient administrations, and coherent notions of local resources coupled with definite development plans, a much-expanded French programme could probably operate with great effectiveness. "In the pre-industrial phase," noted the OECD 1963 aid *Review*, "a country may have very limited absorptive capacity. However, as infrastructure is built, manpower trained, markets broadened and organizations established, opportunities for investment may increase rapidly."[20] Perhaps useful "French" aid in the first period could not exceed seven or eight million dollars a year; in the second, limits would not be traced by recipients' immaturity, but by Canada's own budget and political priorities.

c. Latin America

Pressures are also exerted to promote a Canadian "presence" through aid in Latin America. Again Quebec opinion tends to motivate such aid in terms of cultural and even religious affinity, recalling mystical ties of Latin civilization and an impressive, if relatively brief, missionary tradition;[21] while English Canadians, when they do not deny the very concept of hemispheric neighbourhood, tend to justify aid to the Latin New World on grounds of political and, characteristically, commercial interest.

[20]*Development Assistance Efforts and Policies: 1963 Review* (Paris), p. 16.
[21]See Marcel Roussin, *Le Canada et le système inter-américain* (Ottawa, 1959); Groulx, *Le Canada français missionnaire*, pp. 331–463; and Claude Ryan, "Le Canada et l'Amérique latine," *Le Devoir*, Nov. 15, 1963, p. 4.

None of these arguments bore fruit in official aid policy until November 1963, when the Canadian government announced "a further [sic] contribution to Latin American development, in close co-operation with the Inter-American Development Bank, through the availability of new and additional lending resources."[22] This aid, starting at $10,000,000 a year, takes the form of long-term, low-interest loans from a $50,000,000 fund, annually renewable, whose creation was announced the same day. Before the scope and goals of any new programme are defined, its implications for Canada's aid policy and global foreign policies deserve frank appraisal.

The alleged advantages of aid to Latin America are well enough known not to require lengthy comment: enhanced influence upon United States policy, deeper understanding of Latin American revolutionary forces, and satisfyingly closer "people-to-people" relations with long neglected nations sharing certain vital qualities of a nascent Atlantic culture. But these benefits are far from guaranteed by aid, and may in part be attainable through traditional means of diplomatic and commercial representation (already reasonably well installed) or by programmes of strictly cultural exchange.

On the other hand, development aid presents at least two dismaying drawbacks. First, if—as is almost inevitable—it includes technical assistance, it will spread still thinner Canadian skills even now demonstrably over-extended. Second, once the principle of giving it is acknowledged, it is apt to expose Canada to intensified demands for an ever-increasing volume of aid. Canada was criticized abroad when she gave Latin America no aid at all;[23] but if experience in donor consortia elsewhere is relevant, a substantial, though modest, Canadian programme to that area may provoke still more insistent pressures, because our contributions will then be judged in a more intimate regional, rather than a worldwide, context. As a result, Canada may at some time face the unenviable choice of raising her total aid level to accommodate current standards of hemispheric equity (no less, by rough comparison with US aid to Latin America in 1965, than forty or fifty million dollars a year for Canada) or of reducing aid to traditional Commonwealth and French-speaking recipients.[24]

[22]Canada, *House of Commons Debates*, Nov. 14, 1963, pp. 4718–19.
[23]See the remarks of Senator Wayne Morse before the Committee on Foreign Relations of the US Senate in June 1963: "Canada . . . is not willing to participate at all in . . . economic aid to Latin America. . . . We must say to these other countries, 'We have to cut back until you come in and do your share.' " (*1963 US Senate Hearings*, p. 490).
[24]One of Canada's best-informed observers of Latin American affairs estimates

Perhaps Canada should have declined outright to enter Latin American aid, pleading that previous commitments made superior claims on her tiny resources. But since the Canadian government has already established formal co-operation with the Inter-American Development Bank, it may only be hoped that the new loan policy can be convincingly presented—with established export credit—as a small and stable token of Canada's necessarily limited concern for Latin America. Any more ambitious programme of grants, beyond perhaps minor and symbolic technical assistance, would in the long run undermine more valuable older relationships. And it might confront Ottawa with heightened inter-American demands for a financial and political solidarity Canada remains unready fully to embrace.

2. PROGRAMME PLANNING

These broad political priorities for recipients can be translated into units of actual aid only through a long and rather complex series of specialized options. Such decisions are reached through conventional techniques of interdepartmental committees, functioning under the chairmanship and co-ordination of the External Aid Office. In theory, this planning process follows three distinct stages: area and country allocation, country programming, and project planning, all mainly relevant to grant aid.

a. Area and country allocation

The first allocation fixes proportions of funds for major regional or functional programmes: Colombo Plan, SCAAP, Commonwealth Caribbean, French Africa, Commonwealth Technical Assistance, Commonwealth Scholarship and Fellowship Plan, and multilateral grants. When a maximum aid level is agreed with the cabinet, the budget is distributed to separate programmes according to the relative importance of each in Canadian foreign policy, recipients' absorptive capacity, pertinent

that "the total cost of membership in the OAS [a logical consequence of aid, and of which cost aid would be the major portion] could turn out to be a fairly uncomfortable commitment for Canada, especially considering its existing and prospective commitments for assistance in other parts of the world." John D. Harbron, *Canada and the Organization of American States* (Montreal, 1963), p. 29. Harbron fixes Canada's initial subscription to the Inter-American Development Bank alone as "perhaps on the order of thirty million dollars or more"; and while admitting that Canada's likely total aid contributions under the OAS are "difficult to assess," he suggests (p. 27) that "even if they were modest in the initial years, they would undoubtedly tend to grow over time."

international factors, and historical seniority. Before Ottawa announced
the general increase in aid in November 1963, it did not determine a
global level in advance, but reached one almost accidentally by the
accumulation of individual programme levels decided for particular
reasons. This somewhat haphazard method, attributable partly to the
need to meet staggered deadlines of pledging conferences, gave way
to a rationally planned global level only in the main estimates for
1964–65, which for the first time placed all bilateral grants except food
aid and disaster relief in a single non-lapsing consolidated fund.

TABLE 2.1

Regional or Functional Allocation of Canadian
Bilateral Grant Programmes*

Programme	Millions of dollars	
	1963–64	1964–65
Colombo Plan	41.5 (with food aid)	32.5 (minus food aid)
Special Commonwealth Africa Aid Program (SCAAP)	3.5	6.5
Commonwealth Caribbean Assistance Program	2.1	4.0
Commonwealth Scholarship and Fellowship Plan	1.0	1.2
Assistance for French-speaking African States	.3	4.0
Commonwealth Technical Assistance Program (since 1964–65, covered by contingency fund)	.02	.3
TOTAL	48.42	48.5

*SOURCE: External Aid Office.

In bilateral grant programmes a further allocation by country is made
virtually in concert with area allocation. Similar factors influence this
apportionment, though here recipients' disparate absorptive capacities
weigh most heavily. Political priorities also intervene, sometimes con-
flictingly: is it more astute to concentrate on large key countries with
high absorptive potential, in the hope that these "islands of development"
will keep afloat smaller and less mature neighbours? Or is it wiser to
invest Canada's limited resources in these smaller extremely backward
nations neglected, with perhaps disastrous political effect, by richer

donors? Canada's answer has varied in differing circumstances. In Asia and Africa, the first reasoning has dictated massive aid to India, Pakistan, Nigeria and Ghana, with lesser emphasis on Malaysia and Ceylon; in the Caribbean, the second argument has led, beginning in 1961, to special attention for smaller West Indian islands previously in the backwash of international aid.

Before 1964, country allocations were publicly defined only for major recipients in the Colombo Plan, and there for capital aid alone. In all other bilateral programmes (except for technical assistance, dispensed essentially on merit, feasibility and timing of requests), allocation took the form of confidential "earmarking" in Canada. This unilateral technique based provisional allocations for SCAAP and the Caribbean on private Ottawa estimates of principal recipients' absorptive potential, past aid use, and political significance. If part of an earmarked commitment appeared impossible to spend before the end of a fiscal year, sums likely to lapse were quietly transferred in mid-year to mature projects in other countries in the same area programme. This could easily occur when an unexpected bottleneck arose either in negotiation or execution of aid; and, since recipients had not been formally promised a fixed amount for a given year, transfer was not politically awkward. Yet however "flexible" this method might appear, it was clearly no more than a desperate and imperfect substitute for stable, officially committed country allocations—crucial for sound economic planning by recipients and for careful, unhurried expenditure by donors. The 1964–65 legislative consolidation of aid funds on a non-lapsing basis now allows Ottawa to make firm public commitments each year to major countries in all Canadian programmes, and so to improve both the efficiency and publicity of Canadian aid.

b. Country programming

Once the volume of a country's allocation is decided, Canadian administrators plan with recipients the country programme's content.[25] The central criterion in fixing programme content is economic need, as defined by priorities of the recipient's development plan. Need, to attract aid, must coincide with Canadian resources, be precisely described and of demonstrable urgency. It is of course a fluctuating factor, changing at each successive stage of development. Education and pre-investment

[25]"Programming" is defined by a leading American authority as "a continuous process from the first proposal of an idea to the design and acceptance of a project, and from the project agreement, the implementation orders, and the contracts to the arrival of technicians and equipment." John D. Montgomery, *The Politics of Foreign Aid* (New York, 1962), p. 169.

resource surveys have thus dominated African country programmes, and communications and transport equipment those of the Caribbean; while India and Pakistan, long eager for project aid in power generation and transmission, requested and received from about 1958 onwards greater industrial commodity aid. When the content of country programmes is determined in general outline by donor and recipient officials, the Canadian cabinet, if it approves, releases a brief description of the coming year's projects for several countries.

c. Project planning

A classical method of increasing the "impact" of aid combines different elements of capital aid, such as equipment, buildings and commodities, with technical assistance, in a single integrated scheme. Alternatively, it may combine various types of technical assistance, such as advisers, teachers and trainees. This concept is known as the "project approach," and its result a "composite project."

The project approach has for over a decade held a notable place in Canadian programme planning, and has been followed increasingly since about 1958. "We are prepared to bring . . . young doctors here," conceded the Director General of External Aid in 1961, ". . . but I would like to see this linked to something that Nigeria or Ghana are doing themselves. . . . We must ask 'where is your health centre, your medical clinic, your hospital?' "[26] Such questions, by seeking to relate isolated requests to coherent, more aid-worthy, comprehensive projects, have often helped Canada save her aid from ineffectual dissipation.

Composite projects have developed in three general types. First is the capital infrastructure project incidentally involving on-site training or higher training in Canada. At nearly all Canadian power projects, at Warsak, Shadiwal or Kundah, for instance, and on aerial surveys in Pakistan, Ceylon and Nigeria, local nationals have been trained in basic skills on the job and, both during and after operations, in advanced disciplines in Canada. Second is the project conceived from the beginning as integrated capital and technical assistance, but this time with transfer of skills emphasized at least as much as—and usually more than—productive exploitation of the capital facility itself. Thus the Canada-India Reactor, while producing small amounts of medical isotopes (not to speak of plutonium . . .), is essentially an instrument for training a scientific élite for a later series of nuclear power stations: a goal underlined by the sending of one hundred young Indian scientists to study, during the CIR's erection, at Chalk River in Ontario.

[26]*Standing Committee on External Affairs*, 1961, p. 158.

The Katubedde Institute of Practical Technology in Ceylon, the Ghana Trades Training Centre, and the Mangalore Regional Engineering College in India were built, equipped and partly staffed by Canada exclusively for teaching. Finally, the project approach is growingly evident in pure technical assistance, in which a team of Canadian advisers or teachers organizes a training project abroad, or a group of recipient nationals study together in Canada in a special course. In 1965 twenty-three French-speaking Canadian university staff were in Rwanda helping to establish a new national university, and three University of Toronto doctors were giving courses in anesthesia in Nigeria; since 1961, the University of British Columbia has been fulfilling a contract to assist, through long-term exchange of staff, a new School of Business Administration at the University of Malaya; and since 1959, Carleton University has been operating special courses for overseas students in public administration. In all these variations of project planning, each element of aid has been made more telling by being joined to a unified attack on a common problem.

But the project approach, while assuring a programme both stability and concentrated impact, is probably not a suitable guide for all Canadian aid. Even though small in volume, Canada's assistance requires, if it is to remain an agile instrument of foreign policy, a substantial margin of flexibility within its project-oriented framework. Sometimes aid must proceed more quickly than cautious project planning allows, to meet an unexpected political or economic change; sometimes a donor may simply wish to explore, through dispersed and diverse operations, a recipient's capacity for larger integrated aid. In both cases, the project approach needs tempering by a willingness to collect a variety of unrelated "scraps" from the numerous, and often worthy, requests always at Canada's disposal.

3. INITIATIVE

The planning process, by trying to match recipients' needs with donors' resources, raises the question of initiative in aid negotiation. Should proposals come from recipients only, from donors, or at different times from both? Sometimes, in the free give-and-take discussions of the programming stage, original initiatives are obscured; but more often they are clear, and carry political or economic implications affecting the value of the aid itself.

By publicly emphasized policy, Canada has always held that donors should remain essentially aloof from initiative. "I would hope," the

Director General advised the Standing Committee on May 26, 1961, "that, as far as possible, we can leave the initiative in the hands of the recipient countries."[27] This policy rests on several persuasive motives. Most important is a desire to strengthen recipients' official development plans, by respecting their priorities and even detailed project definitions. Donor proposal of unscheduled aid tends to disrupt rational planning and, if tolerated, can cause disjointed or chaotic progress. "To-day most of the developing countries have their own national development plans," reminded the Director General on December 12, 1963, ". . . closely examined by a consortium . . . and the projects within that development plan have been approved. . . . we have only financed projects . . . within that plan."[28]

Donor initiative also risks political resentments against what recipients frequently regard as doctrinaire and unsuited advice. Western concepts of financial orthodoxy, administrative efficiency and private incentive are usually implicit in donors' offers, which may therefore offend recipients whose culture and political philosophy find such notions inapplicable.[29] Or again, recipients may deplore a proffered gift if they suspect it hides a commercial or economic calculation in the donor's exclusive interest. Finally, for a practical reason, donor initiative is hazardous because it supposes a knowledge of recipients' economic and political problems at least as intimate as that of recipients themselves. Canadian field administrators on two-year postings abroad can rarely arrive at such deep understanding during their mission—especially when, as now, they have extra duties of political reporting or trade promotion.

In reality, however, the simple rule of recipient initiative does not fit by any means all patterns of negotiation. There are, in both capital and technical assistance planning, numerous situations favouring an enterprising, indeed leading, role for donors.

Donor initiative in capital aid, for instance, is sometimes defensible when a recipient either has no plan at all, or an incoherent or unrealistic one; it is often necessary to help new recipients formulate project

---

[27]*Ibid.*, p. 165.
[28]*Ibid.*, 1963, p. 67.
[29]The Secretary of State for External Affairs, Mr. Green, recognized this problem when he told the Standing Committee in 1960 that "the one thing these [Asian] leaders are conscious of is what they think should be done to improve their own countries. They are not often asking for suggestions from us as to how we think they should develop their countries: they have their own views and we try to fall in with those views, provided they make sense." *Ibid.*, 1960, p. 81.

requests that correspond with Canadian resources; feasibility studies are recommended not only to verify recipients' proposals but eventually to develop new, more appropriate projects (about 3 per cent of Canada's capital grant aid is spent on feasibility studies); or general surveys of a recipient's needs may be urged by donors to allow a concerted approach to gaps in development: in July 1961 a tripartite Canadian, British and American mission toured the smaller West Indian islands to define and co-ordinate uncharted aid requirements. Further, when recipients' aid-worthy project lists are formally approved by international consortia, donors can, to suit their own domestic economic needs, bid for specific projects not formally or by priority offered to another donor.

In technical assistance, a common and readily accepted type of donor initiative is that wielded by foreign advisers sent expressly to analyse problems and recommend solutions. Initiative here is in fact the principal function of the adviser, and its imaginative (though informed and realistic) exercise is indeed a measure of his success. Most of Canada's integrated field training projects, like Katubedde and Mangalore, have grown in this way. Another standard technique is the "general offer" system of training or education. Approved and encouraged in particular under the Colombo Plan—whose Bureau often distributes offer announcements—this method allows donors to open at their own con-venience special training facilities for overseas visitors. Canada first made such offers in 1959, for group courses in community and town planning, seed improvement, public administration, and co-operatives. In some of these courses, candidates were hastily chosen because advance notice by Canada was too short; but in the main, instruction proved better adapted to recipients' needs than many courses designed purely for Canadian students.

From all this it emerges that aid negotiation inevitably invites donor and recipient to view initiative as flexible and reciprocal. Most aid relationships, especially within the Commonwealth, mature into a certain easy informality and confidence that permit initiative to be blurred, or at least underplayed. The only firm ground rule demands that donors' initiatives be based on close scrutiny of recipients' published plans of development. Within this limit donors can, and sometimes must, point to neglected but happy coincidences of their own resources and recipients' needs. It is hardly true, as some cynics would have it, that "if they know what they want and how to ask for it, they don't need it;" but in a broad and unpatronizing sense, tactful, timely donor initiative is a form of aid itself.

4. INTERNATIONAL CO-ORDINATION OF AID

None of the above problems can be envisaged in isolation from a global aid effort that year by year dwarfs the scope and dominates the use of Canada's aid. In earlier post-Korea days, national aid programmes, few in number and recipients, could attack their several goals with little co-operation or even consultation among donors. Each programme was at bottom experimental, and each experiment so novel and distinctive that common problems were scarcely visible. But as West European and Japanese prosperity flowered from the ashes of war and whole continents burst forth in indigent freedom, aid took on a perplexing and cumbersome magnitude. "All these factors," the Director General explained to a conference of the Canadian National Commission for UNESCO in March 1963, "—an increase in the number of recipient countries, a growing number of donor countries, and expanding levels of total assistance—made clear the need for international co-ordination so that overlapping of efforts, duplication of programmes and wastage could be avoided."[30]

Although co-ordinating machinery multiplied spectacularly in the early 1960's, some of its methods were forged more than a decade before. These methods were at first those of the United Nations and the Colombo Plan; later they were strengthened by more formal and specialized techniques of the World Bank, the Organization for Economic Co-operation and Development, and the Inter-American Development Bank.

a. The United Nations
Since the UN began its aid programmes shortly after the War, it has carried on with Canadian aid authorities a day-to-day association that both sides insist is of extraordinary mutual profit. Canada and the UN aid agencies co-operate mainly in technical assistance activities, Ottawa lending its services to arrange UN training programmes in Canada and to recruit Canadian advisers for UN service abroad. Canada benefits, through close personal contact of its officials with colleagues in New York, from the UN's incomparable experience in all aspects of aid administration, as well as from public and confidential UN reports. Since 1960, co-operation has extended to capital aid; about once a

[30]H. O. Moran, "New Purposes and Methods of International Assistance," *Dialogue 1963* (Ottawa), p. 64.

month, the UN Special Fund forwards its internal reports on pending and unfinished projects to the External Aid Office, which reciprocates at suitable intervals. This constant exchange of documents, and daily consultation by letter and telephone not only prevent duplication of project review, but also foster a flow of technical information of the utmost value in current operations.

b. The Colombo Plan

The Colombo Plan is perhaps the best known and least understood of Canada's co-operative associations. Despite its title, the Plan does no planning at all, and does not, as many think, "channel aid through Colombo." It is perhaps best described as a form of consultative bilateralism, a loose and pragmatic sharing of ideas and information by nations giving or receiving aid in a series of distinct, two-sided relationships. Like many British-inspired institutions, the Colombo Plan counts more on atmosphere than on rigid and rational machinery. "In no time at all," Andrew Shonfield writes, ". . . the British were able to create something of the atmosphere of a club. . . . There is here a sense of active participation on the part of the underdeveloped countries, who sit round the same table with . . . the donor nations . . . as equals."[31]

The major agency of high-level contact is the annual meeting of the Colombo Plan Consultative Committee. Held each year in a different member capital, this meeting usually assembles top aid officials for about two weeks, the last three or four days of which are distinguished by the presence of ministers not required by more pressing business. The officials submit summaries of their country's progress in giving and/or receiving, to be included in a thick and uncritical public report. When this important work is done, the ministers—if present—each make a speech commending their own country and the others for their efforts, and, if possible, announcing some increase in their nation's aid. (In November 1963, the Ottawa cabinet managed the extraordinarily sensitive feat of announcing its aid increase the day *after* the Director General made Canada's ministerial speech in Bangkok.) The consultative value of these formal proceedings, one Canadian official confided succinctly in August 1963, is "not worth a damn." But the private bilateral meetings in the wings of the conference do make possible a good deal of concrete, if not detailed, negotiation; and it is as a pretext for such encounters, rather than as a forum of supposed multilateral co-ordination, that the meetings are justifiable.

At lower levels, consultation is assured by two agencies situated in

[31]Andrew Shonfield, *The Attack on World Poverty* (London, 1960), p. 185.

Colombo itself. The Colombo Plan Bureau is a small clearing-house for common publicity and statistics, which it receives from member governments and publishes monthly without critical comment. Supervising the budget and policies of the Bureau is a Council for Technical Co-operation, composed of members' diplomatic representatives accredited to Ceylon. Apart from circulating general offers of training and defining common questionnaires for technical assistance requests, the co-ordinating role of these agencies is marginal.

c. The World Bank
The International Bank for Reconstruction and Development (IBRD or "World Bank") has in recent years placed its unparalleled aid experience behind committees of donors known as "consortia" and "consultative groups." Each type aims to co-ordinate levels and quality of aid to specific regions, though through slightly different methods and with varying ambitions.

As of April 1965 the Bank had organized three consortia (for India, Pakistan and the Indus Basin—the latter group, interested in a specific project, is usually called a "Club"), all of which included Canada as well as other major donors. On the basis of the Bank's expert assessments of recipients' development plans (a service not required in the Indus Basin Club), donors pledge both grants and credits under two-year commitments. Excluding food aid, these commitments are related to projects identified by the Bank and the consortia themselves as significant contributions to economic development. Following submission to the Bank of each recipient's development plans for the coming commitment period, a first meeting is held at which the Bank advises donors and recipients of its criticisms. Out of ensuing discussions a consensus evolves on projects or other aid that consortium members may usefully support. Later a pledging conference is held, at which donors try to achieve—usually with limited success—a fair sharing of the aid burden. The whole process, suggested a Canadian participant during an interview in December 1963, is "one of the most useful forms of co-ordination there is: it guarantees that Canadian aid is of high development priority, and stops both recipients and Canadians from using aid for secondary or propaganda aims."

The Bank's consultative groups are similar in principle to the consortia, but involve no pledging and are more flexible in concept. Also as of early 1965 the Bank had formed four of these groups, for Nigeria, Sudan, Colombia and Tunisia. Canada, as a Bank member, has the right to attend any of these groups' meetings, but in practice is active mainly in the Nigerian and Colombian groups. Such committees are limited to recipients having acceptable development plans; and, with the aim of raising aid levels through better co-ordination, they serve primarily to exchange economic information between donors and recipients, and confidential assessments of projects and plans among donors. They also benefit all concerned by affording access within a common framework to the advice and worldwide experience of the Bank's own professional development experts.

d. The OECD Development Assistance Committee

Part of the newly organized OECD's mandate in 1960 was creation of a Development Assistance Committee (DAC—initially the Development Assistance Group or DAG) "to consult on methods . . . for expanding and improving the flow of long-term funds and other development assistance"[32] to developing countries. In particular, DAC hopes to secure "some harmonisation of aid efforts and policies," underlining increasingly the importance of quality as well as volume of aid. Through three distinct but interlocking techniques, DAC has become undoubtedly the central and decisive organ of Western aid co-ordination.

The heart of DAC's co-ordinating task is the Annual Aid Review. Based largely on tested OEEC and OECD methods of "confrontation," the Review groups all significant Western donors in a series of searching interrogations on policies, aid levels, administration and operations. Early in each year the DAC secretariat in Paris circulates a detailed questionnaire to members asking information and views on the volume, types, terms and conditions of aid given. Written replies, with critical comments by secretariat experts, are then circulated to members for preliminary study. In May or June, a high-level meeting is held in Paris, during which each donor submits to a session of courteous, though quite unrestrained, questioning by its colleagues—three of whom are expressly appointed to lead the probe. The Director General of External Aid habitually conducts Canada's formal defence, while his close collaborators remain to question other members. By all reports, these highly confidential meetings are testing, substantive and utterly frank. "While questioning is severe," assured a Canadian official in December 1963, "it is not an unpleasant experience unless you're really quite naughty." Formal niceties are respected, he added, but the moving force of the confrontation is "shame tactics"—not through bitter and overt criticism, but through pointed questions and all the arsenal of unspoken displeasure of which professional diplomats hold the secret. Following the

[32]*Development Assistance Efforts and Policies: 1963 Review*, p. 4.

formal meetings the DAC Chairman produces a report, usually one of the most instructive and realistic documents available on current aid.

Parallel to the Annual Review are a number of Working Groups on common problems such as "terms and conditions of aid," "tied aid," and "technical assistance." Finally, Regional Co-ordinating Groups of great flexibility have been created to study special difficulties of individual countries or regions, such as East Africa, Thailand and Latin America. These groups "are not necessarily concerned with getting together additional financial contributions. They might concentrate on making sure that existing aid contributions are dovetailed properly, ensuring that technical assistance is adequate to back up financial help or on encouraging participation by foreign private enterprise."[33]

e. The Inter-American Development Bank

Thirteen months after Mr. Martin announced Canada's "soft loan" programme, Ottawa signed the agreement then foreseen with the Inter-American Development Bank (IDB). This arrangement enables Canada to co-operate with the Bank in financial and administrative matters without accepting the obligations—including a subscription—of formal membership.

In brief, Canada delegates to the Bank nearly all routine planning and negotiation, while retaining ultimate control of funds. Ottawa exerts its control by consultation with the Bank at every stage of project development, and through its right to approve, reject or modify final contracts. The Bank, explained the press release announcing the understanding on December 4, 1964, has "the primary responsibility for selecting and processing loan projects and for establishing the terms and conditions for the loans in accordance with the provisions of the agreement. . . ."

This arrangement offers Canada convincing advantages. To begin, at no expense to Canada, it opens to Ottawa a unique fund of economic, administrative and political expertise on Latin America. This allows Canada efficiently to allocate her relatively small yearly contribution of $10,000,000 to projects of high continental priority. Then, indirect negotiation of contracts by a mainly Latin American staff spares Canada the political dangers of dealing with recipients notoriously resentful of bilateral aid relationships. Finally, the Bank serves as a buffer between the External Aid Office and Canadian business firms seeking to develop competing projects. Against these benefits, of course, must be placed a possible loss in specific publicity for Canada as a donor.

[33]*Ibid.*, p. 46.

In the first months after its signature, the agreement seemed to promise happy results. By April 1965, Canadian administrators believed that they and the Bank staff had established a "good working relationship;" after four months, they were close to agreement on four loan contracts absorbing almost the entire first year's allocation. The arrangement will be worthy of interest not only for this technical success; but because, over the years, it will give the measure of Canada's ability to co-operate with Latin America without necessarily submitting to the burdens and pressures of the inter-American system.

In the broad perspective of international aid since the War, the trend toward co-ordination of effort is striking. Recent reports of established co-ordinating groups, moreover, confirm that this sensible and overdue discipline will spread much deeper to include formal co-operation in field administration and on projects themselves. It is perfectly clear, from further review of Canadian administrative and operational procedures, that intensified co-ordination at all levels is the only attainable solution for many, if not most, of Canada's problems as an independent donor.

III. The Rationale of Selection

An effective aid programme grows primarily from wisely chosen operations. "No amount of efficiency at the later stages," warned the 1963
DAC *Review*, "can make up for a fundamentally wrong choice of aid-
financed project or activity."[1] As the heart of applied policy, this selection process translates donors' objectives into action; consequently,
more than any other principles of policy, the criteria guiding the choice
of activities decide the ultimate quality and impact of aid.

Selection of Canadian aid activities appears to rest on five major
factors, usually considered in the following order: Canadian content;
contribution to the recipient's economic development; recipient's absorptive capacity; political effect; and Canadian export potential.[2] Since each
activity and each recipient economy is in some ways unique, this list
is by no means immutable; yet it does define questions that must be
asked, sooner or later, of almost every aid proposal.

1. CANADIAN CONTENT

Whatever the type of aid requested, the first, and generally absolute,
condition of Canadian acceptance is Canada's ability to furnish it. "On
capital projects," the Director General assured the Standing Committee
on May 31, 1961, "certain criteria are applied to make certain they are
within Canadian capabilities. From the beginning of the Colombo Plan

---

[1]*Development Assistance Efforts and Policies: 1963 Review*, Paris, p. 59.
[2]For obvious reasons, these criteria apply only to bilateral grants and "soft"
loans. Under bilateral export credit on conventional commercial terms, only tied
procurement is an indispensable condition; and grants or loans to multilateral
agencies usually escape donors' direct control altogether.

it has been the policy to supply only commodities which are produced in Canada. In the technical assistance field . . . it has been the practice to send out as experts only Canadians, and in our training programmes to place trainees only in Canadian . . . institutions."[3] "Our programs continue," he confirmed to the same committee on December 12, 1963, "to operate on the basis of procurement in Canada."[4] Traditionally, Ottawa has estimated the proportion of its bilateral grant funds actually spent on Canadian purchases at some 95 per cent.[5]

For many years, it has been fashionable to decry such "tied" aid as somehow less unselfish and valuable than grants or loans that recipients may use without restriction as to source of procurement. This argument is understandably popular with those countries which, while having no or small aid programmes of their own, stand to increase their exports through untying of other countries' aid. But it also draws currency from persuasive technical criticisms which display specific "circumstances where aid tying is harmful. It may prevent the buyers," complained the 1963 DAC *Review*, "from buying at the best price or may cause delays in the execution of projects. In the case of loans, the effects of higher prices will continue to be reflected in higher capital and interest payments. Imports of lower priority may be preferred because they can be readily supplied by the donor country."[6] Similar thinking led in July 1960 to the "Bonn agreement," which committed major donors, in a marvellously ambivalent exhortation, to "move toward untied aid,

[3]*Standing Committee on External Affairs*, 1961, p. 174.
[4]*Ibid.*, 1963, p. 52.
[5]*Standing Committee on External Affairs*, 1956, p. 189. This estimate may be slightly high. It is true that commodity aid, representing 45 per cent of the total bilateral grant programme between 1950 and 1963, is invariably bought in Canada. But project aid and technical assistance, by nature complex, are less easily "tied" to national sources. Administrators considering ostensibly Canadian-made capital equipment can rarely assess with accuracy the full extent of its foreign-made components; and in practice, they cannot measure the sums Canadian contractors spend abroad privately to buy construction machinery. Overseas transportation costs, while initially paid to Canadian agents, mainly benefit foreign carriers, which alone maintain routes to Africa and South Asia; and a substantial portion of advisers' salaries always remains in host countries to supplement local allowances. These exceptions probably reduce the global Canadian content of Canada's bilateral grant aid to a level of 85 or 90 per cent. Still, while distinctly below official estimates, even these figures are high enough to illustrate that Canada's policy of domestic procurement is intentional and, as far as technically possible, rigorous.
   The External Aid Office applies a "rule-of-thumb" requiring that at least 80 per cent of each purchase be of Canadian origin. "If a bid falls below that," explained an EAO officer in January 1964, "we look at it pretty closely before going any further."
[6]*Development Assistance Efforts and Policies: 1963 Review*, p. 37.

having regard among other factors to their balance of payments situation and the international payments position."[7]

For reasons known to every donor, however, the crusade for untied aid has failed, and is unlikely soon to achieve meaningful success. Most compelling is the argument that tied aid—by providing domestic employment—induces public opinion in donor countries to support a much higher level of aid than otherwise acceptable. Spending aid funds at home also ensures tighter administrative control: Canadian aid is not converted by recipient countries into "concubines and . . . Cadillac cars," the Director General promised the Standing Committee on December 12, 1963, "because . . . our moneys are used solely to provide Canadian goods and services."[8] Further, untied aid funds subsidize the exports of trading rivals frequently offering less generous aid. Why should Canadians, for instance, finance competing German or Japanese products—and thereby aggravate the problems of Canada's own balance of payments? If Germany and Japan produce an item more cheaply, should not the aid request be directed to them, not to Canada? Indeed, since there are now more donors offering more varieties of aid, does not the whole case for tied aid lose much of its essential relevance?

To this general defence of tied aid may be added distinctively Canadian justifications. Canada's aid is not tied to a limited range of projects or activities (excepting Colombo Plan wheat quotas, abandoned in 1964), but only to procurement in Canada. Recipients thus enjoy a wide freedom of choice allowing them to invest their allocations flexibly, and therefore efficiently. In any case, many development imports can be purchased most economically in Canada: Canadian prices for power generation equipment and transport aircraft are at least competitive; and for some industrial commodities such as nickel, asbestos and aluminum, they largely determine world prices. Other Canadian prices which are high, moreover, are lowered by careful pre-selection study of costs and quality, and by purchasing on tender. Finally, the "Buy Canadian" policy itself leaves a reasonable margin for off-shore purchase of equipment "not made in Canada but nevertheless essential to the completion of a project."[9] Diesel motors for the Bombay State Transport project, for instance, a trawler for the Ceylon fisheries project, and control equipment for several power stations were bought in the United States or Europe.

[7]*Ibid.*, p. 36.
[8]*Standing Committee on External Affairs*, 1963, p. 59. A gallant inference . . .
[9]*Ibid.*, 1956, p. 189. The witness is the Colombo Plan Administrator.

In this light, Canada's tied aid policy seems less vicious than its detractors would suggest. In principle, no doubt, it imposes burdens on both the planning and administration of aid; and in practice, particularly during times of heavy Canadian unemployment, Ottawa has applied it with somewhat narrow zeal. But few can dispute that it represents, given Canada's chronic economic problems and the reluctance of other donors to untie procurement, a realistic and even inevitable condition of aid. The policy is not ideal; but it is a measured definition of the politically possible.

2. CONTRIBUTION TO ECONOMIC DEVELOPMENT

A second criterion judges the benefits that a proposed aid activity may confer on the recipient's economy. Presumably the long-range economic aim of aid is to eliminate the underlying need for aid; if aid is seen as merely a perennial and ever growing welfare programme, shunning goals of basic self-sufficiency and lasting improvement in productivity, its impact will surely diminish with each increase in the recipient's population. "Whether this increase," reminded the Colombo Plan Council's Report for 1959–60, "should be counted as additional pairs of hands to produce new wealth or merely as mouths to be fed and bodies to be kept alive depends upon the opportunities now being opened up for new development. . . ."[10]

In assessing a proposal's likely stimulus to economic growth, Canadian planners normally consider its priority in the recipient's plan for development, and its so-called "multiplier effect" as a contribution expanding beyond the immediate time and place of transfer.

Realistic development plans grant highest priority to aid directly assisting self-sustaining economic progress, both industrial and agricultural. "Infrastructure" projects, which lay the indispensable groundwork for secondary development, are the backbone of these plans, and cover such cardinal fields as power, irrigation, transport, communications, heavy industry, mining, agriculture and rural development. Social or welfare services, as planners realized their essentially palliative role when not tightly linked to basic economic growth, have been increasingly downgraded: allocations to social services in the public sector of the

[10]*Technical Co-operation under the Colombo Plan: Report for 1959–60 by the Council for Technical Co-operation in South and South-East Asia* (Colombo, 1960), p. 8. Hereafter cited as *1959–60 Colombo Plan Council Report*.

first three Indian Five Year Plans have been successively 32, 23, and 14 per cent[11]; and in Pakistan's three Five Year Plans, allocations for roughly equivalent services fell from 31 to 28 to 21 per cent.[12]

Although difficult to prove from published figures, it is probably true that Canada defines "economic development" rather more strictly than most large donors. In general, Canada believes that development should be pursued principally through activities making a substantial contribution to self-perpetuating economic progress; ancillary welfare and current consumer aid are assigned marginal or even doubtful value.

Of course, Canada has given ample and varied aid in education, health and nutrition—activities economically defensible only in the uncertain measure that an educated, healthy and well-fed population is necessary for economic growth. But Canada's emphasis, with few notable exceptions, has been on deep and permanent development. "We have tried," explained the Colombo Plan Administrator in 1957, "to enter into projects of a fundamental nature. . . . we are dealing with very poor agricultural countries. . . . The need is to diversify their economies, to provide employment and to process their agricultural output and to enable them to exploit their natural wealth."[13]

The expression "multiplier effect" describes the inherent capacity of an aid activity for producing benefits beyond its initial purpose. International agencies constantly remind donors that aid-generated growth must be not only basic, but self-perpetuating. And Western donors themselves increasingly emphasize, as the Director General of External Aid pointed out in March 1963, that aid should "build stable societies and economies capable of self-sustained growth."[14] Rapid achievement of this goal plainly demands that aid contain a built-in catalyst to development.

The choice of high-priority infrastructure activities itself guarantees some degree of extended impact. But serious assessment of a proposal's "multiplier effect" requires expert, imaginative review of its background and potential. In judging capital aid requests, for example, Canadian planners have asked whether a projected power plant would stimulate the growth of facilities for agricultural or industrial production; whether

[11]I. Sundaram, *A Critical Analysis of the Third Five-Year Plan* (Delhi, 1960), p. 17.

[12]Government of Pakistan Planning Commission, *Outline of the Third Five-Year Plan* (Karachi, Aug., 1964), p. 6.

[13]*Statements and Speeches*, no. 57/29, p. 4.

[14]H. O. Moran, "New Purposes and Methods of International Assistance," *Dialogue 1963* (Ottawa), p. 64.

trade expansion was likely to result from the supply of locomotives or railway ties; whether resource surveys might point to new crops and industries; or whether a fishing trade assisted through gifts of trawlers, small-boat motors and refrigeration plants might open new, specialized foreign markets.

Predicting the long-range usefulness of technical assistance is more hazardous; the possible ramifications of each of many thousand human experiences are innumerable. This complexity of estimating the multiplier effect is sharply underlined by standard questions recommended in the 1959–60 Report of the Colombo Plan Council for Technical Co-operation:

Will the training given to this trainee enable him to raise productivity on a lasting basis in his particular field? Will he be able to pass on his knowledge or skill to others on his return and so increase the number and efficiency of local people productively employed? Will the services of the expert lead to the finding of new resources (not forgetting human resources) or to greater production from existing resources? Will the extra skill which he can be expected to bring with him continue to exist and to grow after he has left? Is the equipment being requested merely to do a job of production, or will it lead to the acquisition of new knowledge and new ideas by the people who will use it so that they can contribute more effectively to economic growth?[15]

All these questions are well known to Canadian administrators. "We try to get key people," said the Colombo Plan Administrator in 1957, "who can return to their various countries and teach others what they have learned. In addition, we send out Canadian experts to set up training centres and to try to solve problems in the area itself."[16] After planting seeds of new knowledge and kindling a spirit of enquiry in strategically placed individuals, planners then rely on the recipients' own continuing initiative to enlarge aid beyond the scope of the original technical mission.

Acceptance of these principles is not enough, however, to ensure their careful application. Doubtless the standards of development priority and multiplier effect guide closely Canadian review of capital aid which, by its high cost and reasonably predictable economic consequences, makes such study both worthwhile and feasible. But lack of trained staff and the pressure of burgeoning programmes have rarely allowed adequate scrutiny of technical assistance proposals. Instead of being probed individually, these requests are increasingly subject to a cursory

[15]*1959–60 Colombo Plan Council Report*, p. 65.
[16]*Statements and Speeches*, no. 57/29, p. 4.

processing in batches. This administrative handicap to a sound policy must soon limit either the quality or the expansion of Canada's technical assistance.

3. RECIPIENTS' ABSORPTIVE CAPACITY

Experienced donor agencies consistently emphasize that external aid can be fully useful only when recipients' economies are structurally and psychologically prepared to exploit it. Canada has accepted this view both by linking its aid with existing indigenous efforts and, where possible, by making aid conditional on such efforts. This policy aims to foster initiative and self-help in recipients, and sees the proper function of aid not as a permanent crutch, but as a temporary and highly selective stimulus. "All our aid is trying to do," stressed the Colombo Plan Administrator at the very beginning of Canada's programme, "is to help these people to help themselves."[17]

Two basic questions must be asked in assessing a recipient's capacity to absorb aid. Is the recipient technically, financially and administratively equipped to extract lasting benefit from the aid? And if it is so equipped, are interested authorities at all levels sensitive to the need for aid and determined to ensure the aid's effective use?

Regrettably, a material inability to use aid often plagues those very nations needing it most acutely. "The overriding problem," complained the UN *Technical Assistance Newsletter* of June–July 1961, " has been to strike a balance between what Africa needs . . . and what it can absorb."[18] This physical obstacle, which is present to some degree in all developing nations, obliges donors to study in detail the support that recipients can give to each requested aid activity.

The evaluation of recipients' absorptive capacity naturally calls upon different standards for various forms of aid. Food aid and industrial commodities are customarily given on evidence of ability to pay international freight charges, and of adequate storage and distribution facilities. Industrial commodities, having few primary consumers and a fairly measurable end-use, present relatively simple options: it is immediately clear, for instance, whether a recipient has productive machinery suitable for transforming aluminum, asbestos or nickel; even levels of production are roughly predictable. Food aid, on the other hand, cannot be traced as easily in its likely distribution, and may

17*Ibid.*, no. 52/52, p. 9.
18"Problems in the Giving," in vol. 2, no. 3, p. 16.

sometimes have to be granted or refused on unavoidably shallow investigation. Technical assistance requests are usually still less severely tested. This is partly because technical assistance is often the obvious key to building a general absorptive capacity; but it also reflects again the profound inadequacy of Canada's field administration: when the annual movement of advisers and trainees is measured in thousands, field administrators find review of individual cases all but impossible.

But it is capital project aid which, by its usual high cost and complexity, best lends itself to detailed requirements of recipient support. Canadian planners examine, for example, whether recipient budgets provide for payment of local currency costs—often, as at Warsak and Trombay, as much as half of total project costs; whether the recipient can mobilize technical staff and equipment to help execute the project and to sustain it after completion; and whether the local administration appears serious and efficient enough to expedite construction, not hamper it through lethargy or incompetence. Budgetary and technical demands are indeed formal conditions of most project agreements; the administrative requirement, while tactfully unexpressed, is shown by experience to be no less necessary.

Clearly, no condition is more central to effective use of aid than the physical ability of recipients to absorb aid. It is this criterion alone, as Professor Nathan Keyfitz wisely observes, that allows aid policy to be rational by allowing it to be finite in its goals. To identify the most able recipients, he suggests, those close to "take-off" into self-sustaining development, and "to study their constitutions to find what ingredients which can be added by donor resources will bring them to the critical point, ought to be the pivot of all thought on foreign aid."[19]

Few donors dispute the hoary maxim of sociologists that sound philanthropy responds only to "felt needs." Canada heeds this principle first by leaving nearly all initiative in aid negotiation to recipients; but more important, she insists on proof that sponsors of an aid request understand their proposal clearly and intend to support its fulfilment with resolution.

It is widely agreed that aid can play its full part only if underpinned by improved economic, fiscal and social policies within recipient countries themselves. Indeed, aid not tied to promise of reform may even, by dulling incentive to urgent change, defeat its whole purpose as a stimulant of, not a substitute for, domestic effort. Yet at this level of recipients' general development policy, Canada has rarely, if ever,

[19]Nathan Keyfitz, "Foreign Aid Can Be Rational," *International Journal*, vol. 17, no. 3 (Summer, 1962), p. 241.

unilaterally and explicitly made her aid conditional on large-scale reforms of self-help. Such demands are never practical for smaller donors, whose slim bait, in a world of multiple and wealthy aid sources, is doomed to be ineffectual unless joined to the more persuasive potential of an international consortium. Not even the richest donors, as American setbacks in the Latin American Alliance for Progress spectacularly prove, seem able to exact basic reforms without unacceptable political risks or resentment. Plainly, Canada's only realistic high-level policy can be to limit her aid to countries well advanced in self-help, and to encourage reformist pressures through the powerful collective action of international donor groups.

At the less controversial level of individual requests, however, Canada can and does demand evidence of local interest on grounds essentially technical. Without necessarily publicizing its conclusions, Canada may wish to determine, for example, whether a proposed irrigation scheme is welcomed by local officials and villagers; whether ministers are likely to forward a commodity shipment to designated factories or a government-protected black market; whether scientists genuinely plan to use a piece of abstruse equipment or want it merely to impress foreign colleagues; whether an adviser or teacher is actively desired by his future collaborators, who must, in addition, be open to reasonable advice from him; and whether a trainee views a Canadian tour as a chance for valuable study, a paid holiday, or an eventual permanent escape from his less affluent homeland. In every case, it must be asked whether the request stems from a specific need, or merely from a general willingness to take anything that is "free"—a kind of "pet-crow" complex.

Assessing local intentions regarding proposed capital projects is usually part of a standard economic and technical feasibility study by short-term Canadian advisers.[20] These painstaking and deeply instruc-

[20]The place of these studies in Canada's general selection procedure was explained by the Director General on May 26, 1961, in these terms:

". . . what factors influence our decision? One of the first tests we apply, if it is a capital project, is whether it is within the capabilities of Canadian engineering consultants and Canadian construction firms. If we are satisfied on that point, we then carry out investigations to see whether the equipment and materials that will be needed are available in Canada. If we are satisfied on both counts, we then apply the normal economic and other considerations to determine whether the project fits into the economic development plans of the recipient country. The next step is to employ a Canadian engineer to go out and make a feasibility study. If, on his return, his report is favourable, and if his estimate of the cost is within our financial limitations, or at least within the financial allocation being made to the country, the government then decides to award the contract to a Canadian construction or engineering firm, depending on the type of services required."

tive on-site surveys are obviously, for both political and technical reasons, not suited to commodity requests. But some adaptation of on-site review to technical assistance requests seems wise, and in a continuously expanding programme, imperative, if the human aspects of requests are to be intelligibly appraised. Once more, widespread reform of Canada's field administration appears the key to high-quality, rationally controlled aid. The costs of new staff and searching procedures are very high; it can be shown, however, that in terms of efficient expenditure and recipients' esteem, they would be quickly and generously repaid.[21]

4. POLITICAL EFFECT

In selecting aid activities, donors pursue two main kinds of political goals. They may seek to influence directly an international situation or a recipient's behaviour; or they may try to create, through favourable publicity, a political climate which will strengthen indirectly their influence on a recipient's policies.

Canada has generally refrained from using aid for direct intervention in recipients' affairs. The inconclusive results of her few discreet attempts at such action suggest indeed that aid is rarely a reliable instrument for promoting well-defined political change. Canada's aid under the Indus Waters settlement, even linked to much larger consortium aid, did not diminish Indo-Pakistani tension more than momentarily; her aerial survey of the Mekong Basin, again associated with a multilateral effort, did not open to the mutually hostile beneficiaries a new era of cordial co-operation; and her two inter-island passenger vessels were impotent to salvage a disintegrating West Indian Federation.

The pursuit of limited Cold War objectives through Canadian aid has been still more prudent. In the very few projects where such goals may be even suspected, the Cold War motive is clearly subordinate to plausible, if not indisputable, economic criteria. The Umtru hydroelectric and irrigation scheme in Assam, for instance, was assisted by Canada partly because, said the Colombo Plan Administrator in 1954, "China has recently taken over Tibet, and if you look at the map you

---

(*Standing Committee on External Affairs*, 1961, p. 160). "These preliminary surveys are often fundamental," he added on December 12, 1963, "and it is perhaps not understood generally by the public that they are routine on every large capital project." (*Ibid.*, 1963, p. 67).

[21]See chap. v for certain proposals to reform Canada's field administration.

will see that Tibet and Assam have a common border."[22] Yet besides serving as a politically valuable "pork-barrel" project for the Indian government in a region of uncertain national loyalty, Umtru was a project of high development priority, worthy of Canadian support on technical grounds alone. Likewise, the gift of the Canada-India Reactor appears to have been partly inspired by an earlier Soviet offer to build an atomic research pile in India. "This is one of those cases," assured the Administrator in 1956, "where we got in first."[23] But anti-communist "one-up-manship" could never have sufficed to justify this highly intricate $15,000,000 project. The reactor was built above all because it gave hope for a long-term solution to India's problems of power generation and because India had the technical manpower to operate it.

The goal of indirect influence through aid publicity is also secondary to economic standards in Canadian choice of activities; but it is pursued with far less reticence. Canada, like most donors, believes that the presence of aid missions in a country affords a practical opportunity to study and shape the recipient's policies. "In countries where we have . . . aid programs," stressed the Director General in 1963, ". . . they are very anxious to carry their problems to the Canadian representative. . . . The right Canadian in a developing country can acquire a position of tremendous influence; he can virtually become an *ex officio* member of their cabinet."[24] Consequently, it is reasoned, if aid can lead to such an advantage, a donor's political influence can be enhanced by choosing aid activities most likely to capture the recipient government's attention.

Impressing governments, even those least responsive to public opinion, means impressing not only officials, but the population at large. As a result, donors often prefer to give so-called "photogenic" aid, large, technically advanced infrastructure projects that serve as both monuments to Canadian generosity and symbols of the recipient's progress. "Such projects as Warsak," affirmed an External Affairs witness before the Standing Committee in 1958, "and the atomic reactor . . . near Bombay, are very startling examples of aid by the West; and people of those countries when they have visitors from the USSR and Communist China I think make a point of showing their visitors these substantial projects. I leave you to imagine the reaction of

[22]*Standing Committee on External Affairs*, 1954, p. 218.
[23]*Ibid.*, p. 207. The suggestion of an anti-communist motive in Canada's acceptance of the CIR was rejected in November 1963 by a high official of Atomic Energy of Canada Limited. This denial cannot, of course, cover the cabinet which, on the Administrator's cryptic but suggestive public evidence, was almost certainly conscious of gaining some Cold War advantage.
[24]*Ibid.*, 1963, p. 59.

say, Chou En-lai, to the atomic reactor given to an underdeveloped country by a country such as Canada."[25] The same political attraction for both donor and recipients is present in a number of Canadian educational projects: the Katubedde Institute of Practical Technology in Ceylon, the Trades Training Centre in Ghana, and the Canada Hall university residence in Trinidad are models of the permanent "prestige" project, and are all the more influential because they will shelter over many years part of the recipients' future technical and administrative élite.[26]

But this alertness to opportunities for publicity has never been an overriding purpose of Canadian policy. Canada has sometimes rejected tempting "political" projects either because they lacked reasonable economic justification or because their urgency did not allow time for a pondered decision. When pressed by Pakistan's new revolutionary régime in October 1958 to supply immediately a pre-stressed concrete plant for a showpiece refugee settlement at Korangi Town, near Karachi, Canada agreed only to start a small pilot plant, insisting on judging the full-scale project against customary standards of economic and technical feasibility. After some eighteen months, Ottawa decided that the larger plant was suited neither to public enterprise nor the type of dwelling envisaged; meanwhile the less squeamish American and British governments had given rapid and generous aid which enabled the grateful Pakistan authorities to complete the vast settlement ahead of schedule. Canada did leave behind, it is true, a monument to her interest: two years later, beside the main trunk road from Karachi,

---

[25]*Ibid.*, 1958, p. 222.

[26]On December 12, 1963, the Director General listed the following "various ways in which the local people can become aware of the source" of "our large capital projects":

"One way is through the engineering consulting firms working on the projects who have their own buildings out there on which there will be a sign saying, for example . . . 'Jones and Associates, Montreal, Canada'; the construction companies do the same thing on the project sites. A second way is that there is usually a bronze plaque erected by the receiving country on the completion of the project to say 'Gift of the people of Canada', or other appropriate wording. The third is the customary . . . hand-over ceremony arranged by the receiving government. In January 1961, I accompanied the minister who went out to inaugurate five Canadian grant aid projects in India and Pakistan. There was a series of quite impressive ceremonies, when it was obvious that the local people knew where the assistance had come from because at intervals along the road they had erected arches with crude printing on them reading 'God Bless Canada'; or you would go into the villages where there would be hundreds of people congregated wanting to shake your hand, and there would be signs saying 'Long Live Canadians' and that type of thing. So they realized the source of the aid . . . on the capital projects." (*Ibid.*, 1963, p. 58).

stood the ruins of her abortive pilot plant—a shredded tent blown to the sand over a pile of crumbling bricks.

Since about 1959–60, moreover, changing demands for Canadian aid have pushed the calculation of publicity potential increasingly into the background. Traditional Asian recipients have requested a higher proportion of industrial commodities which, being both less durable and less prominently displayed than project aid, lend themselves to publicity hardly more satisfying than an uninspiring and quickly forgotten dockside photograph. "Take copper," suggested the Director General in 1963, ". . . the Pakistani peasant who goes to the bazaar and buys his copper pot has very little idea that it was Canada that made that pot possible. That is why I say that commodities are anonymous."[27] Further, the emerging states of Africa, lacking the material capacity to absorb large capital projects, have required mainly technical assistance —a form of aid that is usually unspectacular, even if it can strongly influence isolated individuals. In a word, the publicity factor in Canadian selection, while never consciously neglected, is at bottom conditioned by the type of aid requested.[28] And by accepting that the forms of aid needed are best determined by those who will use the aid, Canada in fact equates good propaganda with the economic good of recipients.

5. CANADIAN EXPORT POTENTIAL

A still less weighty, though not negligible factor in selection is Canada's commercial advantage. Already certain widespread claims that aid stimulates donors' exports have been dismissed as extravagant; clear examples of aid-generated trade are both too rare and, as a percentage of Canada's total aid and GNP, too small to encourage any systematic attempt at using aid for export promotion.[29]

Yet domestic political pressures from business executives and a chronically underemployed labour force oblige Canadian planners at least to be alert to trade opportunities that aid may occasionally embody. In practice, this means that between two requests of comparable merit

[27]*Ibid.*, 1963, p. 58.
[28]The Director General has summarized the political benefits of major aid forms as follows: ". . . of the three types of assistance I would say capital projects very clearly are the things from which the most national credit results. Commodities produce almost none; while in technical assistance it depends to a large degree on the personality and conduct of the individual." (*Ibid.*, 1963, p. 59).
[29]See chap. I, sec. 3 on "Economic Aims."

and cost, preference will normally be granted to that promising some expansion of Canadian commercial exports. Were a recipient to propose as projects of equal priority a steel plant and a hydro-electric scheme, the latter—for which Canadian equipment might be more competitive in world markets—would probably be favoured as a possible foothold for later commercial orders.

In technical assistance, there is no room for even this slim margin of commercial preference. In spite of a popular belief that trade follows the adviser now that it can no longer follow the flag, donors cannot, in practice, deliberately seek commercial openings in a multitude of personal exchanges. All advisers are prone, of course, to recommend equipment from their homeland; and trainees may sometimes come to prefer a Canadian product over a similar foreign one. But no single choice of a person or field can ever predictably offer benefits in larger trade. The commercial factor must therefore be considered an extremely irregular and secondary influence on Canada's selection policy. In technical assistance, it has virtually no place; and in capital project or commodity aid, its function is always eclipsed by the much more decisive criteria of feasibility and recipients' priorities.

Out of this questioning emerges the conclusion that Canadian aid, while conceived and allocated essentially in terms of Canada's own political interest, is ultimately fashioned by non-political criteria of the recipients' interest. Far from baring a contradiction in the objectives of aid, such an inference merely emphasizes that sound policy must rely, in its execution, on sound technical judgment. This is not a defence of technocracy. It is, as a review of Canadian aid administration and operations will show, but a reminder that lucid and coherent policies are illusory without a corresponding investment in competence.

PART TWO / Administration

IV. The First Decade

It is a truism, and sometimes an excuse, of policy-makers that even the most enlightened programme is only as successful as those who administer it. Certainly the well-publicized misadventures of Western, communist and United Nations aid administrations have offered politicians comfortingly rich evidence that their wise policies are more often thwarted than supported by civil servants. Not surprisingly, the latter have been known to hold that administration, good or bad, is always a faithful image of sound or vicious policies. Of course, the debate between these opposing determinisms is a perennial one among public administrators, ending usually in the satisfying, if indefinite view that, somehow, policy and administration are Siamese twins.

This broad consensus is therefore a fairly uncontroversial standard for assigning—or indeed disguising—responsibilities, and it will usefully guide assessments of past and present aid administration in Canada. But these assessments are possible only after a review of aid machinery in the early years; for in many ways, the practices of the decade following the 1950 Colombo Conference have shaped indelibly the outlook and methods of today's administrators.

1. HISTORY

a. Before and after Colombo (1945-51)

For five years following the Second World War, Canadian development aid flowed only through the multilateral channels of United Nations Specialized Agencies. During this time, there was no central Canadian office to receive and process requests for aid. Grants to UN agency funds were studied by the Department of Finance, in consultation with the

Bank of Canada and the Department of External Affairs; while administration of UN training programmes in Canada and recruitment of
Canadian experts for UN service grew empirically, on lines of ministerial specialization: FAO dealt directly with the Department of Agriculture, ICAO with Transport, WHO with National Health and Welfare;
the Information Division of External Affairs handled UNESCO
requests, and the Economic and UN divisions of the same department,
having a general political interest in aid, administered, or distributed
to qualified ministries, requests from the UN Technical Assistance
Administration. A further complexity resulted from the practice of
certain UN agencies in carrying on direct recruitment of experts in
Canada.

Following creation in 1949 of the United Nations Expanded Programme of Technical Assistance (EPTA), high-level interdepartmental
meetings were held in Ottawa to decide upon machinery to co-ordinate
these widely dispersed operations. The Colombo Conference in January
1950 gave greater urgency to this need, and in September that year the
interdepartmental group, chaired *ex officio* by a senior official of
External Affairs, established a five-man Technical Co-operation Service
(TCS) in the Department of Trade and Commerce. This unit was to
arrange programmes for Colombo Plan and UN trainees, and to recruit
Canadian experts for missions abroad. It had no jurisdiction over UN
grants, which remained a function of the Department of Finance.

Meanwhile, in December 1950, a permanent Interdepartmental
Group on Technical Assistance (IGTA) was formed to create and guide
a new central agency for both technical and—under the Colombo Plan
—capital assistance. This committee was to consider regularly future
Canadian resources, policies and procedures in technical assistance, a
mandate clearly demanding a variety of competence. Under the chairmanship of an External Affairs officer were some twenty members,
notably from the Departments of Finance, Trade and Commerce,
Labour, Agriculture, Mines and Technical Surveys, and National Health
and Welfare, as well as the Bank of Canada.

In fact, the delicate and crucial choice of a department to house the
enlarged central unit fell mainly to the principal candidates, External
Affairs and Trade and Commerce.[1] External Affairs, while naturally
keeping broad control of aid policy, was not anxious to burden itself
with detailed current administration; and finally, it was thought sensible

---

[1]The Department of Finance showed no interest at any time in absorbing day-
to-day administration, contenting itself with ultimate control of expenditure
through interdepartmental committees.

by all to leave the main administrative office in Trade and Commerce. The readiness of External Affairs to relinquish this practical task rested on two distinctively realistic motives, summarized frankly by a senior participant in the meetings: "In External Affairs we were relieved to have T. & C. set up a unit and look after these things. [We] had [before TCS] one officer in UN Division doing everything, and we were well aware that the Department was not equipped to deal with recruiting engineers and such creatures. We had qualms about the implications of having this under T. & C. [presumably the fear that Canadian aid would appear to have a commercial motive], but the practical advantage of a proper office, and most of all, the patronage of C. D. Howe in the Cabinet, seemed more important."[2] The East Block's finesse in recruiting the grey eminence of the St-Laurent régime as a vested-interest supporter of aid is an unchronicled, but surely significant, proof of post-war maturity in Canadian diplomacy.

Whatever the tactical calculations of the moment, both this ministerial patronage of the new agency and Canada's bilateral aid programme itself were generally regarded as strictly temporary arrangements. "We all thought," recalled another participant, "that aid to Asia would last no more than two or three years."[3] Of course, as often happens, what began as temporary in theory survived to become permanent in fact. This "crash programme" mentality is partly explained by immediate communist threats in Korea and Indochina, as well as by the approaching, and successful, end to North American reconstruction aid in Europe. It must also have been simply an intuitive, defensive reflex against indefinite commitments to as yet unmeasured, though clearly gigantic, demands from the emerging underdeveloped world. Not unnaturally, it will be seen, this deliberate short-term view of aid led to a nearly disastrous failure—far from overcome today—to attract competent career aid administrators.

b. The years of improvised expansion (1951–58)

The new agency, called the International Economic and Technical Co-operation Division (IETCD), began functioning in the autumn of 1951. During the seven years of its life were laid the foundations of Canada's bilateral aid programme and its administrative machinery.

[2]Note to the writer, July 1963. Another External Affairs representative in these meetings added in an interview on October 29, 1963, that his department had no desire in 1950 to endanger security precautions in the East Block by having "a lot of foreign trainees milling about there."

[3]*Idem.*, Oct. 29, 1963.

An outstanding part at this pioneering time was played by the IETCD Administrator, Mr. Nik Cavell. Mr. Cavell, after a lifetime as a company executive and administrator in Asia, brought to his task practical common sense, a sensitive feeling for Asian psychology, and a persuasive enthusiasm for overseas aid. While during his tenure a number of acute administrative problems appeared, his eloquence was as prominent in rallying public support for aid in Canada as was his judgment in promoting a capital aid programme of substance and sophistication.

As agreed by the high-level study group, however, the central policy role rested in a standing interdepartmental committee. The original IGTA almost immediately split into two specialized committees, one remaining identical in personnel, powers and name to IGTA and supervising technical assistance; the other, a smaller but senior group, directing the far more costly capital aid operations. Both committees had the specific function of recommending project allocations, and the new Interdepartmental Group on Capital Assistance (IGCA), or Colombo Plan Group, also recommended to the cabinet annual allocations by country.

Membership of the Colombo Plan Group never exceeded twelve persons, and gradually major decisions were taken by about five senior officials of the agencies permanently represented: External Affairs, Trade and Commerce, Finance, the IETCD (usually the Administrator), and the Bank of Canada (normally the Deputy Governor, who was also an Executive Director of the World Bank). Other departments were invited to attend meetings when the Group considered projects requiring their specialized knowledge. As in the IGTA, meetings were chaired by the External Affairs representative, whose preeminence reflected the overriding political interest of his department. As usual in such committees, discussion was free, though each member theoretically offered a fairly distinct professional outlook. The delegate from Finance, for example, assessed the economic wisdom of project proposals; the two Trade and Commerce members argued technical and administrative aspects, frequently on the engineering advice of the Crown corporation, Defence Construction (1951) Limited (DCL); and the Bank member, naturally, represented Canadian monetary policy, as well as the valuable experience of rigorous "banker's charity" practised in project review by the World Bank. Working informally and flexibly, this small committee also functioned with notable effectiveness. The consistently high standard of its judgments during the early years exerted a stabilizing influence which compensated in great part for administrative unevenness that weakened both the IETCD and the agency succeeding it.[4]

The IETCD, a purely administrative organ, had not made an unpromising start. During 1952, key personnel were recruited, notably a seconded officer from Health and Welfare to re-organize the Technical Co-operation Service, and a full-time Chief for the new Capital Projects Section. This section became the special responsibility of an Assistant Administrator, who also directed the entire division during his superior's frequent field visits.

Within six months of the first appointment, technical assistance administration was re-organized on lines that remained basically unchanged until the reforms of the External Aid Office in 1961. All administrative aspects of technical assistance were concentrated in the division, and advisory panels were established in competent departments (such as Agriculture, and Health and Welfare), as well as in various private organizations (such as Ontario Hydro and the universities). These panels, which soon operated as an informal "old-boy network," ensured the regular collaboration of interested outside bodies, and proved a remarkably efficient method of mobilizing and co-ordinating expert technical judgment at little, if any, cost to the government.

Within the IETCD itself, distinct Training and Recruiting Sections were formed, respectively for overseas trainees and Canadian technical experts. Work of training and recruiting officers was specialized by profession, each officer handling all requests, bilateral or multilateral, within a given field: engineering, health, agriculture or other discipline. Financial and travel arrangements were rationalized; policy and procedural manuals for office staff were begun; an attempt was made to assess, and inform recipient governments of, Canadian technical and educational facilities; and a system was developed for recording statistics and progress reports. Regrettably, much of this sound preparation was not properly exploited. Eight years later, the manuals had still not been approved; definitions of "experts" and "equipment" were not in harmony with those of the Colombo Plan Bureau, to Canada's discredit in published comparisons of national aid statistics; and the idea of up-to-date project summaries—essential for close programme planning—was still-born. Nevertheless, when the seconded Chief of TCS returned to

[4]For a very careful account of the role of interdepartmental aid committees and the early years of aid administration in Canada, see Joan Matthews, "Canadian Foreign Aid: 1950–1960," unpublished MA thesis, McGill University, 1962, pp. 96–117.

Health and Welfare in the autumn of 1953, the indispensable ground-work of technical assistance administration had been laid, and later experience was to show that most of it had been laid well.

A noticeable deterioration in technical assistance administration began at this time, partly owing to a constant and unsettling turnover in TCS staff. The first and gravest loss was that of the TCS Chief himself. Shortly after, two of the six other TCS officers departed, and one new officer remained less than a year. When the new TCS Chief was posted to Karachi in February 1955 to administer technical and certain capital aid in the field, TCS split into two distinct units, Training and Recruiting Sections now reporting separately to the Administrator. Meanwhile, lacking a full-time co-ordinating officer, procedure definition and record-keeping suffered badly, and the technical assistance programme as a whole proceeded in an atmosphere of improvisation and even some confusion. Little was done to perfect reliable techniques of selecting and "briefing" experts or trainees; detailed, up-to-date reporting on field conditions as well as long-term estimates of needs and resources were largely unknown. Inadequacy of field reporting was in part the fault of diplomatic missions abroad, some of which were less than keenly interested in what they considered the professionally unreward-ing drudgery of aid administration. But the source of many problems was simply the persistent difficulty of locating qualified staff. The Civil Service Commission failed regularly to recruit personnel requested by the IETCD; and the Administrator himself, absent three or four months each year to investigate projects in Asia, was unable to devote continuous attention to this urgent need.

In 1956, the resident aid officer in Karachi returned to Ottawa as Chief of a reunited TCS, and his experience in field administration was judged useful enough to justify a permanent TCS posting in Pakistan.[5] Between 1955 and 1957 several transfers and additions fundamentally recast TCS personnel, bringing the total IETCD complement in the spring of 1957 to sixteen. However, as a result of hasty reforms and

[5]See *Standing Committee on External Affairs*, 1956, p. 132, where the IETCD Administrator explains the value of this experiment:

"The object in sending [a resident officer to Pakistan] was to give him practical experience of these countries. One of the great difficulties in my shop has been to find people with this practical experience, and since we cannot find them we must try to create them for ourselves as opportunity offers. [Our returned resident officer] . . . has now had this experience and is therefore vastly more valuable to our operation than he was before. He has seen for himself the nature of the conditions which he is helping to remedy, he has visited schools and educational establishments in the area, has talked to the officials who are trying to improve them and has sat in one of the countries . . . as a working officer. . . . As time

uncertainty in technical assistance policy and methods, staff continued to be shifted and replaced almost without interruption. Looseness of policy seemingly grew as the IETCD itself gradually assumed the broad policy function of the IGTA. For some time, in fact, this unwieldy body had given way to the IETCD, which came to consult External Affairs and Finance only when indispensable and to deal with other occasionally interested departments at a junior level. In April 1957 the IGTA disbanded, leaving the IGCA or Colombo Plan Group as the single, though powerful, interdepartmental policy committee.

Paradoxically, by far the greater administrative energy was spent on the policies and machinery of technical assistance, an activity consuming less than 3 per cent of total aid funds. Two facts explain this apparent imbalance. First, capital aid, dealing in easily measurable products, can be administered by a much smaller staff, dollar for dollar, than can technical assistance, concerned unavoidably with imponderables of human conduct. Two million dollars in wheat can be given virtually by the stroke of a pen, while the same amount invested in trainees would demand months of interviews and correspondence by dozens of carefully trained officers. Secondly, since much day-to-day capital aid administration was carried on outside the IETCD, a study limited to that body obscures the true complexity of capital project aid. Besides the technical assistance "old-boy network" which often advised also on capital aid, scores of persons in other government departments and in private firms administered parts of the capital programme in liaison with the IETCD. While numbers of staff obviously varied year by year, and some officers worked on aid only part-time, the following figures are representative: five engineers in the Foreign Projects Section of Defence Construction (1951) Limited, and a half-dozen administrative officers handling tenders, contracts and financial arrangements; four economists in the Office of International Programmes and Contributions in the Department of Finance (this office also reviewed special relief grants and grants to UN agencies); a handful in the Treasury Office and Central Pay Office; five officers in the Canadian Commercial Corporation (CCC), the official government procurement agency, purchasing equipment and commodities; six Foreign Service Officers in the Economic Division II of External Affairs, studying political aspects of

---

goes on, . . . I would like other of my officers to have similar experience in the area."

In spite of this unqualified approval, the resident officer technique was never imitated by Canada outside Pakistan, and was terminated in Karachi by the External Aid Office in 1961 due to increased personnel requirements in Ottawa.

unfinished and proposed projects, scrutiny requiring close acquaintance with every stage of field administration—particularly the delicate details of housing, local purchasing and contractors' responsibilities. Finally, Canadian contracting firms themselves carried a heavy burden of current project administration, both in Canada and at site. Plainly, the IETCD's role in capital aid was that of co-ordinating a fundamentally decentralized system. As a result, the small capital aid staff of three or four officers in the IETCD, while operating with sometimes excessive casualness, was able to supervise a large, and reasonably efficient, programme.

In early 1958, the IETCD Administrator was posted to Ceylon as High Commissioner, where he served until his retirement in 1960 as Canada's *ex officio* member of the Colombo Plan Council for Technical Co-operation. A new central administrative unit, the Economic and Technical Assistance Branch (ETAB), was created within Trade and Commerce in December 1958, with elevated standing above the division level in that department's hierarchy. ETAB inherited from the IETCD a remarkably mature capital programme and the valuable policy guidance of the Colombo Plan Group; it was also the dubious beneficiary of its predecessor's increasingly dangerous administrative disorder.

c. Interregnum (1958–60)
After some nine months during which the Assistant Administrator ran the IETCD, a former senior officer of the Civil Service Commission, Dr. O. E. Ault, became Director of ETAB on December 1, 1958. In reality, ETAB was little more than a rebaptized IETCD, a purely administrative unit under the policy direction of the Colombo Plan Group.

But soon ETAB broke new ground in several directions, with immediate effect upon its structure and staff. Most notable were a marked emphasis on technical assistance, and a corresponding pause in initiation of large capital projects. This stress on technical aid doubtless owed something to the Director's background as an eminent educator; but it also followed inevitably from cabinet decisions to create three new area programmes implying a high proportion of technical assistance: the Canada-West Indies Aid Program (later expanded to cover the Commonwealth Caribbean), Commonwealth Technical Assistance Plan, and Commonwealth Scholarship and Fellowship Plan. In 1959, 528 trainees arrived under Canada's bilateral programmes, compared to 408 the previous year; numbers of departing experts in the same period rose from 64 to 74. Reduced project activity resulted mainly from three factors external to ETAB's own orientation: the new Prairie-inspired Conservative ministry decided to include a higher level (though a lower percentage) of surplus wheat in enlarged capital programmes; a great part of current funds was necessarily devoted to completing large projects, such as the Warsak and Kundah dams and the Canada-India Reactor, launched under the IETCD; and both India and Pakistan were reaching a temporary stage in their development at which new projects were needed less than substantial imports of industrial commodities allowing full exploitation of existing production facilities.

The internal administration of ETAB also evolved, partly under the pressure of these political and technical influences. Early in 1959, owing perhaps to decreased activity of the Colombo Plan Group in capital project review, ETAB tried to play a more creative role in policy-making by establishing a Programme Planning Division. Further, some worthwhile experiments were started in specialized field administration (in India and Pakistan), and in the project or group approach to training. Unfortunately, many of these imaginative reforms suffered from a breakdown in lines of communication within ETAB, and from a general sluggishness in its administration.

These defects, it seems, grew both from hesitant internal policies and from the frequent shifting of staff accompanying or promoting these policies. During the rest of 1959 and in early 1960, ETAB, and notably its technical assistance administration, was shaken by a series of damaging and demoralizing upheavals. Before the end of 1959, four officers —including the former IETCD Assistant Administrator, the Chief of the Technical Assistance Division (a renamed TCS), and the Chief of the new Programme Planning Division—resigned. Soon after a new Chief of Technical Assistance was borrowed from the Department of Public Works, a Civil Service Commission survey recommended abolition of both this post and the Technical Assistance Division itself. Consequently, separate divisions for training and experts were again created, and the deposed Chief was transferred to the Programme Planning Division—with special authority for technical assistance. Another outsider was borrowed from the Ontario government as a special adviser and as Chief of Programme Planning. An officer from Trade and Commerce was seconded to ETAB as Assistant Director, but only on a temporary basis.

In these conditions, responsibilities tended to be unstable or, at best, unclear. Within a few months, the Assistant Director, the Chief of Programme Planning, and a newly appointed special adviser on education left the Branch. Shortly after, a new Chief of Programme Planning was seconded from Defence Construction (1951) Limited, though only for capital aid; technical assistance planning was transferred back to the Technical Assistance Division, which once again had risen, phoenix-like, from its ashes. In fact, this reunion remained theoretical, for training and experts sections continued to function independently, with little practical liaison.

For at least a year before the end of this era, it was apparent that the growing volume and complexity of Canada's aid programmes demanded both a strengthening of administrative staff and machinery and a tighter control by policy-makers over administration. ETAB itself had proposed, in a memorandum of February 1959, to assume the major role in policy-formation; but meanwhile, the Colombo Plan Group, observing delicately that "existing arrangements were no longer entirely adequate,"[6] had produced a scheme for a semi-autonomous body centralizing all aid administration under the minister responsible for aid votes. This proposal was accepted by cabinet on August 24, 1960, and next day the Prime Minister's Office announced that "the administration and operation of aid programmes" would, from September 1, be "placed under one head" in a new agency called the External Aid Office (EAO). The first Director General of the EAO would be a career diplomat, Mr. H. O. Moran, reporting directly to the Secretary of State for External Affairs.

2. AUTOPSY

The extraordinary instability of staff and structures since the mid-1950's suggested plainly that Canada's aid administration was floundering. Difficulties of aid execution underlined this decadence, even while the financial volume of Canadian assistance increased significantly. As frequently happens, criticism of administrative leadership focused more on obvious or alleged weaknesses of individuals than on the difficult concrete problems they faced. Doubtless, the personnel and administrative policies, as indeed the professional talents, of chief officials, were not always best suited to aid administration. But the underlying causes of the general malaise could be imputed only to the inherent complexity of foreign aid itself, and to cabinet policies fixing the scope and framework of administration. These major defects in cabinet direction were, on one hand, a deliberate short-term view of aid and, on the other, a divided political responsibility for its administration.[7]

[6]H. O. Moran, "New Purposes and Methods of International Assistance," in *Dialogue 1963*, Ottawa, p. 63.

[7]Some of the ideas in this and the following chapter were outlined by the writer in an article entitled, "The Administration of Canadian Colombo Plan Aid," *International Journal*, vol. 16, no. 2 (Spring, 1961), pp. 169–82.

a. A short-term perspective of aid
The refusal of Canadian governments until 1960 to adopt an explicit long-term view of aid and its administration was the central and decisive fault in Canada's early programme. There was, it is true, no valid precedent in 1950–51 for large-scale intergovernmental development aid, particularly in the form of projects. There had been massive programmes of relief and reconstruction in Europe: but relief in Asia could be at best a palliative and at worst a soporific; while reconstruction on the Marshall Plan model was a clumsy misnomer when recipient states lacked both the industrial base and technical élite at the heart of Western Europe's post-war renaissance. Donors had to improvise, particularly those, like Canada, which offered substantial capital aid but little Asian or colonizing experience.

Yet this absence of a relevant example, and the plausible guess that the urgency of aid would subside fairly soon with presumably limited threats in Indochina and Korea, were no excuses for abandoning normal processes of creative policy-making. At no time during the ten years after Colombo can one identify a serious official attempt to assess underdevelopment as an entirely fresh challenge, demanding a global review of priorities in allocation of foreign policy resources. Never, in a lucid and systematic way, did governments try to fix attainable goals for Canadian aid, or study its practical integration with other instruments of foreign policy. Never did they envisage—and proclaim—aid as the primary strategic vehicle of Canadian policy in the developing world for probably the rest of our century. At first, cabinets seemed unaware that Canadian foreign policy had indeed entered a fundamentally new phase; later they appeared caught in a paralysed and self-congratulatory fascination with a few politically "photogenic" capital projects. At all times, their view was on the immediate, visible results of aid; never on those deep and distant, if sometimes intangible, objectives that alone can rationally promote the abiding national interest.

Fatally, this persistent myopia was bound to undermine the aid administration. Called to execute tentative and shadowy policies, civil servants could do little more than stumble hopefully from budget to budget, responding peristaltically to each sporadic batch of project requests. Throughout the decade, the effect on staff recruitment was disastrous. When the IETCD sought in 1951 and 1952 quickly to mount a competent core of personnel, few departments were ready to release any but the redundant or unwanted; departments interested technically in aid resented what they regarded as "empire-building" by an intruding outsider, for a shaky and fugitive political operation in Asian welfare. When cabinets failed year after year to assign to aid an officially permanent and key role in external policy, the early reputation of aid as a career for transients and misfits was confirmed: those most able to run an imaginative programme—the adventurous though experienced, relatively young middle- and upper-grade officers— shunned the aid administration as a professional dead-end. Since aid remained in the backwash of government policy, a vicious circle of mediocrity made it practically impossible for the administration to recruit above its own proven level of competence. With no stated cabinet perspective of aid, the very notions of programme planning, procedure study and career development lost all relevance.

In fairness, it must be noted that this short-sighted view of aid was shared during the post-Colombo years by nearly every donor country.[8] Only in the years 1960–63 did Canada's aid-giving partners, the United States, the United Kingdom and France, begin to place aid on a longer-term footing through consolidated aid administrations. Even now executive appeals for aid funds in the United States are subject to hostile Congressional scrutiny that annually challenges the very existence of the aid programme.[9] It is also true that there are stubborn constitutional, political and economic obstacles in Canada to promises of large fixed levels of aid for prolonged or indefinite periods. Finally, recognition is due to several multi-annual commitments made by Canada (always subject to Parliamentary approval) in addition to normal five-year extensions of the Colombo Plan system accepted by all members: in 1958, a total of $10,000,000 over five years was promised to West Indies islands in the Commonwealth; in 1959, a commitment was made to give $50,000,000 annually over three years under the Colombo Plan; and in 1960, a total three-year commitment of $10,500,000 was

[8]Though more often legislatures, than governments, were responsible. See John D. Montgomery, *The Politics of Foreign Aid* (New York, 1962), p. 207:
"Whenever the [US] executive branch has been successful in rallying Congress, its efforts have borne the characteristic odor of crisis. Carefully considered arguments designed to gain support for longer-term commitments to foreign aid, either in funding or programming, have met with monotonous failure. In part, this has been due to a persistent view that foreign aid was an emergency program rather than a long-term government operation, and that when the Axis had been defeated, the war damage repaired, European productivity restored, and regional defenses installed, the United States could withdraw and allow normal processes to do the rest."
[9]See Representative Otto E. Passman (sometimes called "the most powerful Congressional antagonist of foreign aid"), "Why I Am Opposed to Foreign Aid," *New York Times Magazine,* July 7, 1963, pp. 16 and 17.

offered to countries in the Special Commonwealth Africa Aid Program (SCAAP).

But none of these highly useful commitments conferred upon Canada's programme the permanent status and prestige needed to assure confident, flexible planning and steady recruitment of competent administrators. If anything, the prestige of aid was diminished by the notorious reluctance of high-ranking ministers to defend aid or even attend Colombo Plan ministerial meetings.[10] Neither the fundamental significance of aid nor its central function in Canadian external policy was fully seized by Canadian ministries in the first decade; and the perilous decay of the aid administration at the end of this stage was no more and no less than the shabby image of cabinet indifference.

b. A divided political responsibility for administration

The other basic weakness of the administration also resulted from a want of cabinet vision. When in 1951 the cabinet agreed to entrust current administration of the External Affairs aid vote to the Department of Trade and Commerce, it theoretically split responsibility for policy and administration between two ministers, each exclusively accountable to Parliament for a distinct aspect of aid. But since within the interdepartmental advisory policy committees the Department of Finance exercised a decisive budgetary control, and since External Affairs kept a quasi-administrative planning and negotiating role through its Economic Division II, administration in fact fell under three departments.

Doubtless, close personal relationships of committee members, particularly among the handful of senior civil servants in the Colombo Plan Group belonging to the so-called "under cabinet,"[11] made harmonization of the three departments' interests easier. But intrinsic differences in outlook and aspirations still divided these ministries, and led each to retard or complicate the work of the two others. External Affairs, as formal sponsor of the aid vote and perpetual supplier of chairmen for interdepartmental committees, rightly wielded a supreme veto inspired by diplomatic motives; but diplomats, seen by pragmatic

[10]Of the first twelve Colombo Plan ministerial meetings only three were attended by the Secretary of State for External Affairs. After sending junior ministers for three years in a row, Ottawa began in 1962 to send only the Director General of the EAO. This recent ministerial boycott follows a trend of nearly all Colombo Plan members, even recipients; as a Canadian official explained in 1963, "they don't get a nickel in Bangkok [venue of that year's Colombo Plan meeting]; but in Washington [home of the World Bank] they're fighting for their lives. That's where the guts of the thing are."

[11]The expression belongs to R. Barry Farrell, "The Planning and Conduct of

technicians from Trade and Commerce, tended to "over-politicize" projects, injecting devious and encumbering political arguments into otherwise straightforward engineering problems; and seen by officials from Finance, they tended to put ethereal diplomatic cavilling before sound economic judgment. Trade and Commerce naturally belittled both political and budgetary factors in favour of technical—and commercial—expedience. And Finance, for its part, invariably brought to bear on its colleagues' proposals a questioning restraint, untempered by field experience in the unkind political and technical realities of aid execution. Necessarily applied after a good deal of preliminary review by the two other departments, such a financial brake slowed, and sometimes disrupted, intergovernmental project planning.

This schema is of course somewhat overdrawn, in the interest of clearly identifying latent conflicts. But in substance it is authentic. Canada's early aid administration was in fact tricephalous, a basic flaw exaggerated moreover by the insistence of each participant on intervening in many minor decisions: mail from the field on strictly technical points, for instance, usually passed to ETAB over a diplomatic desk in Economic Division II, where it often remained for an extended *visite protocolaire*. Further, the fundamental ministerial separation was compounded by the "farming out" of most engineering and purchasing functions to two entirely distinct Crown corporations.

Fragmented among at least five agencies, three of which shared control of its policy, and without a lasting cabinet commitment to its future, Canada's aid administration in 1960 was divided, confused and deeply demoralized. Worse still, it was demonstrably outdated. Constantly rising levels of assistance and an ever-expanding number and diversity of recipients posed demands on personnel and techniques that could only disrupt irreparably the old machinery. To overcome during the second decade the aid programme's two underlying weaknesses, the cabinet endorsed the concept of a centralized administration with greatly enhanced status. The remedy was timely and potent; it was not a panacea.

Foreign Policy in Canada," unpublished doctoral thesis, Harvard University, 1952, p. 68. Cited in James Eayrs, *The Art of the Possible* (Toronto, 1961), p. 33.

V. New Machinery and New Men for the Sixties

1. POLICY WITHOUT PEOPLE

The External Aid Office (EAO) represented a bold attack on the political and structural defects of the early administration. By raising aid to a semi-autonomous footing under the immediate direction of the Secretary of State for External Affairs, the cabinet recognized aid as a momentous activity of long-range Canadian diplomacy. Concentration of policy and administrative functions in a single powerful agency seemed to end at a stroke the awkward disarray of the old three-headed machinery, replacing a tired and paralysed Gulliver by an able, unchallengeable Leviathan. At last aid appeared to command the coherent ministerial supervision and rational management demanded by an alert, effectual foreign policy.

Broadly speaking, the EAO in its first five years has realized these lofty hopes. Firm administrative leadership and unified political control of aid allocation have marked the whole programme with unaccustomed and stimulating clarity of purpose. Upon the strong organization now laid down, any foreseeable growth in Canadian aid operations could be, if not automatic, at least orderly.

But the deep-rooted failing of earlier days—inadequate recruitment of qualified staff—is still far from overcome. While a brief sketch of the Office's structure as of May 1965 reveals notable success in attracting certain senior officers, efforts to build a permanent core of competent administrators at other levels appear less fruitful. Further analysis suggests that this fundamental debility can be cured only by drawing from the long-term nature of aid practical conclusions the government has so far been unwilling to accept.

a. A centralized hierarchy

Although officially announced for September 1, 1960, the External Aid Office began managing aid operations only in mid-November of that year. For about a year more, studies were made by the Director General and other experienced officers seconded from External Affairs and Finance to shape new policies and machinery. In July 1961, the Treasury Board approved the EAO's first personnel establishment, including nine positions carrying a salary of at least $12,000. Beginning in the spring of 1962 the new system came gradually into effect, and three tightly co-ordinated elements appeared: the External Aid Board, the EAO itself, and a number of auxiliary agencies performing specialized tasks in liaison with the EAO.

(i) *The External Aid Board.* This small high-level interdepartmental committee replaces the Colombo Plan Group in broad policy co-ordination among ministries principally concerned with aid. The Board differs from its predecessor, however, in two significant aspects: first, by specifically comprising deputy ministers (or alternates) of Finance, Trade and Commerce, and External Affairs, as well as the Bank of Canada Executive Director of the IBRD, and the Director General of External Aid, it has greater authority; second, the chief aid administrator, the Director General, is no longer a mere observer or ordinary member in the group, but its *ex officio* chairman.

Like any interdepartmental committee, the Board has a purely consultative function, related mainly to "basic policy questions."[1] In practice, this includes reviewing all major submissions to cabinet on bilateral aid: country allocations, proportions of each aid type, and capital projects. The Board is also frequently invited by the Director General to advise on current EAO operations; but its principal task is to harmonize in advance of cabinet meetings differing departmental views on the aid programme's general orientation and content.

As a result, the Board's meetings follow a deliberate will to compromise rather than rigid debate sanctioned by recorded voting. In fact, much of its work is settled informally by telephone or in bilateral encounters of individual members with the Director General. After each full meeting, the Director General prepares a summary memorandum, which is circulated to other members for verification and for preliminary briefing of respective ministers. The draft thus revised—and usually unanimously approved—is forwarded by the Director General to the Secretary of State for External Affairs, who can then present the

[1]*Standing Committee on External Affairs*, 1961, p. 155.

final submission to cabinet knowing that its recommendations will rally the informed understanding of his most intimately concerned colleagues. Since some ministers are known to examine aid proposals with the commendable earnestness of amateur engineers or economists, this careful preparation of a pre-cabinet consensus is an effective technique for developing, and ratifying, politically acceptable programme lines.

The system clearly assigns a pivotal role to the Director General. It is he who calls Board meetings, prepares provisional agenda, background notes and memoranda, and reports to the minister responsible to Parliament for aid. In practice, the Board allows him great autonomy of decision; limits to his day-to-day initiative are traced not by explicit regulation from the Board but by his own judgment of what his committee colleagues are likely to endorse. Not only does he have, as Director General enjoying the status of a deputy minister, a direct channel to his minister completely outside the External Affairs hierarchy, but, under his hat as Board Chairman, he interprets to the minister the sometimes opposing arguments that lead to Board recommendations— arguments that may still be raised in cabinet. And while continued debate in cabinet can, and occasionally does, modify original EAO proposals, the Director General remains unmistakably the central figure in the Board itself, as in the office for which he is immediately answerable.

(ii) *The External Aid Office.* The duties of the Director General in relation to the EAO were summarized in the Prime Minister's press release of August 25, 1960:

(*a*) The operation and administration of Canada's assistance programmes covered by the general aid votes of the Department of External Affairs;

(*b*) To keep these programmes under constant review and, as appropriate, to prepare recommendations on them and related matters to Cabinet; to prepare submissions to Treasury Board on financial questions relating to economic assistance;

(*c*) To ensure co-ordination in the operations of other Departments and agencies of government concerned with various aspects of economic assistance programmes;

(*d*) To consult and co-operate as appropriate with international organizations and agencies;

(*e*) To consult and co-operate as appropriate with Canadian voluntary agencies active in underdeveloped countries;

(*f*) To co-ordinate Canadian efforts to provide emergency assistance in case of disasters abroad; for this purpose to achieve the necessary liaison with the Canadian Red Cross Society and other appropriate Canadian organizations;

(g) To be responsible for the internal administration of the External Aid Office; and

(h) To perform such other duties as may be required in relation to Canada's external assistance programme.

As questions of members of the Standing Committee on External Affairs showed in June 1961, the expression "general aid votes" in reality meant only bilateral grant aid and "a working relationship with the United Nations and its Specialized Agencies"[2] in recruiting advisers and receiving trainees under UN programmes. In 1965, the EAO also took in hand the new soft loans. But since export credit is handled by the Export Credits Insurance Corporation and multilateral grants remain the responsibility of External Affairs, the EAO—and indeed the External Aid Board—still do not regroup all Canadian programmes "under one head," as implied by the preamble to the above enumeration. Nevertheless, the EAO does unite organically policy and administrative functions of virtually all programmes "operated" by Canada, a reform long demanded by awkward separation of the Trade and Commerce aid unit from the close policy control of External Affairs.

The EAO's internal organization has absorbed only those functions of outside agencies that it was felt could be performed more conveniently and economically in the Office itself. Tender purchasing of commodities and equipment, for example, is still entrusted on commission to the Canadian Commercial Corporation; and the EAO budget is included in the External Affairs estimates, even though this context has sometimes led to confusion regarding EAO autonomy.[3] On the other hand, the Foreign Projects Division of Defence Construction (1951) Limited was transferred in early 1962 to the EAO, at an estimated annual saving of $40,000. Owing to this pragmatic policy and low staff overhead in the EAO's own establishment, the office's identifiable administrative costs of $1,251,600 in 1965–66 represented slightly less than 1 per cent of total appropriations for bilateral grants and soft loans.

Divisions within the office are of course organized by broad function, though further specialization by area distributes tasks in all divisions and sections except the Finance and Administration Division.

[2]*Ibid.*, pp. 209–10. Uncertainty as to EAO functions undoubtedly arose from an erroneous statement a month before by the Secretary of State for External Affairs to the effect that the Office dealt with all bilateral and multilateral programmes (*ibid.*, p. 50).

[3]*Ibid.*, p. 209. The Glassco Commission suggested in 1963 that legislation might be enacted to define "more explicitly the degree of [the EAO's] independence from the Department" of External Affairs (See *Report of the Royal Commission on Government Organization* (Ottawa, 1963), vol. 4, p. 131).

CHART 1. EXTERNAL AID OFFICE
(June 1965)

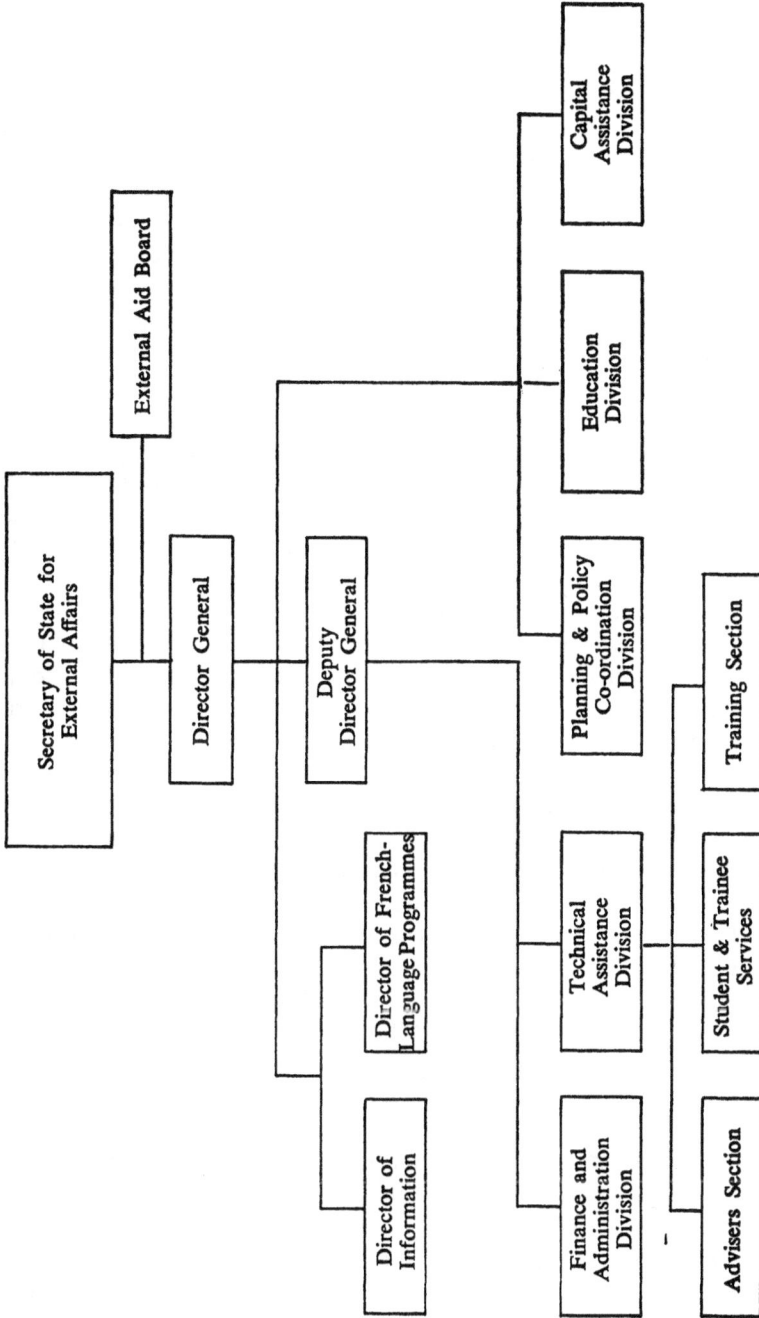

External Aid Board

Secretary of State for External Affairs

Director General

Deputy Director General

Director of French-Language Programmes

Director of Information

Planning & Policy Co-ordination Division

Education Division

Capital Assistance Division

Technical Assistance Division

Finance and Administration Division

Student & Trainee Services

Training Section

Advisers Section

Source: EAO Finance and Administration Division.

The central EAO organ is the Planning and Policy Co-ordination Division which, working closely under the Deputy Director General, acts as a kind of general staff for all aid operations. Ten officers with widely varied backgrounds plan country programmes, make preliminary assessments of project requests, establish procedures, and co-ordinate activities of all operational divisions. It is here that theoretical unity of policy and administration is translated into concrete terms.

The other novel EAO unit is the Education Division, one of the few federal government offices concerned directly and exclusively with education. This Division was formed in 1961 to anticipate the unprece-dented demands that numerous freshly independent African states were to pose in every field of academic education, in particular at the primary and secondary levels from which Canada had previously remained aloof. While this Division's teacher and scholarship programmes appear to duplicate administrative functions already performed by well-established sections for advisers and trainees, little confusion of tasks in fact occurs. The great number of persons moving in academic programmes—many more than under all technical programmes combined—now easily justifies development of administrative methods to suit the unique prob-lems of education; briefing of Canadian teachers, most of whom depart together in September, can be organized into formal courses in a way impossible for technical advisers, who leave at all times of the year as sporadic requests are received; and a similar difference distinguishes scholarship-holders—who usually arrive *en masse* in August and Sep-tember—from technical trainees, whose reception must still often be planned individually, in response to unpredictable needs.

In broad function, the other divisions do not differ significantly from their embryonic antecedents in the IETCD or ETAB, except that the Capital Assistance Division now exercises much more detailed and authoritative control over execution of projects. Two special posts with immediate access to the Director General underline the EAO's concern with aid publicity and reception of overseas visitors in Canada. How-ever, no distinct machinery exists for either programme evaluation or liaison with Canadian voluntary agencies: evaluation indeed seems ignored except in an impressionistic or accidental way, although it surely merits an independent division staffed with two or three experts in economic development and international politics; while liaison with voluntary groups, which occupies a good deal of the time of senior officials, might profitably be entrusted to a special officer, perhaps in the Planning and Policy Co-ordination Division.

(iii) *Associated agencies.* In addition to the Canadian Commercial Corporation which, through the Department of Defence Production, handles tender purchasing for bilateral programmes, various other offices and departments maintain regular, more informal liaison with the EAO. Defence Construction (1951) Limited is still consulted on engineering problems; the Finance Department International Programmes Division (which, with the East Block, also reviews multilateral contributions) advises on financial problems; the External Affairs Economic Division, though often by-passed on details, channels advice on political matters; the Wheat Board co-operates in surplus grain shipments; and many other specialized departments or agencies such as Mines and Technical Surveys, Transport, Health and Welfare, and Atomic Energy of Canada Limited, supply expert advice on technical problems within their competence. On a similar flexible basis, provincial government departments, universities, private firms and voluntary bodies are constantly consulted. Sometimes consultation is achieved through standing advisory panels, as in earlier years; more often, it takes place outside any formal channel, simply as an easy exchange by telephone or letter to solve a peculiar difficulty.

b. *The persistent staff crisis*

But it is still the EAO that carries the primary burden of bilateral programmes, and it is there that the continuing scarcity of administrative personnel must be reviewed. Naturally, initial efforts in recruitment were aimed at filling senior positions, and within two years of the EAO's creation most of these posts were occupied by men of outstanding accomplishment. By March 1963, the Director General was able to say: ". . . we have for the first time professional economists, persons from the academic world, skilled administrators and trained political officers who have served in the underdeveloped areas, devoting their full time to the planning and operation of Canada's six bilateral aid programmes."[4] This was a noteworthy improvement over the EAO's plight two years earlier, when he had deplored both the feeble numbers and quality of his staff in terms bordering on despair: ". . . for the moment, in the External Aid Office, we do not have people, period."[5]

In spite of this conspicuous progress in raising the general level of staff competence, gaps remained in May 1965 in certain senior posts,

---

[4]H. O. Moran, "New Purposes and Methods of International Assistance," *Dialogue 1963*, Ottawa, p. 63.

[5]*Standing Committee on External Affairs*, 1961, p. 176.

in French-language personnel, and in the lower ranks of officers who might eventually form the cadres of a professional service of aid administrators.

First, at the higher level, the key position of Director of Planning and Policy Co-ordination was open, though in practice it was covered by the Deputy Director General; also without incumbent was the much less powerful but sensitive position of Trainee Liaison Officer, or Chief of Student and Trainee Services.

Although present in greater strength than two years earlier, French-Canadian officers were still too few to meet the needs of a French-language programme increased (by allocation, if not expenditure) thirteenfold. After a long unsuccessful search, the EAO had by then armed itself with two high-level French-Canadian officials: a Director of French-language Programmes and a Deputy Director of Education. These two experienced men were helping to attract younger French-Canadian administrators; nevertheless, the proportion of French-Canadian officers to the total EAO officer staff remained low: eight out of fifty-six.

The even less impressive participation of French Canadians in the aid programme before 1965 had for some years led Quebec nationalists to use the EAO as a textbook model of Anglo-Saxon domination. In 1963, Jean-Marc Léger delivered himself of a front-page editorial in *Le Devoir*, in which he took the apparently English names of the EAO's twelve chief officers as *prima facie* evidence of discrimination against both French-speaking recipients and administrators: "La composition du Bureau est éloquente, normale d'ailleurs dans l'optique d'Ottawa et contribue, avec beaucoup de faits analogues à expliquer l'orientation de notre assistance à l'étranger et de notre politique extérieure en général."[6] Other explanations, notably French-Canadian preference for private careers and the exalting attraction of a post-Duplessis Quebec régime, are well known if less emphasized.[7]

But even with more English-speaking officers learning and using French in their work, the EAO in 1965 had not overcome its earlier handicap: an educational and technical assistance programme designed to mobilize Quebec's resources for French-speaking countries was being run without a fully adequate corps of native French-Canadian adminis-

[6]"Un Bureau canadien de l'aide à l'étranger entièrement unilingue," *Le Devoir*, Montreal, July 26, 1962, p. 1. The EAO's total officer staff in November 1963 was forty-one, five of whom were French Canadians, all at lower levels.

[7]See Guy Dozois, "L'Administration publique dans un pays bilingue et biculturel," *Canadian Public Administration*, vol. 6, no. 4 (December, 1963), pp. 414–23.

trators. Canada's inability to spend even one third of her 1964–65 allocation of $4 million for these countries owed much to normal delays in the
"pipeline" of aid expenditure and much more to recipients' inability to
absorb aid; but the EAO's own weakness in French-speaking staff at
home and in the field must be counted as at least a significant factor.

Finally, the Office suffered, though less acutely than in other years,
from a general shortage of young university graduates able to build
a specialized career service in aid administration. Since in the long run
this weakness must define the gravity of the other two, its possible
remedies should be sought in an analysis of personnel development as
a whole.

2. ATTRACTING THE ABSENT ELITE:
A PLEA FOR A CAREER SERVICE OF AID ADMINISTRATORS

Before assessing supposed obstacles to a career service, it may be helpful to summarize the general advantages of such a system and its effect
upon field administration abroad and in Canada.

a. The principle: pragmatic empire-building
The logical consequence of viewing aid as a long-term policy is
obviously the formation of a career service of External Aid Officers. A
permanent instrument of diplomacy cannot be wielded coherently and
sensitively with temporary staff; the special work of aid administration
requires special people, new officers to spend a lifetime in a third, distinct
foreign service. Why must such a corps of "development diplomats"[8]
be independent of the two older services of trade promotion and classical
diplomacy?

First, because aid administration demands specialized knowledge that
cannot be absorbed and usefully exploited by men whose primary career
in trade or diplomacy imposes a series of triennial uprootings from
posts entirely dissimilar in conditions of living and work, or whose
secondment to the EAO is by definition transient.

Second, as a matter of practical psychology, only a specialist aid
administrator—combining technical understanding, a gift for public and
personal relations, and an uncommon instinct for sound initiative—has
a clear professional interest in conscientious performance of aid duties.
However great the skill and devotion of present overseas administrators,

---

[8]The term is Eugene Black's, *The Diplomacy of Economic Development*
(Cambridge, Mass., 1960), p. 24.

many of them understandably view aid work as an annoying impediment to the pursuit of their principal career.

Third, long-term career possibilities offer the most convenient solution to a nearly universal lack of overseas experience on the part of EAO staff dealing with technical assistance and education. Indeed, briefing of advisers, trainees and scholars is still handled almost entirely by officers who, through no fault of their own, have no direct experience in developing nations at all. Plainly, this lamentable gap invites some scheme of alternating postings between Ottawa and recipient countries, in the manner of the diplomatic and trade services. Administrative and technical judgments cannot be made in isolation from the peculiar economic, political and social realities of underdeveloped nations; and only a professional career service could afford to train officers abroad in these unique problems on a systematic basis.

Lastly, an External Aid Service would simplify communication between EAO staff in Ottawa and Canadian aid administrators abroad. The latter, at present controlled by either External Affairs or Trade and Commerce, are in constant touch with the EAO—and indeed many of them now spend a few weeks there before going abroad; but they cannot always appreciate sympathetically the problems and methods of their Ottawa correspondents. The reverse is also true. If EAO home staff had thorough personal acquaintance with conditions in developing areas, the quality of exchanges between Ottawa and the field could improve measurably: fresh ideas could pass with minimal distortion from their country of origin and eventual implementation to those ultimately directing their execution: and Ottawa's greater understanding of field difficulties would allow planners to send field administrators and technicians directives both more precise and uniformly realistic.

b. Field administration abroad: "les absents ont toujours tort"
Even more than in Ottawa, a career service could transform field administration overseas. Much, if not most, foreign aid administration can be carried on with maximum effectiveness in recipient countries, rather than in Canada at desks, however intelligently manned, ten or twelve thousand miles away. Regrettably, present field administration is inadequate in numbers, type and authority of personnel.[9]

Two kinds of overseas appointments deserve consideration. For capital aid, full-time engineering attachés could be posted in every country

---

[9]Cf. Walter R. Sharp, *Field Administration in the United Nations System* (New York, 1961); also John D. Montgomery, *The Politics of Foreign Aid* (New York, 1962), pp. 159–82.

receiving large-scale project aid—for instance, in India, Pakistan, Ceylon, Malaysia, Nigeria, Ghana and Jamaica[10]; or alternatively, small teams of engineers could reside in major project-aid regions—say, in South Asia, Southeast Asia, East and West Africa, and the Caribbean. Such men, who could move quickly to sites of active and prospective projects, would not make decisive feasibility studies of proposed projects, but would furnish far more rapid and competent assessments of these than can diplomatic or trade staff. Above all, they would keep Ottawa and field technicians informed of each other's problems and, where appropriate, settle recurring field difficulties: costly delays in shipping and customs clearance, on-site personnel problems, and interpretation of intergovernmental agreements. For these tasks, they would of course need sufficient rank to extract decisions from host governments, and sufficient power to act, when needed, with quick independence.

Field specialists in technical assistance administration could also enable great savings in Canadian funds and prestige. They could ensure careful interviewing of training and scholarship candidates; serious investigation of requests for demonstrating equipment (calling in *ad hoc* experts when required); and verification that "felt needs" for advisers and teachers are not only felt, but are really needs. These administrators, like their engineering colleagues, would also travel widely and constantly in countries of service. Obviously, both types of appointment would magnify Canadian administrative budgets perceptibly; but the enlarged outlays, by allowing much more effective administration and supervision, would soon realize both for Canada and recipients economies many times greater in actual high-quality aid. Rivers of sterile correspondence on administrative trivia would dry up; delays on technical decisions would cease to invite recipients' despair or derision; and Canadian technicians abroad, freed from the tedious and humiliating trials of begging for promised local support, could apply untrammelled energies to their professional missions.

c. Field administration in Canada: corollary of an ungovernable geography

Not only would career officers of an External Aid Service work in Ottawa and abroad; they would staff regional offices for technical assistance and publicity throughout Canada. External aid administration,

---

[10]This formula was tried with recognized success in Pakistan during work on the Warsak Dam, and was repeated in 1963 for a number of projects in the West Indies. Both officers, however, held only *ad hoc* postings, with no permanent status as career administrators abroad.

like every other federal government activity, faces the formidable barrier of Canada's continental geography. Both recruitment of Canadians for service overseas and reception of foreign guests have suffered incalculably from the EAO's discouraging physical remoteness.

Technical assistance administration—so utterly dependent on direct personal contact—must somehow be decentralized in Canada. The EAO could with immense profit establish three or four regional bureaux in large cities outside Ottawa having a high recruitment potential and numerous resident visitors: certainly in Toronto, Montreal and Vancouver, and perhaps in Winnipeg and Halifax. Such offices could interview Canadian candidates for overseas missions; and not only brief scholars and non-itinerant trainees, but give them the constant, intimate and sympathetic attention they deeply need. Regional offices could exploit fully recruitment facilities of provincial governments, universities and professional bodies, and strengthen liaison with voluntary groups promoting the welfare of trainees and scholars. The Montreal bureau might indeed be given practical control of all French-language technical assistance, possibly under some form of shared jurisdiction with the Quebec government. By moving the mountain to Mohammed, this would overcome the reluctance of competent French-Canadian administrators to work in Ottawa, and give the Quebec government—which is, after all, the largest reservoir of French-language expertise in Canada— an inherent stake in the French programme. All the offices would conduct public information programmes through talks, films, seminars, documentation and other suitable techniques. Finally, they would fulfil a vital function that Ottawa has virtually ignored until now: the evaluation of study in Canada by trainees and scholars, and serious surveillance of their problems of maintenance and acclimatization. None of these requirements has been or can be efficiently met from Ottawa alone. Either the EAO must branch out to the sources of its human activity, or resign itself to administering more or less blindly columns of increasingly meaningless statistics.

d. The unreal obstacles

Common objections to a career aid service do not appear well-founded. First, it is argued that such a service would not be large enough to offer openings to young men of ambition or to justify creation of new civil service classifications. But even the minimum staff outlined above would demand from thirty to forty new specialized officers, a number which would multiply continually as capital, and especially technical, assistance programmes grow. And in the same way that officers of the trade commissioner and diplomatic services are partly interchangeable, so could procedures be imagined to allow reasonable transmigration between the older services and an External Aid Service. Since all three services would compete for similar candidates through a common foreign service examination, equivalent ranks and basic promotion criteria could facilitate passage from one specialization to another; young officers would then have before them career openings far broader than those of any single initial service.

Second, it is said that there would not be enough applicants for a career aid service, even if lateral openings to the senior foreign services could be arranged. Yet numerous recent university graduates—the kind, for instance, likely to volunteer for the Company of Young Canadians—are interested in neither political reporting nor trade promotion; many of these would welcome a career in aid, but only if assured of a stable long-term future in this field.

Finally, it is held that in most recipient countries the current volume of Canadian assistance does not warrant permanent postings. This argument ignores both the likelihood of rising aid levels and the relation of administrative staff needs to different types of aid: the presence of five Canadian advisers in a country with a primitive or unusually corrupt bureaucracy may easily occupy a conscientious aid officer full-time. Dollar value of aid is no standard of reasonable administrative requirements.

The career service is therefore an urgent and logical imperative of an expanding Canadian aid programme. Long ago this wise investment in human resources was understood by the United States and other large donors, even though excessive professionalism and bureaucratic sclerosis have marred some of their efforts. An External Aid Service is the only important administrative conclusion remaining to be drawn from the government's professed faith in the long-range perspective of aid; until this reform is achieved, aid policy itself will be shackled— not by the public's refusal of increases in aid, but by the administration's growing impotence to exploit them.

PART THREE / Operations

VI. Projects

The task of judging the success of Canadian policy from over three hundred capital aid transactions and several thousand technical missions is, to say the least, challenging. Economists no doubt can claim that the obvious goal of aid is development, and persuade themselves of having discovered objective standards for assessing it through decimals of increase in productivity, gross national product, or per capita income. But for the student of politics, the path toward meaningful evaluation of aid is obscured by confusion in both aims and criteria. Is the goal of aid peace, anti-communism, the promotion of exports, or simply relief of the donor's conscience? Is the right yardstick stability, liberal democracy, support for the donor's diplomacy, or some combination of these? How, indeed, can such ambiguous standards be applied in practical terms? In the absence of a satisfyingly rational political theory of aid, answers to all these questions are apt to be less scientific than dogmatic.[1]

Perhaps the most instructive method of assessing the political results of aid is to analyse operations by function, measuring presumed objectives against experience in the field. However academic this approach, it can help to identify the difficulties of each form of aid clearly and systematically. Such an analysis must first gather information through a variety of techniques: questionnaire surveys, interviews, the study of

[1]The few serious attempts to make these answers scientific cannot, however, be ignored. See George Liska, *The New Statecraft* (Chicago, 1960), for a tightly argued debate on the theoretical foundations of aid policy; Charles Wolf, Jr., *Foreign Aid: Theory and Practice in Southern Asia* (Princeton, 1960), on the techniques of allocation and measurement; and John D. Montgomery, *The Politics of Foreign Aid* (New York, 1962), for a reasoned analysis of field operations. The following assessments of Canadian operations primarily consider political and administrative problems, and do not pretend to offer economic evaluations based on possible alternative allocations of resources.

documents, and direct observation; then the assembled data must be organized, through case studies and statistical generalization, to bring real and representative problems into focus. Only by defining concrete problems and by judging their effect on the usefulness of each type of aid activity can the total influence of an aid programme be weighed realistically.

The functions of various aid activities may best be explained by starting from the established distinction between capital aid and technical assistance. Briefly stated, capital aid includes funds, materials, equipment and associated services which contribute to the permanent economic and social infrastructure of a recipient country; while technical assistance represents the transfer of skills and knowledge required to operate the recipient society's vital services. In practice, the two forms of aid often meet in common projects; but in theory, their functions differ radically, and each can therefore be understood better by remembering this difference in concept.

Within the scope of capital aid there are three general types of assistance: projects, commodities, and financial aid. Capital projects and commodities are the characteristic instruments of Canada's bilateral grant programme, which is historically the main vehicle of Canadian aid policy. But financial aid, being composed of dollar grants, loans, and export credit, is administered outside the External Aid Office (excepting soft loans) and so is not fully integrated into general aid policy.

All of Canada's commodity aid and over 90 per cent of her project aid since 1950 have been given to one area, the Colombo Plan region of South and South-East Asia. And to ensure further effectiveness through concentration, both have been limited to fields in which Canadian resources and recipients' fundamental needs coincide. These fields are shown in Table 6.1.

"Project assistance," explained the 1963 DAC *Review*, "is generally understood to mean assistance for a clearly specified purpose, such as the construction of a power plant."[2] A capital project then, as distinct from a technical assistance project, is infrastructure aid whose precise shape and use are agreed upon by donor and recipient. Almost always, capital projects comprise manufactured rather than raw materials, although commodities are sometimes supplied simultaneously to pay ancillary local costs in the recipient country.

Canada's contribution in capital projects may be assessed most intelligibly, perhaps, by reviewing its role in each of the major fields of

[2]*Development Assistance Efforts and Policies: 1963 Review*, Paris, p. 60.

TABLE 6.1

Allocation, by Fields, of Canadian Projects and Commodities (1950–March 31, 1965)*

	Canadian dollars	Percentage of total allocation
PROJECTS:		
1. Power and irrigation	137,110,881	24.5
2. Communications and transport	59,023,423	10.6
3. Natural resources	26,333,608	4.7
4. Health, welfare and education	23,751,390	4.3
5. Industry	9,849,734	1.8
(Total: Projects)	(256,069,036)	(45.9)
COMMODITIES		
1. Industrial raw materials	154,772,336	27.7
2. Foodstuffs	146,035,000	26.4
(Total: Commodities)	(300,807,336)	(54.1)
GRAND TOTAL	556,876,372	100.0

*Statistics in this table and tables following it in this chapter were supplied by the External Aid Office in June 1965. Since some of these figures represent primary allocations based on estimates, they do not necessarily reflect final disbursements. Allocations of counterpart funds to each field of development are not included here, but are discussed in chapter VII.

development listed in Table 6.1: power and irrigation; communications and transport; natural resources; health, welfare and education; and industry.

1. POWER AND IRRIGATION: THE WARSAK DAM

This vital field of economic infrastructure has absorbed more than half of Canada's bilateral grant aid in projects; and the variety of Canada's power and irrigation schemes is correspondingly impressive. As in each field to be discussed, it will be helpful to begin with a complete list of Canadian projects. Then within this perspective, a typical project will be studied in some detail, with passing reference to other relevant experience.

Although several of these projects could lend themselves to illuminating case-studies, the Warsak Multi-Purpose Project probably offers the most comprehensive illustration of the political, administrative and technical problems of this kind of aid. Taking Warsak as a point of departure, it will be possible to point to similar or peculiar difficulties in other such schemes, and thus to judge fairly coherently Canada's whole effort in the field of power and irrigation. The analysis of Warsak will examine four aspects of the project: its purpose, planning and negotiation, execution, and early results.

TABLE 6.2

Canadian Capital Projects in Power and Irrigation (1950–March 31, 1965)

Country	Project	Allocation (Canadian dollars)	Year
ASIA			
Ceylon	Gal Oya Transmission Line	1,349,575	1952–62
	Portable Irrigation Units	136,696	1953–54
	Gal Oya Agricultural Development Scheme	209,590	1954–55
	Inginiyagala-Badulla Transmission Line	2,275,000	1958–60
	Gal Oya Secondary Distribution System	125,000	1962–65
India	Mayurakshi Hydro-Electric and Irrigation Project (West Bengal)	1,299,763	1951–53
	Umtru Hydro-Electric Power Development (Assam)	1,813,717	1953–63
	Diesel Electric Generating Sets	3,007,372	1954–55
	Kundah Hydro-Electric Power Development (Madras State)	43,994,637	1955–65
	Electric Power Equipment	2,800,000	1963
	Idikki Hydro-Electric Power Project	8,200,000	1963–65
Malaysia	Perak River Hydro-Electric Feasibility Study	900,000	1963
Pakistan	Warsak Hydro-Electric and Irrigation Project	37,757,518	1952–59
	Shadiwal Hydro-Electric Power Development	3,126,820	1953–58
	Ganges-Kobadak Project (Thermal Plant for Irrigation Pumps)	2,592,963	1954–55
	Dacca-Chittagong-Karnafuli Transmission Line	5,769,620	1954–59
	Goalpara Thermal Station (Khulna)	2,062,610	1955–56
	Bheramara-Ishurdi-Goalpara Transmission Line	4,400,000	1957–63
	Sukkur Thermal Power Plant	11,415,000	1958–64
	Comilla-Sylhet Transmission Line	5,100,000	1961–63
	Sangu Multi-Purpose Scheme	355,000	1961–63
CARIBBEAN			
West Indies	Water storage and distribution	405,000	1962–64
AFRICA			
Guinea	Hydro-electric study	15,000	1964–65
Total		$137,110,881	

a. Purpose

The Warsak Dam is located on the Kabul River some nineteen miles northwest of Peshawar, near the Afghan border of Pakistan.[3] Its setting

[3]Much of the factual material for this case-study was drawn from two articles in the *Engineering Journal*, Nov. and Dec. 1960, by C. G. Kingsmill (Angus Robertson Limited) and J. H. Ings (H. G. Acres and Company). Several more popular reviews have appeared in *External Affairs*, the monthly publication of the Department of External Affairs, Ottawa. Various aspects of the project were studied by the writer during a two-week stay at the site in February 1960.

is an extremely desolate and arid region, populated by nomadic tribesmen whose harsh existence on the barren hills of the North-West Frontier had traditionally forced them to marauding and war. The Warsak
Multi-Purpose Project had four objectives: (1) to produce electric
power on a scale large enough to stimulate industrial growth in this
backward area, to overcome power shortages in southern industry, and
to reinforce the planned West Pakistan grid; at first, four turbine units
would generate 160,000 kilowatts, and provision would be made for two
more units, as needs dictated, to bring the total installed capacity of
the power station to 240,000 kilowatts; (2) to irrigate about 100,000
acres of the dry plains of Peshawar through a three and one-half-mile
concrete-lined irrigation tunnel channelling up to 500 cubic feet of
water per second; (3) to train up to 10,000 tribesmen from the sur-
rounding hills as a semi-skilled labour force for use in future development construction; and (4) through this salaried employment of local
workers, to pacify and stabilize the area's turbulent tribal society—a
result the completed project was designed to consolidate, as irrigated
farmland and electrified industry rooted the wandering Pathan tribesmen
in fruitful sedentary occupations.

All of these objectives suited well the avowed aims of Canadian
policy. Economic development in West Pakistan could be speeded
through an enlarged power capacity, increased domestic food supplies,
and the training of a large workforce. The project would help to
strengthen Pakistan's control of a strategic boundary in danger of
disintegration through Soviet-encouraged Afghan plans to unite the
Pathans of both nations in an independent "Pakhtoonistan." Canadian
industry could supply efficiently—and profitably—all the skills and
materials needed beyond local supplies. And the size and complexity
of the project made it an impressive permanent reminder that Canada
had placed her great resources and advanced technology in the service
of Pakistan's progress. The dam, a massive concrete gravity overflow
structure almost 750 feet long and 220 feet high, would stand prominently in the eyes of inhabitants and in the Pakistan government's plans
for development. In nearly every respect, the project seemed to fit both
Canada's aspirations as a donor and Pakistan's needs as a recipient.

b. Planning and negotiation[4]
Canadian consulting engineers first studied the feasibility of the Warsak

---

[4]Many of the problems outlined in this and the following section were raised
in the "Critical Report on Canadian Aid" circulated privately by the Pakistan
Government Foreign Aid Review Committee in July 1957.

project during a visit to the site in the autumn of 1952. This technical and economic investigation is a standard preliminary to Canadian approval of all major schemes. Some recipients, such as Pakistan in the cases of Warsak and Shadiwal, have regarded this procedure as an unnecessary delay to implementation of already well-planned projects; but Canada's view is that close preparatory study by the donor can save time, in the end, by avoiding costly bottlenecks during construction.[5]

The consultants' recommendation in favour of Warsak was approved by the Canadian Colombo Plan Group and the cabinet, and a consulting engineering firm from Niagara Falls was appointed to design the project and supervise its construction. A general contract for civil construction was then awarded to a Montreal company, and discussions on an Intergovernmental Project Agreement were opened with Pakistan to define the participation of each country and the precise responsibilities of each Canadian contractor.[6] The final Agreement stipulated that Canada would pay all foreign exchange costs, including those for foreign supervisors, technicians, materials and equipment; while Pakistan would pay all local rupee costs, mainly for Pakistani manpower, locally produced materials, housing, office accommodation, and all the energy requirements of construction. It was allowed that Pakistan could recover these local costs from counterpart funds generated by the sale of Canadian-donated wheat.

As in many Canadian projects, however, work on Warsak began several months before the Agreement was officially signed. Canada's willingness to anticipate planning and construction, to some extent on good faith, has usually been appreciated by recipient governments as evidence of a friendly and businesslike attitude. Many months have been saved on important projects by proceeding with work before the

---

[5]Not only recipients have doubted the value of these sometimes costly feasibility surveys. In one Asian country, best left unnamed, a local Canadian aid administrator expressed the view that some consultants—not necessarily Canadians—only "drank gin, copied the old British Army reports, and recommended extension of their own contracts." He agreed that, under the circumstances, the first two liberties might often be justified.

A good example of the usefulness of these surveys was given by a Canadian engineer who had observed the work of the Warsak survey group. Comparison of Warsak with Karnafuli, a project in East Pakistan rejected by Canada, showed a wide difference in production costs: Warsak power was to cost approximately Rs. 1,250 per kilowatt of installed capacity; and Karnafuli power was estimated to cost Rs. 4,500 per kilowatt of installed capacity.

[6]Appointment of both Canadian companies was by direct cabinet selection. Soon after, the government adopted the present policy of directly selecting only consulting engineers and architects, leaving all civil construction contracts open to bidding.

exact borders of power and responsibility have been settled. Yet in other cases, such as Shadiwal, considerable time and even goodwill have been lost from delay in signing agreements. In the absence of formal agreements, procedures of procurement and technical support have remained unclear, and the personal authority of Canadian supervisors contestable, sometimes long after the early stages of construction. Not surprisingly, local purchases and customs clearance of vital equipment have often been slowed; and ill-defined chains of command have led to psychological tensions between technicians of the host and donor countries. In the case of Warsak, Canada's early start on work at the site probably meant a net gain of several months. Since Canadian engineers reached Peshawar shortly after the award of prime contracts, the complicated problems of field administration could be attacked well before the arrival of the main Canadian work force, heavy equipment, and project installations. At the same time, this quick action conveyed to Pakistani officials an excellent impression of eager efficiency.

c. Execution
The implementation of a large capital project tests a donor's policy at three levels: technical, administrative and sociological. The answers given to problems in each of these fields determine the effectiveness of every project and of the programmes as a whole.

Technically, the Warsak Dam is judged by qualified experts to be an engineering feat of great boldness.[7] The design and construction of massive, yet precise, engineering works in an almost inaccessible hill region lacking water and power supplies, skilled labour, and even simple housing, would be trying enough for local contractors in Canada; the same task complicated by the need to lay lines of supply and communication over 10,000 miles to an area of hostile climate and unknown society, approached the Herculean.

Warsak was completed, it is true, well over a year behind its original schedule. But this delay was due less to faulty calculation than to the difficulty of penetrating unforeseen rock formations to pierce the diversion tunnel. And the need to work out administrative procedures also slowed early progress. Both donor and recipient had to learn the new art of transferring foreign aid; and, as one of the first really large projects, Warsak was a test-bed for practical international co-operation.

Apart from occasional shortages of cement and spare parts, the

[7]This view was expressed not only by Pakistani and Canadian engineers, but by representatives of American and multilateral agencies in West Pakistan. See again the above articles in the *Engineering Journal*.

gravest technical problem of Warsak during construction was the lack of trained Pakistani workers. Soon after work began, almost twice the planned number of Canadians had to be imported; this brought the total permanent crew of skilled Canadian tradesmen to over one hundred, in addition to some fifty Canadian consulting engineers and supervisors. The tradesmen, mainly electricians, welders, carpenters and, later, turbine specialists, performed routine operational jobs, served as foremen for the roughly 10,000 Pakistani labourers, and trained the tribal workers in several trades.

The use of these skilled Canadian tradesmen speeded construction significantly. The vigour and industry of the Canadian workers, and the sense of urgency of the Canadian contracting firms, visibly impressed Pakistani observers; as a group, the Canadians established a pace and quality of construction that stimulated all the participants.[8] From the standpoint of technical efficiency in completing the job and in training a large, primitive work force, the Canadian tradesmen were necessary. And they contributed vividly to the immediate symbolism of Warsak as a joint endeavour of two friendly peoples—even though, as it will be shown, the psychological problems they raised left in some doubt the wisdom of mingling cultures at this level.

Many of the most severe problems during construction of Canadian projects are administrative. A first difficulty may arise, it has already been hinted, from slowness in signing an intergovernmental project agreement setting out the administrative and technical responsiblities of participating governments and contractors. On some Canadian projects—including Warsak—engineers have suffered serious frustrations because the project agreement was not signed before work began. One Canadian project manager in Asia, after complaining in a March 1958 confidential report of his lack of documented authority over local labour, and of the host country's slowness in reimbursing local expenses, explained his trouble in these words: "Unfortunately the Agreement still remains unsigned even though we have been resident at site for one and a half years. Our position will be slightly strengthened when the Agreement is signed because occasionally we are told by junior officers,

[8]The Pakistani Chief Engineer of the project and several other Pakistani officials believed that this example of Canadians—even university-trained engineers —working with their hands, side by side with Pakistani workers, was one of the most valuable technical and psychological lessons of Warsak. One year, when monsoon rains threatened to delay progress, the Canadian staff worked even on Christmas Day, showing a zeal that deeply impressed their devout Moslem colleagues.

overseers, etc. that we are here in an advisory capacity."[9] By December 1959, the Agreement for this project had still not been signed. In a letter to his company, the same project manager stressed then that the absence of a formal Agreement had caused both misunderstanding and delay, adding, "it is very desirable that this agreement be completed before the project gets under way and especially before representatives of the consulting engineers are sent to site. The main point of contact between the Canadian representatives and [those of the host country] is at the project site. It is therefore important that both parties be clearly aware from the outset of their duties, responsibilities and authority." Recognizing this need, the External Aid Office decided in 1961 to delay on-site work on future projects until agreements were signed. The reform has generally tended to reduce conflicts of jurisdiction during work; but the urgency of completing projects—and, in Africa and the Caribbean before 1964, the danger of annually lapsing funds—have often forced Canada to relax this rule.[10]

Even if a project agreement has been signed in advance, a Canadian project manager usually faces three administrative problems during construction. The least costly, though often the most vexing physically, results from unsatisfactory housing and transport for Canadian personnel. Normally these facilities are supplied by the recipient country; but since definitions of "adequate comfort" and "convenience" differ widely for peoples from two continents, Canadian engineers frequently waste much time debating improvements in these conditions with local officials, or in persuading disgruntled Canadians that available services are indeed suitable.

At Warsak, Pakistan built a modern and comfortable "colony" for its Canadian guests, and the Canadian government and contractors added

[9]No agreement was signed for another project, the Dacca-Chittagong transmission lines, until two years after work began. Some six months of intergovernmental negotiation were then required to settle the retroactive payment of local costs. Even when the agreement had entered into force for Warsak, debate over payment of local costs such as spare parts, housing, and internal travel continued. To resolve these arguments Canadian and Pakistani authorities established a so-called "knock-for-knock" account under which the costs of disputed items (Canadian air-conditioners and Pakistani pumps, for instance) could cancel each other out. At the end of construction, however, 546 audit objections were left to confuse this imprest account; and in April 1964, over three years after Warsak's inauguration, more than thirty of these still remained unsettled.

[10]Work on Sukkur, for example, began in August 1961, while the project agreement there was not signed until March 1962. The Nigerian aerial survey also began before an agreement was approved, for the compelling reason that unfavourable weather threatened to delay flying for several months.

recreational facilities that made life, if not work, most bearable, even in 120-degree heat. Other projects have not always provided Canadian tradesmen with such pleasant accommodation; but Canadian workers have usually accepted what was offered, as long as those on each project enjoyed reasonably equal privileges. Such equality has not always existed. Before the EAO assumed the administration of engineering contracts in December 1961, different Canadian contractors on the same job were allowed to supply varying benefits additional to the host country's contribution. As a result, Canada's participation in certain projects was marred by unnecessary rivalries and conflicts among Canadians themselves. On one large project engaging several Canadian companies, the bitterness among Canadians over differences in housing, transport and family allowances supplied or supplemented by Canada did not escape Asian colleagues. The deplorable impression left by such quarrels, which are harmful on any construction job but humiliating in an external aid programme, is easily imagined.[11]

A second problem is local purchasing. Usually Canadian purchases on local markets are handled by an agency of the host government which, through tender, buys on behalf of the Canadian contractor. This formula is adopted because the host authorities are eventually charged with local costs, are more familiar with local markets, and can theoretically procure items more quickly and at lower prices. Canadian project managers and stores officers frequently feel, however, that direct purchasing by Canadians would be faster and cheaper, being free from prolonged tendering procedures and alleged "baksheesh" arrangements. Even if items purchased directly were more costly, they argue, the time gained would allow great savings by reactivating idle equipment and manpower. At Warsak, a special agency of the Pakistan Government, the Warsak Dam Project Organization (WDPO), handled all local purchases, and maintained clean and orderly stores for locally produced necessities. A parallel Canadian stores department maintained stocks of Canadian spare parts and equipment, and passed on requests for local

[11]Asian hosts at the above project were treated to the curious spectacle of Canadian workers "high-jacking" jeeps from other Canadian companies thought to enjoy superior transport facilities. At least once this involuntary sharing of vehicles led to a high-speed road chase by the high-jackers and their pursuers in plain view of their astounded hosts. Other discontent grew from unequal rights to bring wives and personal automobiles to the recipient country—in both cases, the risk of high-jacking being fraught with consequences too distressing to contemplate.

Inter-company rivalries were infrequent at Warsak, although turbine specialists there unsuccessfully threatened to strike on one occasion over alleged inequalities in canteen allowances.

purchases to the WDPO. In some ways, this arrangement was sensible. At the same time, it was natural that the urgent needs of a Canadian construction team should often be difficult to reconcile with the stringently regulated Indian Civil Service type of procedures of the Pakistani WDPO.[12]

Many Canadian project managers in like circumstances have desired wider discretion in local purchasing, with control of a standing fund in local currency to permit rapid procurement of the small but vital items that can occasionally tie up an entire job. At the end of 1959, one Canadian project manager in Asia reported:

We have lost a lot of time due to the want of minor items such as welding rod, acetylene and oxygen, small tools and so on. These items have been available in the local market but their purchase has sometimes not been made due to the forgetfulness or lack of organization of the . . . Executive Engineer. In some cases purchases have not been made, with the mistaken notion of trying to save money.

A glaring example at . . . has been the lack of oxygen and acetylene. This is produced in . . ., 80 miles away by road, but it took 2 years negotiations to persuade the Executive Engineer to return the cylinders by truck instead of rail. The trucks have been supplied by Canada as part of the aid but the argument ran that the cost of the gas was greater than the cost of the rail freight. We estimate that we have lost not less than one month on the construction schedule due to the lack of oxygen and acetylene.

Each party to such disagreements is legitimately conditioned by his own training and responsibilities. Yet technical staff cannot settle problems rooted in long-established government administrative techniques without risking political complications. In the interest of rapid economic progress, some of these techniques certainly need streamlining. Still, the co-operative concept of international aid and the basic obligation to respect the political authority of recipient nations demand that some variation of the bilateral purchasing formula be preserved. But in no event should resulting administrative troubles be allowed to engender harmful conflicts among technicians of the participating countries.

A third administrative problem results from delays in the recipient country's procedures for customs clearance and shipping. Equipment supplied as foreign aid is normally liable, as are all imported goods, to customs duties. These duties, as well as clearance charges and internal

[12]The Director General of External Aid called the appointment of the Pakistani Chief Engineer of Warsak as head of the WDPO a "mistake" that should not be repeated on future projects. (*Standing Committee on External Affairs*, 1961, p. 161). A colourful, and admittedly coloured, view of the trials of Asian administration was conveyed by William Stevenson in "The Babu-cracy of India," *Globe and Mail*, Toronto, Jan. 23, 1961, p. 7.

transport for Canadian aid are paid as "local costs" by the recipient government. On nearly all Canadian projects, some delays have occurred because machinery for unblocking bottlenecks at points of entry and shipment was ineffective. The Pakistan Foreign Aid Review Committee reported the delay in Karachi of some small consignments to Warsak for more than one year, partly owing to faulty distribution of shipping documents. Some emergency air-freight shipments of spare parts from Canada were held in Madras for several months because no suitable procedure existed there to speed clearance to Kundah.[18] Such delays obviously cause substantial increases in project costs both for Canada and the recipient: Canada must spend extra aid dollars to maintain her staff for every day wasted, and the recipient government must pay demurrage charges—charges which make release from customs still more difficult, because they disrupt usually rigid project budgets.

The Warsak Project established its own "clearance expeditor organization" in Karachi in the first year of construction, and this led to real improvement. Yet even then, the Canadian High Commissioner had occasionally to intervene at cabinet level to secure release of goods or allocation of special rail cars. Other projects have not been as fortunate. Frequently, customs clearance and transport of goods to site within the recipient country take longer than sea freight from Canada. Equipment for the Maple Leaf Cement Factory in West Pakistan, for example, was held in Karachi for months because Canadian representatives could obtain neither rail wagons of proper size nor permission from railway authorities to cross low-roof bridges with bulky machinery. The Ganges-Kobadak Project was similarly retarded by lack of heavy barges for river transport. Sometimes, important equipment has been delayed because of simple misunderstandings that a special expediting agent at ports of entry could easily avoid: shipments of dynamite and grease guns (mistaken for "guns from Greece") were held up by one country for issue of arms permits. Some of these delays have exposed Canadian materials to costly pilfering and vandalism, acts which have frequently caused still greater financial losses in construction time.

Such frustrations understandably provoke friction between Canadian technicians and their colleagues of the recipient country. While often admiring the Canadians' initiative and energy, officials of host countries instinctively feel that foreigners who wish to change established methods of administration are not—as the Canadians invariably think—strengthening the recipient's ability to absorb aid, but only undermining its public

---

[18]Most Canadian equipment for Kundah, however, entered India through the west coast seaport of Cochin, where special expediting machinery did ensure a smooth flow of supplies.

order and sovereignty. Many Canadians, for their part, view the recipient's administration as the root of nearly all technical problems, and as a formidable obstacle to economic development. One typical Canadian project report complained that

The responsibilities and sanctioning powers of each level of authority [in the host country] are defined rigidly by the Public Works Department Rules, a "Bible" built up over the past 100 years. Each officer in the chain of command will only contact or write the officer immediately above or below him. Moreover each officer wants an order from his superior or request from his subordinate in writing before taking action. This "action" may consist only of passing the order or request up or down the chain of command. With this set-up it is hardly surprising that action is slow, as it is bogged down in administrative and organizational procedures.

. . . As a consequence I have had to adopt an attitude of polite and persistent persuasion, and the whole problem has taken a disproportionate amount of my time.

It is true, of course, that this debate recalls poignantly the classical conflict of government works administrators and private contractors in Canada. But inevitably this natural functional disagreement is mistaken on aid projects for distrust between nationalities; and its political effects are therefore potentially far more dangerous.

The chief sociological lesson of Warsak questions the wisdom of sending abroad large numbers of hastily selected and relatively unsophisticated tradesmen. Doubtless some of these men have proved better diplomats than certain of their more educated superiors; examples of "ugly Canadian" workers befriending and helping local colleagues in their spare time are far from unknown. But the great majority of skilled Canadian workers have had difficulty in adapting to the deep changes of culture and status imposed by overseas service. Many express their reaction through insatiable complaints about material accommodation; others exhibit more extravagant symptoms of "culture shock."[14]

This maladjustment cannot be blamed merely on the workers' usual inexperience in alien environments. While their Canadian superiors generally maintain warm and easy friendships with their foreign counterparts, Canadian tradesmen meet a double handicap to such relations in the structure of the local society: the educated but highly class-conscious local officials who do speak English tend to despise any workers lacking formal higher education; and the non-English-speaking local labourers

[14]C. G. Kingsmill, in his article in the *Engineering Journal* (Nov. 1960, p. 46), showed in a detailed chart, however, that the turnover in Canadian employees at Warsak compared very favourably with that on a normal project in Canada. This record may owe something to the deterrent of financial penalties incurred by workers terminating contracts ahead of schedule, but still more to high wages—usually 25 per cent above similar Canadian rates, and tax-free.

share neither language nor Westernized customs with their Canadian colleagues. These social and linguistic barriers were sharply evident at Warsak where the harsh tribal *mores* of the Pathans struck many Canadian workers as archaic, repugnant and disconcerting. Not surprisingly, this reaction, too often ill-concealed, led native workers at Warsak and on some other jobs to complain privately of the Canadians' unnecessary roughness and lack of understanding. The unwillingness of some Canadians to sympathize with local religious customs, notably daily prayers and Ramadan, and their habit of addressing local workers in pungent barracks epithets (invariably still more offensive in literal translation) were indelicacies that the proud and puritanical tribesmen could not easily forgive.[15]

It would be unfair to condemn the Canadian technicians alone for this result. Canadian companies must recruit men who are above all technically competent; and they cannot reasonably expect that every skilled man engaged will be a master of international diplomacy. Trained workers are interested primarily in doing a job well and quickly, and are naturally impatient with customs, methods or persons that appear to slow progress. In the interest of satisfactory relations between Canadian and host country technicians, therefore, it would seem wise to send overseas only high-level Canadian consultants and supervisors, leaving ordinary contracting work to entrepreneurs of the recipient country. Where this formula has been followed—on the aerial surveys and, with attenuations, at Kundah, Gal Oya, Shadiwal and Ganges-Kobadak—Canada's name has been better served by the presence of men respected for their minds, as well as their skills. The use of a large crew of tradesmen at Warsak was necessary to complete that vast project in a reasonable time. But the experience should not be repeated unless the selection, briefing and supervision of Canadian workers can be much more closely controlled by the Canadian government.

[15]The bad feeling engendered by such behaviour was apparent in several villages near projects employing Canadian tradesmen. While villagers recognized that most Canadian foremen were correct, they agreed that few were actively sympathetic to the local workers' problems. Occasionally these workers accused individual Canadians of using physical violence (one Canadian—not at Warsak—confided that he regularly "biffed" his local workers to ensure obedience), though fortunately the delinquents were not usually regarded as representative of Canadian staff.

One egregious Canadian who did, however, endear himself to his men was an amateur equestrian known by legend at Warsak as "Harry the Horse." Fiercely admired by the warrior Pathans for his defiant preference of cantering to dam-building, Harry ended his days on the North-West Frontier after riding a horse into the dining-room of a hotel in Peshawar to prove a claim that the food there was unfit for man or beast.

Two marginal benefits of the large Canadian colony at Warsak, however, were the school and the hospital equipped and partly staffed by Canadian authorities. Many of the psychological disadvantages that Canadian policy may have suffered from the "golden ghetto" appearance of the Warsak colony were offset by the fine impression left by these two institutions. Pakistani engineers and their families enjoyed full use of Canadian recreational facilities, of course, and apart from a few unfortunate incidents, these arrangements encouraged happy fraternizations.[16] But the international school and hospital evoked from most Pakistanis respect and gratitude. For the children of Canadian personnel, the Canadian government provided a two-room primary school staffed by Canadian teachers and based on the Ontario Public School curriculum up to Grade Eight. The school was open to the children of Pakistani engineers, several of whom accepted this invitation. Of much wider service was the modern, 50-bed hospital operated for all the 11,000 persons associated with the project, Pakistani and Canadian. This self-contained institution had an operating theatre, an X-ray room and a laboratory; its Canadian medical staff included two doctors and three nurses, while its Pakistani staff comprised two doctors, thirty nurses (including eight girls—a startling innovation in Moslem tribal territory), and four laboratory technicians. This small but efficient clinic probably won for Canada the gratitude of more ordinary foreign nationals than any other single Canadian project. For the first time, thousands of tribesmen and their families enjoyed, free of charge, the most up-to-date medical care available. Through this care, the tribal folk obviously understood in simple human terms the message of international solidarity that the great concrete dam itself was partly intended to convey.[17]

[16]Comradeship in bowling and outdoor sports was warm and vigorous. International dancing parties, however, proved a disappointment, at least for the men. Since Pakistani engineers usually left their wives at home in *purdah*, a lively and at times unseemly competition for Canadian lady partners often put the on-site solidarity of Pakistani and Canadian technicians to the most elemental of strains.

[17]The following statistics on the hospital's record in 1959 were supplied by the Director, Dr. D. M. Goode of Fredericton, N.B.:

	Pakistanis	Canadians	Others	Total
Admissions	542	179	47	768
Babies		16		16
Out-patients	48,489	4,524		53,013

The Warsak Hospital, with all its equipment and trained Pakistani staff, was taken over on completion of the project by the Pakistan public health authorities.

On no other project has a full-scale Canadian medical facility been established, such care being normally supplied by the recipient country. But if Canadian policy hopes to express aid in ways that will help directly, and be understood by, the average inhabitants of recipient nations, perhaps other Canadian hospitals should be attached to projects employing a sizable Canadian staff. Resident Canadians would thereby enjoy probably more satisfactory treatment, and a valuable human touch would be added to the impersonal transfer of goods and equipment.

d. A provisional assessment

What, in sum, has been the contribution of Warsak to the achievement of Canadian policy aims? The major technical goals of Warsak were of course entirely realized, though not without some delays through miscalculation. The full capacity of the four installed turbines was not exploited for several months after completion, for Pakistan had been unable to erect transmission lines on schedule. And probably Canada could have speeded Pakistan's take-over of exclusive control by training in advance larger numbers of power plant operators. Since this take-over, furthermore, the slowness and inaccuracy of some Canadian suppliers of spare parts have caused Pakistan's engineers at Warsak considerable inconvenience. Yet none of these mistakes diminishes the enormous immediate impact of Warsak in doubling West Pakistan's 1954 installed capacity for electrical generation, and in breathing life into 100,000 acres of formerly infertile dust. Monthly reports from Warsak in 1964 confirmed that Pakistan's engineers were continuing to run the plant at a highly efficient level. When increased demand overtakes present generation, there is no doubt that Pakistan will wish to acquire the two final turbines to bring the total installed capacity up to its full potential of 240,000 kilowatts.

In addition to these general economic benefits, Warsak and other projects like it have brought hope and comfort to great numbers of individuals. Probably forty to fifty thousand Asians employed on Canadian power and irrigation projects have learned semi-skilled or skilled trades, found a measure of personal economic stability, and, through spending their relatively high salaries, assured their villages an unaccustomed prosperity. Salaries at Warsak, for example, were well above prevailing wage levels: clerks began at Rs. 150 per month, foremen at Rs. 210, and supervisors (70 per cent of whom were illiterate) at Rs. 300. The villagers near Warsak, Shadiwal and Kundah were obviously enjoying during construction a standard of living never approached by their ancestors. Whole families could for the first time eat enough, educate their children, and buy bicycles or other desiderata of economic progress.[18] Four or five million villagers will benefit from irrigation and lighting from the Kundah Project; industrial workers in Madras, West Bengal, Assam, East and West Pakistan, and Ceylon, will be directly aided by Canadian electricity, power lines or irrigation; and the secondary effects of new power and food supplies will be felt permanently throughout local economies in new employment, spending and development.[19]

Not all Canadian projects, of course, have succeeded as encouragingly as Warsak. Nine of twelve pumps supplied to the Gal Oya Agricultural Development Scheme, for instance, were idle for over a year because of a change in planning priorities by the Ceylon government; and two years after completion, Canada's thermal plant in the Ganges-Kobadak Scheme was not used for driving the planned irrigation pumps because the related commitments of other aid agencies had not been met. But even in these cases, no irremediable loss occurred. Ganges-Kobadak later greatly increased East Pakistan's food production; and the Gal Oya pumps were suitable for use on other similar projects. In general, then, Canada's investment in power and irrigation has achieved its economic objective of stimulating lasting increases in productivity.

In the measure that generous publicity is a fair standard of success, power and irrigation schemes have also served well the political aims of Canadian policy. Most Canadian projects in this field have received gratifyingly wide coverage in the press and official statements of recipient countries. At the opening of the Kundah Power House No. 1 in March 1960, Prime Minister Nehru personally attended ceremonies to congratulate Canadian workers and the Canadian High Commissioner—as did President Ayub Khan when Warsak was inaugurated in January

[18]The *Morning News* of Karachi, on April 14, 1957, told of Warsak tribesmen owning automobiles, trucks, scooters, and business concerns in Peshawar, saying that they (probably the village *Maliks*, who received special grants for inducing their fellows to work) "are now living a happier, healthier and more contented life." The same newspaper on July 16, 1957, estimated that labour conditions (salaries, canteen, shops and medical care) at Warsak were "the best obtainable anywhere in the Pak-Bharati sub-continent."

[19]Regrettably the benefit of Warsak to power consumers was diminished by a substantial rise in electricity rates soon after the dam's inauguration. Although the increase resulted from the creation of a single West Pakistan rate based on higher costs in the south, and from the relatively short amortization period decided on by the West Pakistan Water and Power Development Authority (WAPDA "purchased" Warsak from the central government), many Pakistani consumers tended to blame the higher rate on expensive Canadian construction techniques.

1961. The *Mail* of Madras and the *Indian Express* of Madurai both gave front-page coverage to Canadian participation in Kundah, and the *Hindu* of Madras published a four-page supplement on March 25, 1960, with a leading article entitled "Successful Indo-Canadian Venture." The dam at Mayurakshi was named the "Canada Dam," and the power houses at Kundah all carried large neon signs reading "Canada Power House." On the other hand, smaller, locally important projects, such as Shadiwal and the Ceylon transmission lines, have enjoyed little publicity. This neglect is partly explained by the modest size of these projects, but also, perhaps, by the constant attention devoted by Canadian diplomatic staffs to larger and more impressive projects. The importance of regular visits to smaller projects by Canadian officials should not be under-estimated. Such visits not only sustain the morale of isolated Canadian workers; they are the easiest and surest way of awakening the interest of both the local press and recipient authorities.

The extraordinary publicity won for Canada by Warsak was due in part, of course, to the project's intrinsic importance; but it owed much also to the work of a full-time Pakistani public relations staff at the site. From this small group, or on its inspiration, flowed an avalanche of publicity that made Warsak and Canada familiar and synonymous throughout Pakistan.[20] Certainly not all of the published articles were the paeans of hired propagandists. In the *Khyber Mail* of Peshawar on June 6, 1957, for example, Arnold Toynbee praised Warsak as being "admirably designed for solving the problem of the frontier that the Pakistanis inherited from the British, and the British, a hundred years back, from the Sikhs . . ." Then, in what one writer has already noted as a characteristic Toynbee analogy, he compared the pacification of the Pathans to that of the barbarian Scots, who had been absorbed "into the Glasgow mills and the homesteads of Upper Canada"![21] But the

[20]Analysis of the press-clipping files of the Canadian High Commission in Karachi in February 1960 showed the following predominance of Warsak in coverage of Canadian aid by the West Pakistan press over a three-year period from January 20, 1957, to January 2, 1960:
1. Articles or editorials on Canadian aid, 303
2. Number of the above concerning Warsak, 222
   —including photographs, 57
3. Above Warsak articles mentioning Canada, 122
4. General surveys of Canadian aid, 18
5. Articles on Canadian technical assistance, 32
   —including photographs, 6
6. Articles on other capital projects (Shadiwal), 13
7. Articles on wheat shipments, 18
   —including photographs, 2

[21]See James Eayrs, *Canada in World Affairs, October 1955 to June 1957* (Toronto, 1959), pp. 208–9, who quotes an article by Toynbee reprinted from the *Observer*, London, in the *Montreal Daily Star*, Nov. 27, 1957.

number and warmth of Pakistani references to Canada at Warsak suggested that the public relations staff had advertised Canadian participation widely and enthusiastically. On September 4, 1957, President Iskander Mirza thanked Canada in the *Times* of Karachi for her "nation-building project," a "colossal undertaking" that would "strengthen the Commonwealth and emphasize its importance as a great family of nations." An editorial of the Karachi *Evening Star* on January 13, 1960, affirmed that "this project will go down in history as a signal example of enlightened co-operation between Canada and Pakistan, two countries of the Free World, situated half the globe apart." The *Morning News* of Karachi on January 20, 1957, said "these solid efforts by the Canadians go a long way in the establishment of world peace and in removing economic and social inequalities." The same journal on November 15, 1959, told why Warsak would be remembered by the ordinary Pakistani workers: "Canadian engineers are still looked upon with awe by tribal workers because they roll up their sleeves and labour with their hands on back-breaking jobs which could have been passed on to juniors in their profession. . . . Deep in the recesses of the tunnel the Canadians can be seen panting, sweating and leading groups of unskilled employees, grimy and black with grease. Small wonder that the tribal workers shovelling sand are amazed that educated foreigners labour with them in the rough earth."

In brief, Pakistani opinion believed that "Canada should be proud," as the Lahore magazine *West Pakistan* expressed it on November 1, 1958, "that a country of seventeen million is able and willing to help . . . Pakistan. . . . [Warsak is] a permanent monument to the industry and the goodwill of Canadians. . . . the benefits derived therefrom will prove a lasting token of friendship. . . ." At least temporarily, Warsak had become a brilliant symbol of Pakistan's national progress. For many Pakistanis, it had become, as an eager writer in the Karachi *Morning News* urged on January 12, 1960, after seeing hundreds of Sunday tourists at Warsak, "our Taj, our Sphinx, our Colossus."

It is impossible, of course, to relate these panegyrics precisely to Canada's diplomatic influence in Pakistan. It is a fact, however, that during the construction of Warsak and other large power or irrigation projects in India and Ceylon, Canada enjoyed a close and trusting relationship with each recipient government that was unequalled by the influence of several more powerful nations. In at least one case—largely, it seems, as a result of daily co-operation with local officials on four important power schemes—the Canadian High Commissioner did indeed almost serve as what the Director General of External Aid later called an "*ex officio* member of the [recipient's] cabinet."

This relative intimacy can in some measure be ascribed to the partial eclipse of former colonial powers, to the developing nations' distrust of the Cold War motives of the United States and USSR, and not least of all to the skill of Canadian diplomatists. But would Canada have commanded such confidence had she not offered generous and fundamental assistance? Probably not. This conclusion does not prove that aid can secure permanent international friendships; Pakistan's pronounced disenchantment with Canada following Ottawa's military aid to India in 1963 shows that the warmest of aid-fostered friendships is not immune to the chilling strains of normal conflicts of interest and judgment.

Yet aid enables Canada to participate in the recipients' nearly all-absorbing national activity, economic development; and it thereby provides a natural pretext for constant, fruitful consultation that should, in the long run, place these conflicts in a perspective of understanding. Canada's aid to power and irrigation, as the backbone of this participation, has vigorously enlivened the spirit of practical partnership that can sometimes translate understanding into conciliation.

2. COMMUNICATIONS AND TRANSPORT: THE ST. VINCENT DOCK

Aid to communications and transport does not increase production directly; rather it liberates existing productive capacity or allows such capacity to be exploited more efficiently. In this function, it nevertheless strengthens a recipient's infrastructure. For while aid to power and irrigation may immediately increase industrial and agricultural output, the new factories and crops thus created are economically imprisoned unless roads, railways, ports and rapid communications bring food and manufactures promptly to consumers. The special role of transport and communications aid is therefore to stimulate production indirectly by making it profitable and socially useful. Its mission is not to create wealth, but to free it and distribute it.

From the donor's viewpoint, aid in this field is often less politically rewarding than the more lasting and massive "monuments" of other categories. It is true that certain types of transport aid (such as the Bombay State buses) are widely seen in recipient countries; but harbour cranes, railway ties or radio-navigation equipment are either hidden from public view or are by nature unexciting. Prestige or propaganda projects are not incompatible with this type of aid. Yet they do not emerge easily from the peculiar and limited resources that Canada is able to offer.

TABLE 6.3

Canadian Capital Projects in Communications and Transport (1950–March 31, 1965)

Country	Project	Allocation (Canadian dollars)	Year
ASIA			
Burma	Highway survey	125,600	1957–58
	Thaketa Bridge	1,440,000	1958–64
Ceylon	Railway ties	183,600	1953–55
	Ten diesel locomotives	1,759,480	1953–57
	Colombo Harbour equipment	647,292	1953–59
	Telecommunications equipment (Ratmalana Airport)	407,000	1954–60
	Katunayake Airport (terminal and runway extension)	3,359,000	1963–65
India	Bombay State Transport (trucks and buses)	4,352,775	1951–52
	Locomotive boilers	1,815,450	1952–53
	Steam locomotives	21,470,045	1953–55
	Railway ties	5,493,593	1957–59
	Diesel shunter locomotives	1,540,000	1959–60
	Meteorological equipment	250,000	1959–60
	Construction equipment	3,500,000	1964–65
Indonesia	Three Otter aircraft	400,000	1958–59
Malaysia*	Equipment for Department of Public Works	517,500	1959–61
	Highway survey	250,000	1962
	Television network	500,000	1962
	Singapore Harbour development	200,000	1964–65
Pakistan	Railway ties	2,770,490	1951–52
	Karachi Port Trust equipment	100,000	1963–64
CARIBBEAN			
West Indies Federation	Two cargo-passenger ships	5,868,095	1960–62
	Port handling equipment	290,130	1961
British Guiana	Road-building equipment	30,000	1962
	Trucks	44,500	1964
St. Vincent	Dock and warehouses	1,008,670	1960–64
Trinidad	VOR System—Piarco International Airport	149,500	1964
AFRICA			
Guinea	Road-building equipment	170,000	1964–65
Kenya	Road-building equipment	127,950	1962–63
	Radio transmitters	38,000	1964–65
Nigeria	Meteorological equipment	117,753	1963
Tanzania	Trucks	75,000	1964–65
Uganda	Trucks	22,000	1963–64
Total		$59,023,423	

*Including Singapore, which withdrew from the Federation in August 1965.

Since much of this aid takes the form of simple transfers of equipment, it generally raises fewer administrative and psychological problems than complex projects engaging numerous Canadian technicians abroad. Consequently, Canadian projects in this category can best be reviewed by dwelling more briefly than before on a single case study, and by emphasizing the variety of experience gained through Canada's whole contribution to transport and communications.

Among the most worthwhile of these projects stands the deep-water port at Kingstown, capital of the British Caribbean island of St. Vincent. Since it called for transferring overseas not only materials but Canadian technicians, the St. Vincent Dock Project is perhaps not entirely typical of most Canadian activities in transport and communications; but as a timely and effective investment of aid funds it sets a standard of careful selection that suggests for this field a rich economic and even political potential.

a. Purpose and planning

The project took shape following a tour of West Indian harbour facilities by two Canadian government engineers in mid-1959. Their survey, undertaken at the request of the British colonial authorities, revealed that handling costs for general cargo in all the ports visited were higher, in terms of cost per ton, than those in nearly all other Caribbean and South American ports. This inefficiency was laid to three factors: (1) the smallness of consignments, reflecting the modest production and demands of each island population; (2) the lack of warehouse space, which left goods unprotected during frequent violent storms; and (3) the absence or inadequacy of mechanical handling equipment.

To help overcome these deficiencies, the engineers recommended two related Canadian contributions. To begin, they proposed that Canada supply to various sites such handling equipment as cranes, motor trolleys and trailers. This aid, costing an estimated $340,000, would benefit several small islands, notably Barbados, St. Kitts, Grenada, St. Vincent, Dominica, Antigua and Montserrat.

The second proposal foresaw the construction of a deep-water pier and two warehouses on the south-west coast of St. Vincent at Kingstown. British engineers had already carried out successful soundings and test borings in Kingstown bay during 1958, and had shown the scheme to be technically feasible at reasonable cost. The Canadian engineers noted also that the suggested wharf promised to stir a lively economic renaissance on the island by enabling ocean-going vessels to pick up and discharge cargo without using lightering services to carry goods in small boats between ships and shore. Since St. Vincent was then served by six major shipping lines and maintained an expanding trade and schooner traffic with the other islands in the West Indian Federation, the project was attractive both economically and politically.

The growing volume of trade in fact made the wharf an economic necessity; and by further intensifying inter-island commerce the scheme would strengthen a Commonwealth political grouping whose internal cohesion was far from assured.

Accepting the Canadian engineers' estimate that the St. Vincent development would probably cost no more than $1,200,000, ETAB recommended the scheme to the Secretary of State for External Affairs on October 5, 1959. The cabinet approved this recommendation shortly after, and fixed the maximum Canadian contribution at $1,000,000, the St. Vincent authorities being invited to pay all costs above this figure.

As at Warsak, both consulting and contracting firms were engaged by Canada. Following established custom, the EAO awarded the consulting contract to a company judged most experienced in the type of work and the country at hand; and the contractors were selected, after suitable announcement in November 1961, by public tender.[22]

b. Execution

Although earlier Canadian misfortunes in Asia had led in theory to a new policy of delaying on-site work until an intergovernmental project agreement was signed, no such agreement was concluded until August 1, 1963, exactly one year after the Canadian contractors reached St. Vincent. Happily, the delays and frustrations met by Canadian project managers elsewhere because of such negligence did not mar work here. From the beginning, Canadian and Vincentian authorities collaborated smoothly; and when the agreement (since mid-1961 called a "Memorandum of Understanding") was signed, it served more to acknowledge adopted practice than to delimit previously doubtful responsibilities.

Exceptionally, Canadian financial participation covered more than the project's "foreign exchange content"; the recipient colonial govern-

[22]Private complaints that certain Canadian ministers have ignored lowest bids and awarded aid contracts for partisan or "pork-barrel" purposes have never been substantiated. Although at one time a very high percentage of capital contracts was awarded to firms in a city containing the riding of the minister responsible for aid, closer investigation showed this concentration to reflect a genuine coincidence of recipients' needs with the specialized services offered by these firms. In a speech before the British Columbia Association of Professional Engineers in December 1963, the Director General explained that the government's policy was to "award contracts in a way that will not only permit a wide distribution of the fees but will also enable the maximum number of competent Canadian companies to gain experience in Asia, Africa and elsewhere." This was "desirable," he thought, "because . . . today a number of competent Canadian firms are in a more favourable position to seek [foreign commercial] contracts through work they have performed and experience they have gained on overseas projects under Canada's assistance programmes."

ment paid only those local costs beyond Canada's fixed contribution of $1,000,000. The Canadian consultants designed the wharf and warehouses, supplied layout drawings for construction, named a project manager with full control of engineering and building, and carried out final inspection. The contractors provided all labour, material and equipment, raised temporary buildings, ensured loading, shipping and customs clearance of project materials, and arranged for all West Indian subcontracts and services. During construction these arrangements produced a maximum work force of 290 Vincentians under the supervision of seventeen Canadian engineers and foremen.

Construction of the pier and two warehouses presented no fundamental technical problems, though some difficulties did retard progress temporarily. First, the leads of the long raker piles proved too short to hold the piles in their completed length, and more time was needed to sink them deeper. Next, following the contractor's decision to reclaim four acres of land by dredging up fill from the bay instead of trucking it from the hills, the dredging pumps were blocked by stones and coral, causing a further brief delay. This deepening of the ocean floor reduced the Canadian cost of the pier by enabling it to be built closer to shore; but the unforeseen clogging, as well as the use of a nine-inch pump for the twelve-inch suction dredge, probably slowed completion by several weeks. Nevertheless, these mishaps—which could easily occur on a normal job in Canada—were minor; and the St. Vincent project was completed well within the planned schedule. That it was built well, moreover, was proved when the partly finished works survived at least one severe hurricane with no serious damage.[23]

Administration of the St. Vincent scheme was likewise remarkably untroublesome. This "incredible lack of problems," thought the consultant in April 1964, owed much to the similar institutions inherited by Canada and St. Vincent from a common British tradition. It also certainly resulted from the project's nearness to Canadian sources of supply, from the informality of customs clearance and the ease of communication on a small island, and from the modest number of Canadians

---

[23]Technical miscalculations are certainly more frequent on aid projects because Canadian engineers are less familiar with foreign soils, climate, materials and equipment. A caisson for the Thaketa Bridge, for instance, upset into the Pazundaung River in mid-1963, causing a delay of five to six months. The consultant at St. Vincent thought that technical skills learned in Canada could sometimes be "almost worthless" on aid jobs unless tempered by previous experience in the tropics. "Our modern machines and our modern methods," acknowledged the Director General before the BC Association of Professional Engineers, "may not always be suitable or workable in the conditions existing in these underdeveloped countries."

resident at the site. Further, the disagreements of all kinds that inevitably arise on intergovernmental projects were greatly softened by the undisguised enthusiasm of the colonial administration itself. "All contractors have been well received," reported the Canadian project manager to his firm in April 1962, "and have had considerable local assistance in investigating such things as availability and cost of labour, location of fill, sand, stone, etc., and all have been pleased with the co-operation which they may expect from the local Public Works."

This co-operation was indeed so close and flexible that the Canadian engineers were able to devise with local authorities during the pier's construction a widely appreciated secondary project; at a cost of only some $16,000 in Canadian aid funds, they installed pipes and pumps that doubled Kingstown's entire fresh-water supply. Doubtless this aid was no more, as the Leader of the Vincentian Opposition told his colleagues in an apt metaphor on January 10, 1963, than "a drop in a bucket"[24]; and Ottawa's long delay in approving what it regarded as a minor, unscheduled project provoked somewhat resentful scepticism from both the Opposition and the Kingstown press.[25] But on an island where some people were "forced to share their source of water with the frogs and vermin," where the health of inhabitants and tourists alike was threatened by a "tragic state of affairs which could easily lead to an epidemic," even a partial and tardy improvement was welcome.[26] This

---

[24]See "Solve Water Problem Now, Says Cato," *Vincentian*, Jan. 11, 1963.

[25]The *Vincentian's* editorial of July 6, 1963, entitled "Urgent Attention Needed," attacked the delay in an effusion of indignant imagery: "Some time ago we heard tell of assistance from Canada which would help in alleviating this question of water. Whatever has become of it? Has this too gone by the board? Or has lethargy set in and the funds are spinning cocoons in some musty ministerial office? It is time that something be done. Let that something be done before it is too late. Do not lock the stable when the horse has already escaped. Urgent attention is sorely needed. For Heaven's sake let it be attended to."

[26]The *Vincentian* on January 9, 1963: ". . . the Canadian Government has again come to the assistance of the Vincentian people, this time . . . in relieving the shortage of water . . . our thanks must be offered in no uncertain way to the Canadian Government for its help to St. Vincent in this respect." The dismay of local inhabitants when water shortages continued even after the Canadian improvements was summarized in rustic idiom by a Montrose housewife who signed her letter to the *Vincentian* of March 26, 1964, as "Fighting Mad." Protesting against a reassuring press release by the St. Vincent authorities, she wrote, "I laughed a mirthless laugh when I heard that the Hon. C. L. Tannis [Minister of Works] found water at the places he visited. . . . When my children want to bathe must I send them to Majorca? When my baby's diapers need to be washed must I send them to Vermount? Or shall I appeal to W.H.O. for water to prepare breakfast on mornings? Will Mr. De Nobriga and Bottlers Ltd. sell me some water to flush my toilet? Now Mr. Editor, don't you see that the 'Release' is like what the bull lets out? . . . my taps are constantly empty . . . whenever I do get anything from the taps it is like liquid mud."

scheme, still more than the dock, helped directly the ordinary citizens of St. Vincent. As a sensitively chosen project reflecting all the supposed humanitarian, economic and political aspirations of Canada's policy, it proved in a simple way that sound aid ultimately relies less on dollars than on judgment.

Personal relations between Canadians and Vincentians were with few exceptions good, and evidently more intimate than on most Asian or African projects. This close understanding was natural, because cultural differences between Canadians and their hosts were less radical than in distant continents; and of course the real, though light, control over the island's affairs by British colonial officials overcame some of the psychological tensions that foreigners often encounter in fully independent recipient nations. Canadians found no difficulty, therefore, in living in ordinary rented quarters among their hosts, from whom they were not segregated by any physical or serious psychological barriers.

As at Warsak, the only sharp personal conflicts occurred (though rarely) between Canadian foremen and local workers; engineers and administrators on both sides collaborated in an atmosphere described by the consultant as "hospitable and friendly." The most damaging incidents took place in January 1964, leading to a brief strike by Vincentian workers and the beating of a Canadian foreman. After a dispute between the foreman and a Vincentian mason, 150 workers left the job in what the Canadian project manager called "strictly a wild-cat walk-out" based on no legitimate complaint.[27] Such events, while they may occur "about every two months" on a normal job in Canada, as one Canadian engineer put it, frequently blend into tension between nationalities on a foreign aid project. Even the most justified criticism or dismissal by a Canadian may thus be taken by local workers as a gesture of contempt for their culture and skill. It is impossible to fix blame with certainty in such cases; but the following letter from the strike leader to the Kingstown newspaper, the *Vincentian*, on January 11, 1964, is a reminder that Canadian engineers abroad need not just the firmness, but the patience, of a diplomat:

. . . my personal opinion is that the unfortunate occurrence was caused by unsatisfactory conditions of work on one hand and want of tact on the other.

From time to time the workers have complained to me of the lack of respectability [*sic*] on the part of our Canadian employers. . . . If it should rain and the workers seek cover they are insulted, abused and called out to work in the rain. Of course we sometimes hear that Canadians work in genial weather but it is a condition to which West Indians have not yet

[27]See "Strike Hits St. Vincent Harbour," *Vincentian*, Jan. 11, 1964.

grown accustomed. . . . One Millar, a foreman finisher . . . was engaged in finishing a portion of floor when a Canadian labour foreman pulled his trowel from his hand with an oath. Millar is a skilled worker. Millar alleges that in this matter of alleged assault to the Superintendent of Works who is himself a Canadian, he not only failed to receive any redress but was further insulted by the Superintendent. Millar apparently resented this and walked off the job . . . supported by his co-workers who all walked off with him. . . . The incident is regrettable and I feel that with a little tact and courteous dealing the matter would have been readily resolved.

c. A provisional assessment

Since the St. Vincent project was officially opened only in July 1964, its economic value cannot yet be fully appreciated. But it is clear even now that it will benefit the island's economy tangibly in several ways. Local authorities estimate that the elimination of lightering services alone will release $300,000 a year for development purposes, a substantial saving for an economy supporting only some 80,000 people. The dock and warehouses have already made possible far more efficient exploitation of the island's principal crop of bananas: storage is greatly enlarged; loading, soon to be mechanized, is faster—and safe from the frequent sinking of lighters in harbour storms; and two new refrigerated ocean ships launched in early 1964 for the UK-Windward Islands trade will now be able to take on and preserve much larger cargos of bananas than previous ships. "The Canadian Government," praised the *Vincentian* on September 14, 1963, has "strong faith in the [banana] industry as a lasting concern which is to contribute to the general welfare of the people in the territory."

Another likely economic benefit will be a rise in tourist spending on St. Vincent. "The Wharf is being constructed to accommodate any two large ocean-going liners," explained the *Vincentian* on May 11, 1963, ". . . the old way of conveying passengers to and from the ships will be at an end; and this alone should contribute to an increase of tourists to the island." Still more affirmatively, the editor assured his readers on January 25, 1964, that the project "could perhaps mean the difference between existence and non-existence in as far as the tourist industry is concerned. . . . the new wharf project . . . will induce many of these tourist liners to pay regular calls. . . ."

Finally, the scheme, like most composite projects, helped to train local workers in basic skills of construction. In a leading editorial on January 9, 1963, entitled "Our Canadian Friends," the *Vincentian* maintained that the island was "greatly indebted to Canada for the deep water project . . . which with their skilled technicians is offering insight to some of our men, who at the close of the project will be the better off for the experience and knowledge gained." As at Warsak, the Canadian training was more than technical. "One thing . . . that Vincentian workers might learn from the Canadians," the article went on, ". . . is the hard work they put into the job, the interest displayed in their work, the ardour and the zeal with which they tackle the problems confronting them. No clock watchers, no delaying on the job, no wasting of valuable time. . . . From this our own people can learn much." Such training, as well as the other benefits already listed, the writer concluded, "will eventually spell profits for St. Vincent."[28]

Apart from doubts raised by the brief strike in January 1964, the political or "propaganda" effect of the project was, for Canadians, deeply satisfying. On May 11, 1963, the *Vincentian's* editorial termed the wharf "a permanent structural record of the generosity, goodwill and friendship of the people and Government of Canada toward St. Vincent," an accomplishment worthy of the recipient's "abiding gratitude." "Posterity will owe a great debt of gratitude to Canada for making this possible," the newspaper echoed exuberantly on January 25, 1964. . . . "We are sure that every true-spirited Vincentian will wish to show their heartfelt gratitude to the Canadian Government, its peoples and to the workers. . . . To Canada and her Sons, —We Salute You!"

It remains to be seen whether this praise will continue after the elimination of lightering services and the mechanization of loading have thrown out of work—at least temporarily—some hundred or more of the former port workers. In the long run, however, any such hardship is likely to be absorbed, if the Vincentians' own predictions are accurate, by a general rise in employment from the island's growing prosperity. Situated in the island's most central and impressive setting, and designed to solve the recipient's primary economic difficulties, the project seems certain to remain for long a symbol of enlightened Canadian concern for an area notoriously neglected by larger aid programmes. This neglect, the ease with which political impact was achieved, and the relative simplicity of administering aid in familiar nearby islands, suggest that Canadian aid to the Caribbean deserves a new and far more generous emphasis.

[28]The following undated item from the *Vincentian* suggests poignantly, indeed, that Canadian foremen may occasionally have pushed their zeal for completing the job to unreasonable lengths: "A 19-year-old St. Vincent bride-to-be fainted minutes after waiting for an hour for a bridegroom who failed to turn up in church. She was later treated by a doctor. . . . [The intended bridegroom] said yesterday 'Only I would understand why I did not marry the girl. I was forced to work on Saturday until 5 p.m. conveying stones to the deep-water harbour.' " The possibility that the worker himself was a diplomat cannot, of course, be excluded.

Apart from two highway surveys in Burma and Malaysia, the Katunayake Airport development in Ceylon, the Thaketa Bridge in Burma and the harbour development in Singapore, other Canadian contributions in this field have consisted of transfers of equipment. These gifts, which have assisted five distinct sectors, represent ostensibly valid investments in infrastructure; but in almost every case the effectiveness of this aid has remained uncertain because of Canada's failure to investigate the use recipients make of it.

Railways have received much the largest portion of such aid. Railway ties in India, Pakistan and Ceylon, for instance, have built stronger road-beds capable of carrying the heavier diesel locomotives being introduced in major rehabilitation programmes. A gift of 120 steam locomotives to India between 1953 and 1955 overcame a crisis in transport caused by the wartime deterioration of rolling stock. An earlier shipment of fifty locomotive boilers removed a bottleneck at the Calcutta locomotive works, bringing into service an equal number of Indian-built engines that were urgently required. Shunting locomotives delivered in 1961 speeded freight-handling in four large Indian ports where vital industrial equipment and perishable commodities had often been dangerously delayed. And ten diesel locomotives sent to Ceylon (which prominently marked each with the name of a Canadian province) provided the core of a modern fleet of heavy engines able to haul longer trains up that island's numerous hills and mountains.

Ports and shipping were assisted through the two passenger-cargo vessels and harbour equipment given to the West Indies, and by heavy cranes supplied to the harbour in Colombo. All have partly served their immediate purpose, though sometimes falling below expectation. In 1964, the inter-island ships in the Caribbean were running at a financial loss greater than anticipated, and consideration was being given their disposal to private operators; and the usefulness of the Colombo cranes was diminished through the weakness of supporting piers, caused by a local contractor's use of inferior cement.

In later years, Canada supplied road-building equipment on a small scale in Africa and the Caribbean; navigational and meteorological equipment for civil aviation in Asia and Africa; and to Malaya, in 1962 for the first time, equipment for a television network.

Yet however valuable these gifts may appear, the absence of serious Canadian evaluation—and, in many cases, of sustained Canadian interest—makes it impossible to conclude that they were employed effectively. Doubtless their immediate economic benefit to Canada is demonstrable; several of them brought short-term employment to skilled

Canadian workers in times of recession. But their contribution to the recipients' economies generally escapes measurement because Ottawa lacks the human resources to verify their use. Of course there are types of aid—such as railway ties—that it is pointless to follow beyond their permanent installation. And for other kinds, clumsy and persistent investigation is quickly resented by recipients as discourteous snooping. Still, machinery for "follow-up" assessments is indispensable if future operations are to be chosen rationally.

This task of periodically reviewing the use of equipment after its transfer is well suited to the function of eventual Canadian aid attachés resident in recipient capitals. These specialists in aid diplomacy could make it their business to study discreetly and tactfully the employment and maintenance of equipment during regular field investigations of new projects. Their attitude would be one of constructive and solicitous inquiry. While asking whether local technicians were satisfied with their Canadian equipment, the attachés could judge whether possible misuse demanded spare parts, further remedial technical assistance or, *in extremis*, a threat to stop additional aid of this type. Whatever their recommendation, Canada could weigh future requests for aid with reasonably accurate knowledge of a given country's ability to absorb it profitably.

Such knowledge is clearly the only basis for an operational policy that is alert and lucid. Lacking it, Canadian planners remain as blind to the true potential of their aid as they have been ignorant of its real contribution in the past. In the long run, these uncertainties are likely to blunt the political and economic goals of Canadian policy by depriving them of the only context that can define them meaningfully.

3. NATURAL RESOURCES: THE NIGERIAN AERIAL SURVEY

Although absorbing less than 5 per cent of Canada's bilateral grant budget, aid to natural resources probably produces more far-reaching benefits than any other kind of Canadian aid. The discovery and improved exploitation of mineral and food resources may not strengthen a recipient's economy in an immediate, spectacular way; but in the long run, they make possible economic self-reliance, diversified production, and rising standards of living.

Since Canada is still deeply engaged in developing her own natural endowments, much of Canadian technology remains geared to seeking and processing primary resources. In this preoccupation, Canadian skills meet directly the needs of backward nations, many of which, through ignorance of their material potential, are unable even to plan their progress. These skills, transferred by advisers, training, and specialized equipment, are the salient mark of aid to resources; the imposing monumental forms of aid are here largely irrelevant.

Often projects conveying such skills cost so little, and their dispersal in numerous small schemes is so wide, that their impact appears dissipated. Yet carefully chosen and expertly conducted, they usually plant the seeds of lasting enrichment. "The surveying and development of natural resources," stressed U Thant in launching the United Nations Development Decade in 1962, are therefore "a crucial area for intensified pre-investment activity."[29]

The most typical—and by far the most fruitful—Canadian activity in this field is the aerial survey. Developed on a vast scale in Canada by the RCAF and half a dozen large companies since 1945, the science of discovering and cataloguing natural resources through aerial photography and magnetometry has provided recipients on two continents with information vital to rationally planned economic progress. Precise knowledge of a nation's physical wealth is always the first prerequisite to planning itself: without accurate estimates of resources, and without reliable maps to guide their exploitation, priorities and goals are not only arbitrary, but illusory.

Yet in spite of their undeniable value in theory, the aerial surveys carried out under Canada's aid programmes have produced benefits of widely varying scope and immediacy. Although some recipients have understood and sought to realize the immense potential of these surveys, others have failed either to grasp the priority of pre-investment inventories or to plan their use with fitting urgency. Likewise the administration of Canada's surveys has been uneven, some projects being remarkably trouble-free while others have mingled confusion with ineptness. Given this diversity of experience, it is hard to choose a single project that represents fairly Canada's survey effort as a whole. A realistic case study must therefore be multiple, taking one project only as a framework for discussing several distinct operations. This framework is conveniently offered by the three-year programme of resources mapping completed in July 1964 for Nigeria.

a. Purpose and planning
The Nigerian survey was the first of the very few major capital projects financed by Canada under the Special Commonwealth Africa Aid Program (SCAAP) announced in 1960. Since Canada lacked the experience of colonial administration in Africa, and since even United Nations

[29]*The United Nations Development Decade: Proposals for Action* (New York, 1962), p. iii.

TABLE 6.4

Canadian Capital Projects in Natural Resources (1950–March 31, 1965)

Country	Project	Allocation (Canadian dollars)	Year
ASIA			
Burma	Photogrammetric equipment for Burma Survey Department	37,011	1955–57
	Equipment for fisheries development	1,985	1957–58
	Prospecting mining equipment	6,968	1957–58
	Workshop equipment, agricultural development	58,835	1957–58
Cambodia	Fish dryers	2,915	1954–55
	Mobile veterinary service clinics	13,634	1954–55
Ceylon	Fisheries development (trawlers, Mutwal processing and refrigeration plant, etc.)	2,170,308	1952–65
	Agricultural station workshop, tools, and equipment	284,000	1953–57
	Pest control equipment	74,999	1953–58
	Aerial and ground resources survey	2,492,450	1955–60
India	Biological Control Station, Bangalore	46,023	1955–56
	Locust control (trucks with 2-way radios)	135,685	1955–56
	Pest control (2 Beaver aircraft)	146,355	1955–56
	Airborne magnetometer survey	227,224	1955–57
	Equipment for Co-operative Movement Training Centre	37,224	1957–58
	Crop-spraying equipment	300,000	1961–62
	Geological survey	100,000	1964–65
Malaysia*	Aerial survey	201,000	1956–57
	Refrigeration units for east coast fisheries	505,000	1959–61
	Natural resources survey	1,000,000	1964–65
Pakistan	Thal Experimental Farm	196,745	1951–52
	Aerial resources survey	3,355,990	1951–58
	Pest control: aircraft, trucks, spray equipment and pesticides	2,193,950	1952–64
	Hatching eggs and incubator	3,106	1954–55
	Biological Control Station, Rawalpindi	55,383	1954–58
	Equipment for Tractor Training School	17,250	1955–56
	Tarnab Farm Workshop equipment	2,277	1957–58
	Aerial survey and forest inventory	625,000	1960–61
	Data-processing equipment for agricultural census	271,810	1961–62
	Chittagong Hill Tracts (land-use study)	500,000	1963–64
	Fishing equipment	3,950,000	1963–65
Mekong River	Aerial Survey	1,300,000	1958–59
CARIBBEAN			
British Honduras	Survey equipment	54,945	1961–64
Dominica	Natural resources survey	34,717	1961–63
Jamaica	Fishing vessels	125,100	1964
	Pipes for water distribution	100,000	1964–65
"Little Eight"	Development surveys	10,225	1961–62
Trinidad	Development surveys	200,000	1964–65

TABLE 6.4 (*concluded*)

Country	Project	Allocation (Canadian dollars)	Year
AFRICA			
Ghana	Agricultural equipment	21,542	1962
	Plant tissue analysis	8,000	1963–64
	Food research	30,000	1964–65
Guinea	Bridge study	25,000	1964–65
Kenya	Forest inventory	750,000	1962–64
Nigeria	Aerial surveys and mapping	3,438,616	1961–65
	Natural gas feasibility study	42,036	1963
	Forest inventory study	300,000	1963–64
Tanzania	Forestry equipment	86,300	1963
	Aerial mapping survey	1,000,000	1963
Uganda	Geological equipment	45,000	1962–63
	Fishing boat	25,000	1963
	Scout cars for survey	4,000	1963
TOTAL		$26,333,608	

*Including Singapore.

experts knew little of the continent's economic potential, resources surveys were at that time a prudent and logical first step. Even before the founding of SCAAP, a private Ottawa-based firm had explored with the Nigerian government the possible advantages of such a study; and, when Canada's new aid funds became available, Nigeria had already prepared with this company a detailed project request.

The need for a comprehensive inventory of natural resources was clearly of high priority in any programme of Nigerian development. Never had the country's geography been adequately mapped to locate all the physical elements required for progress: mineral deposits, forests, arable land, waterways, and likely sites for power schemes, irrigation projects, roads, and railways. The few modest attempts at aerial photography in the past had always foundered on technical obstacles when existing equipment proved unable to overcome peculiar problems of climate and topography. When Nigeria gained her independence in October 1960, a survey of her resources by the most modern techniques seemed to promise the indispensable blueprint for rapid, co-ordinated economic growth.

Following the project's acceptance by Canada in mid-1961, an initial contract was awarded that autumn to the interested Ottawa firm which, while sharing the work with a Vancouver company, kept full technical and administrative control. This contract, costing $1,350,000, called for aerial photography, ground control surveys, and photogrammetric compilation destined to produce five-colour topographical maps at a scale of 1:50,000 for 28,400 square miles in Central and Western Nigeria. In December 1962 the contract was increased by $500,000 to embrace aerial photography of 60,000 square miles in all, as well as an airborne magnetometer survey of 13,000 line miles for a minerals inventory, and additional topographical mapping of 8,400 square miles in the heavily-populated Lagos-Ibadan area.[30]

b. Execution

Canadian aerial survey companies, often half of whose work is on overseas contracts, are accustomed to adapting equipment and methods to difficult foreign fields. Nigerian climate and living conditions were in some ways less arduous than those on other Canadian surveys; but technical difficulties were at least as challenging. First, navigation on survey flights was hampered by a lack of adequate maps. Next, tropical rain forests and hazardous terrain slowed ground control parties verifying the indications of aerial photographs. Then heavy clouds, which formed early each morning between 3,000 and 6,000 feet, threatened much of the time to spoil the photographs themselves. And finally, even when these clouds partly dispersed during the afternoon, aerial photographers faced a thick, translucent barrier called Harmattan Haze—a mixture of Sahara sand and moisture droplets that hangs permanently over Nigeria between 12,000 and 20,000 feet.[31]

The solutions found to each of these problems were combined to produce an accurate and integrated mapping system of great originality. The lack of usable maps to guide survey flights was overcome by use of Radan-Doppler electronic navigational aids. These instruments, which operate free of ground stations, control flight on a preset course, verify the overlap on flight lines, and maintain the fixed distance between film exposures. As a result, engineers were able not only to navigate precisely and to scale stereo-models correctly, but to eliminate most of the rigorous and costly ground expeditions usually required to check air

[30]Information on Canadian aerial surveys under aid programmes was supplied by Hunting Survey Corporation Limited of Toronto, and by Spartan Air Services Limited and Canadian Aero Service Limited of Ottawa. Technical data for the Nigerian survey is taken from the Canadian Aero publication *Survey* (Winter, 1964) and from a report written by a company engineer, J. M. Zarzycki, entitled "Aerial Survey in Nigeria: An Application of New Techniques" (submitted by the government of Nigeria to the July 1963 UN Regional Cartographic Conference for Africa).

[31]Haze and adverse weather were obstacles on nearly all Canadian surveys in tropical countries; several months were lost on the Mekong survey, for instance, because of monsoon rains. In addition, ground parties were often greatly slowed by poor telephone communications, primitive roads and—notably in Kenya—wild animals.

navigation. The cloud and haze problems, potentially the most harmful to the mission, were successfully met by a novel grouping of specialized instruments, including cameras using infra-red film. Through employing a super-wide-angle lens, in particular, the aerial surveyors achieved photography at the required scale of 1:40,000 from an altitude of 11,600 feet—just below the heaviest part of the Harmattan Haze. But none of this intricate instrumentation could have pierced the haze lying below this altitude without the use of infra-red film. While panchromatic film could at best render photos of doubtful clarity, infra-red was known as a tropical film of almost ideal efficiency: it swept away most of the haze, heightened differentiation, and sharpened contrasts between water and land—contrasts essential for hydro and irrigation planning. The combining of these refinements into a single system, wrote the company scientists in 1964, "cut ground control costs by upwards of 30% and reduced survey time by many months."[32] When the final proofs for printing maps were delivered to Nigeria in July 1964, the contractors had proved a new system of air photography of certain value to other developing nations.

Compared to other Canadian surveys, the administration of the Nigerian contract was remarkably straightforward. Relations between the two Canadian firms in the field were greatly simplified because the prime contract gave one company exclusive technical and administrative authority. This arrangement avoided the constant and often acrimonious disputes between contractors that had marred the Mekong River project because inter-company responsibilities were unclear.[33]

Similarly, co-operation with Nigerian officials lacked the frustrations common on other jobs—largely, it seems, because the local administration understood the project very well and supported it enthusiastically. Even though the project's Memorandum of Understanding was signed only in December 1961, some two months after work began, no significant problems arose between Canadians and Nigerians. Once details of the agreement were approved, assured the Canadian project

[32]*Survey* (Winter, 1964), p. 5. An FAO technical expert attached to the Western Nigerian government wrote to the Canadian project manager in July 1963 to assure him that his Ministry had "used all the available new photography. . . . the use of infra-red photography has been amply justified. . . . it lends itself to finer recognition of forest types than . . . normal photography."

[33]Six independent companies collaborated on the Mekong project. While they agreed to negotiate the intial contract collectively in order to strengthen the whole Canadian air survey industry at a time of depression, differences soon arose in the field over the types and amount of work allotted to each. These disagreements were sharpened by the financial difficulties of one of the major contractors and by costly delays forced by bad weather.

manager in April 1964, "the Nigerians applied the letter of the law; they bent over backwards to support it." This support, almost invariably a source of some conflict on an aid project, applied to both the technical and personal needs of the Canadians. On their arrival in Nigeria, the first Canadians found, for instance, that their requests for ground vehicles—seven new Land Rovers, four Bedford trucks, a Volkswagen minibus and a stationwagon—had been scrupulously fulfilled. And the Canadians' housing was not only ready and adequate, but generously comfortable: accommodation for the permanent Canadian staff included four six-room houses with servants' quarters, a half-acre of land for each and, in some cases, frontage on the Lagos lagoon. Such pedestrian matters, while secondary to the project itself, are never unimportant to technicians in the field. The happy experience in Nigeria and less successful ones elsewhere prove that satisfaction of such basic needs and the technical effectiveness of foreign experts are inseparable.[34]

The smoothness of Nigerian-Canadian administrative co-operation owed something, no doubt, to the Canadian contractors' freedom in hiring local staff and making local purchases without reference to the host government. By thereby placing the potentially most contentious issues in the hands of the Canadian contractors alone, the project agreement left few substantial problems to be settled internationally. Another factor in easing co-operation was the presence in the Nigerian administration of expatriate British civil servants. Yet in most of the day-to-day decisions such as customs clearance, training appointments and reimbursement of local costs, the Nigerians themselves showed an eager competence that unmistakably heartened the Canadian effort. This competence was by all accounts distinctly more polished than that of most other African administrations co-operating with Canadians in development projects.[35]

Such relatively untroubled administrative relations were in fact reported by several Canadian aerial survey companies doing aid work, notably on contracts in Pakistan, Ceylon, Malaya and Kenya. All agreed that the wide independence necessary for aerial survey contractors on missions in distant, isolated areas strengthened goodwill not only by diminishing abrasive contacts with local administrators but by forging bonds of respect and comradeship with local technicians. For in nearly every case, as the following document from a former officer of surveys in Pakistan reveals, the most natural friendships between hosts and

[34]See chap. IX on the problems of Canadian advisers and teachers abroad.
[35]The main problems in other countries were payment of local costs and provision of ground transport.

visitors were cemented, far from bureaucratic formality, in the dust and sweat of simply shared experience in the field:

When the aerial survey had progressed sufficiently a dozen or more [Canadian] geologists arrived complete with transport and enough tinned stuff to sink a battleship. I may say that old officers of the Geological Survey of India, like myself, looked with amazement at all this. No wonder, since we had done our field-work in six-month spells using whatever transport we could find locally, sometimes camels, sometimes mules or donkeys, sometimes men or even women, and often bullock carts—but never motor lorries. The galaxie of wonderful tinned stuffs made our eyes pop out of our heads because Indian geologists are accustomed to live on the country and might well have been reduced to dried locusts, *lassi* (a sort of buttermilk made from goats' milk), dates, or great cakes of unleavened bread. What was good enough for John the Baptist was surely good enough for us, and anyway, we made up for such minor food worries by living in Calcutta in the lap of luxury for six months each year. Our stirrings of envy soon passed when we got our noses into wonderful dishes of bacon and ham which were, of course, unobtainable in a Muslim land like Pakistan . . .

I am bound to admit, however, that the elaborate equipment and copious supplies made possible the completion of the field work in exceptionally fast time and probably with a high degree of accuracy. Equipment and supplies are useless without the personnel to use them. All the geologists of the Canadian party, whether Canadian or not, worked with great enthusiasm and courage. Supported by the excellent organization at their base in Quetta, they were able to complete their huge assignment in the remarkably short space of two and a half years.[36]

Such friendly respect, of course, never prevented hosts and visitors from disagreeing on technical standards and methods; in Nigeria, for example, local engineers argued firmly and successfully with the Canadians to print maps with British typographical symbols. But these differences were easily lost in an overriding trust; and on most surveys, international relations between professional colleagues were at least as cordial as those between Canadians themselves.

c. A provisional assessment

In spite of their enormous potential value, Canadian aerial surveys have not always been exploited by recipients in a manner Canadians would consider rapid. Pakistan, for reasons of external security, forbade public distribution of maps and reports on Canada's $3,300,000 surveys of West Pakistan soils and geology; although the contractor produced 450 sets of maps and commentary in 1960, the Pakistan government in 1962 had been content with taking ten—and of these, estimated a

[36]From the preface by H. Crookshank to *Reconnaissance Geology of Part of West Pakistan*, Hunting Survey Corporation Limited, Toronto, 1961.

Canadian observer, "very few appeared to be in use." "The Pakistanis did not understand either the purpose or results of the survey," he continued, "and seemed to distrust it." Given declared or latent threats from India, China and Afghanistan, Pakistan's qualms were not wholly irrational. And it is true that *bona fide* development agencies, such as the United States and the World Bank, did have free access to pertinent information from the Canadian surveys. Still, early use of the maps and reports was disappointingly restricted, with the consequence that much of their immediate potential must have been unrealized.

Likewise, Ceylon was slow to use the results of the $2,500,000 survey of its resources. Here distribution was completely open, but printing of reports was unreasonably delayed. While the Pakistani maps and reports were printed in Canada, those for Ceylon were left in 1962 by the departing Canadians in the form of corrected proofs. Seemingly because the Ceylon government did not consider their publication urgent, the first of the three major reports appeared only two years later. Doubtless, temporary mimeographed copies had been circulated to several Ceylonese departments during the Canadians' stay, and these had led to a number of specific new projects; but for full-scale development planning only the complete printed versions could be considered fully accurate.[37]

Certainly the scope of these surveys is so broad that their use or neglect can be adequately judged only over two or three decades. The many new resources—and needs—unmasked by surveys must be carefully translated into co-ordinated national plans, and governments must budget funds to suit revised priorities. Yet even in the years immediately following a survey it is fair to expect that recipients take preliminary steps toward these goals; at the least, they can seek urgently and deliberately to apply survey results to generally approved schemes for which funds exist. By this standard, Nigeria's early use of her survey was encouraging. By May 1964, two months before delivery of the final maps, the Nigerian government had exploited survey data in planning year-round navigation of the Niger River; in accelerating a country-wide forestry inventory; in locating bridges and roads in the Western and Northern regions; in planning a new iron and steel industry; in enlarging the sugar-cane industry; and in planning new dams on the Niger for flood control, irrigation and hydro-electric power.

[37]The typographical and photographic quality of the Ceylon reports appears to be distinctly inferior to that of the Pakistan survey. While there may be a danger of making reports somewhat less useful by having them printed by recipients, it is argued that part of integrated survey aid should be local training in map reproduction in order to build the recipient's technical self-sufficiency.

Regrettably, the twenty Nigerian technicians who received training during the survey were not employed efficiently at the time of completion; neither Canada nor Nigeria had provided a photographic laboratory large enough to absorb them. Training on many Canadian surveys, particularly those in Ceylon and Kenya, was however of great and immediate benefit to recipients. In all cases, on-the-job training of local technicians proved the surest way of inducing within the recipient government a lasting and informed enthusiasm for using the surveys effectively.

Canada's own immediate interest also appeared well served by the Nigerian survey. On March 17, 1964, the prime contractor was able to report to the Secretary of State for External Affairs that his company had developed seventy-eight separate jobs worth $989,426 in seven African countries—all "either directly or indirectly through its presence in West Africa on the large-scale mapping project for the Government of Nigeria."[38] This is one of the very few fully documented cases of commercial benefit accruing to Canadian firms through aid contracts.

Further, in the measure that local publicity may contribute to a donor's political prestige, the Nigerian survey seemed a gratifying investment, though it was not nearly as popular as the permanent "monument" types of aid. Occasional articles in the local press explained the basic purpose of the survey and reported on unusual incidents such as the gift by the contractor of a stereo-plotter to the government of Eastern Nigeria. But the most impressive tributes came from representatives of the Nigerian federal government itself. "For the first time in our history," the federal Minister of Finance told Parliament in his 1962 budget speech, "an effort is being made to look at the resources and the priorities from an all-Nigerian perspective." And in President Azikiwe's speech on October 1, 1963, celebrating the anniversary of independence and proclamation of the republic, Canada's survey was the only foreign aid project mentioned.

It would be wrong, however, to judge the political value of surveys, as indeed their economic value, from clippings and speeches alone. Their true worth will emerge only from the use made of them over many years. If their results are constantly and widely applied, the political and economic advantages to Canada may be appreciable; if they are not applied—and the evidence shows that this is often the case —surveys are obviously a waste of money.

[38]Letter from J. W. Strath, Vice-President of Canadian Aero Service Limited, to the Hon. Paul Martin. The writer is grateful to Mr. Strath for providing this interesting evidence.

Canada's primary concern should be therefore to find suitable means of ensuring that surveys will continue to be exploited long after missions are officially ended. A still greater emphasis on training surveyors in recipient countries would help; but even more urgently needed are economists and engineers trained to interpret and project surveys into detailed plans. Perhaps a Canadian experienced in such work should be stationed in the recipient country, for some years after field work is done, to guide and tactfully goad the recipient government into prompt action. Again one can denounce this "following-up" of projects as unseemly and meddlesome. Yet without such a continuing practical interest, surveys are not likely to be—as they are potentially—the most valuable and fundamental of any foreign assistance; they may be merely an elaborate and abortive promise of progress.

4. HEALTH, WELFARE AND EDUCATION: THE CANADA-INDIA REACTOR

The inclusion of so-called "social" aid in programmes of economic development has always provoked debate. Many economists, for whom the sole function of aid is to build infrastructure, view social assistance as a wasteful palliative: why squander funds on temporary help to a handful of individuals, they argue, when the same amount could implant permanent productive capacity of lasting benefit to thousands or even millions? To this partisans of social aid can reply that aid properly conceived should seek not merely to inflate long-term statistics, but to care now for human beings. Did not Bentham urge that happiness be measured for its immediacy and intensity, as well as for its scope and duration?

It is not easy, in practice, to reconcile outlooks so opposite. Yet practical arguments can be marshalled to show that social aid and economic aid are fundamentally complementary. People, as a labour force, are an integral part of economic development; for lasting increases in productivity are achieved not simply through technical innovations and capital, but through a healthy, trained and reasonably contented population. Social aid is also useful in rallying popular support for economic aid that may be politically uninteresting: while public opinion in donor countries wants to be hard-headed in allocating its aid, it often likes to feel soft-hearted in giving it—and in Canada, at least, humanitarian appeals still seem to pry open the public purse most successfully. Likewise, many forms of social aid allow donors to take on an appealing philanthropic mantle in the eyes of beneficiaries; as long as such aid is not patronizing or disruptive of cherished customs, recipient peoples tend to understand and admire it more than economic aid, usually distant and impersonal.

Yet all of these arguments seeking to defend social aid demonstrate at the same time that it is essentially subsidiary to economic aid. Social aid is clearly almost worthless in the long run unless given in close support of attacks upon the roots, mainly economic, of social evils. The great bulk of aid must continue to be devoted to long-term economic construction; for recipients will find salvation not in a wider distribution of immediate comforts and ideas, but in a rising permanent capacity to produce. Social aid deserves a modest place in a balanced programme on grounds purely utilitarian. It is ultimately defensible only if related directly to the primary business of aid which is economic development.[39]

TABLE 6.5

Canadian Capital Projects in Health, Welfare and Education (1950–March 31, 1965)

Country	Project	Allocation (Canadian dollars)	Year
ASIA			
Burma	Textbooks for University of Rangoon	1,013	1955–56
	Equipment for Permanent Training Centre, Rangoon	19,014	1955–56
	Cobalt beam therapy units	109,000	1955–63
	Rangoon Technical High School equipment	53,298	1956–57
	Radium Needles for Mandalay Hospital	15,000	1963–64
Ceylon	Equipment for University of Ceylon	21,003	1953–54
	Equipment for Institute of Practical Technology, Katubedde	309,412	1953–58
	Mobile cinema vans and visual aid equipment	33,166	1954–55
	Equipment for Junior Technical High School, Galle	16,831	1954–55
	Film strips for technical education	1,958	1954–55
	X-ray maintenance equipment	14,705	1957–58
India	Film kits on geology, geophysics, etc.	275	1954–55
	Co-operative Film Training Scheme	49,215	1957–58
	Cobalt beam therapy units and replacement sources	1,108,594	1957–65

[39]A careful review of Canada's social aid, both public and private, is made in two brochures published in 1963 by a temporary body called the National Committee on Canada's Participation in Social Development Abroad, closely linked to the Overseas Institute of Canada. The first, entitled *Background Papers* (mimeographed papers separately numbered) was prepared for a workshop conference on this subject and the second, entitled *Canada's Participation in Social Development Abroad* was the workshop's final report.

TABLE 6.5 (*continued*)

Country	Project	Allocation (Canadian dollars)	Year
India	Calcutta Milk Scheme	130,000	1958–59
(*concluded*)	Canada-India Atomic Research Reactor, Trombay	11,418,773	1958–65
	Metallurgical equipment, Banaras Hindu University	3,000	1963–64
Indonesia	Gresik Cement Plant library	306	1956–57
	Books and journals for Academy of Public Administration, Malang	2,000	1957–58
	Shipment of scientific literature	689	1958–59
Malaysia*	Equipment for University of Malaya	5,000	1956–57
	Equipment for Singapore Polytechnic School	50,000	1956–57
	Textbooks for Junior Technical (trade) School, Kuala Lumpur	556	1957–58
	Small tools, Electrical Department, Technical Institute, Kuala Lumpur	1,580	1957–58
	Textbooks, Technical Institute, Kuala Lumpur	1,317	1957–58
	Trade School equipment, Jesselton	1,451	1957–58
	Workshop equipment for Small Industries Services Institute	7,278	1959–60
	Stereo plotter, University of Malaya	10,000	1959–60
	Soil science equipment, Department of Agriculture	5,500	1959–60
	Technical Education equipment for rural trade schools and secondary vocational schools	186,221	1959–61
	Equipment for fisheries schools and fisheries	60,000	1960–61
	Electrical workshop equipment	50,000	1962–63
	Cobalt beam therapy units	125,000	1963–64
	Technical education equipment	275,000	1963–64
	Mobile laboratory, University of Malaya	20,000	1963–64
	Equipment for 53 technical schools	3,000,000	1964–65
	Equipment for Montfort Boys' School	35,000	1964–65
Pakistan	Mobile dispensaries	11,795	1955–65
	Books on cost accounting for Pakistan Institute of Industrial Accounting	15,000	1959–60
	Equipment for Rawalpindi Veterans' Hospital	25,000	1963–64
	Lahore Refugee Housing Scheme	2,000,000	1963–64
	Cobalt beam therapy units	75,074	1963–64
South Vietnam	Laboratory equipment, University of Dalat	5,700	1957–58
Thailand	Cobalt beam therapy units	85,000	1963–64
International	Medical book scheme	220,000	1958–63
	Small projects†	25,000	1958
CARIBBEAN			
Jamaica	School equipment	91,000	1963
	Vocational training equipment	50,000	1963–64
"Little Eight"	Vocational school equipment (St. Kitts)	29,499	1959
	Improvement of water supply (St. Vincent)	16,331	1962

TABLE 6.5 (*concluded*)

Country	Project	Allocation (Canadian dollars)	Year
	Primary schools and warehouses		
	(Grenada, Antigua, Dominica)	1,475,000	1962–63
Trinidad	University College residence	696,423	1961
	Dominion Law Reports	2,000	1963–64
	Fire trucks	25,000	1964
West Indies			
Federation	Film contribution	10,000	1958–59
AFRICA			
Cameroun	Textbooks	1,000	1963
Dahomey	Textbooks	44,000	1963–64
French-speaking			
African States	Audio,visual equipment (Cameroun,		
	Central African Republic, Congo-		
	Brazzaville, Dahomey, Ivory		
	Coast, Morocco, Niger, Togo,		
	Upper Volta)	138,043	1963–64
Ghana	Trades Training Centre, Accra	900,000	1962–64
	Agricultural education equipment	80,000	1963–64
Kenya	Paper for Literacy Campaign	35,000	1963–64
Malagasy	Paper for Literacy Campaign	6,000	1964–65
Nigeria	Rural water development surveys	75,000	1963–64
	Data-processing equipment,		
	Board of Education	25,000	1963–64
	Dominion Law Reports	4,544	1964–65
Rwanda	Library equipment	15,000	1963
Sierra Leone	Boys' secondary school	216,752	1962
Tanzania	Motion picture projectors	14,414	1962
	Mobile film vans	9,500	1963
	Ambulances (Zanzibar)	13,757	1963
	Audio-visual equipment	74,902	1964–65
Uganda	Cinema vans	68,000	1963–64
	Handicraft equipment	31,501	1964
Total		$23,751,390	

*Including Singapore.

†"Small Projects" include equipment, almost invariably educational, supplied to support Canadian advisers and teachers in the field, or even, occasionally, foreign trainees studying in Canada. This equipment, which is counted by most other donors as technical assistance, is authorized under an Order-in-Council delegating discretionary power to the Director General for amounts up to $1,000. Such aid is now paid for out of country allocations.

Canada's largest project in this field—and indeed the largest aid project of its kind in the world—is the Canada-India Reactor (CIR). Although the CIR can scarcely be called typical, the variety and originality of the problems it raised make its study unusually worthwhile.

a. Purpose and negotiation

Unlike nearly all Canadian aid, and in contradiction with frequently defined policy, the CIR grew from an initiative by Canada. Recognizing

India's proved competence in atomic science and her desire to obtain a high-flux reactor for advanced research, the Canadian government offered in April 1955 to provide Indian scientists with a reactor of the NRX type used at Chalk River since 1947. The CIR was to be built at the principal Indian atomic establishment of Trombay, some six miles from Bombay. It would operate at a maximum thermal power of 40 megawatts and, like the NRX, would be fuelled with natural uranium, moderated with heavy water, and cooled by ordinary fresh water. Providing a high neutron flux over a large volume, it would serve as a tool for fundamental research, produce fissile and radioactive materials for medicine and industry, test engineering concepts, and train staff to design and operate larger reactors, particularly the power reactors planned to overcome India's shortage of conventional energy sources.[40]

When specifications had been worked out by Indian and Canadian scientists to adapt the NRX to India's special needs and physical environment, full-scale planning began in Canada at the end of 1955 and excavation at Trombay started in February 1956. Two months later, on April 28, the formal project agreement was signed, estimating the total cost at $13,500,000, of which Canada's share would be $7,500,000. The reactor, its supporting equipment and a special steel dome would be supplied by Canada, as well as scientific advice and engineering supervision. India was to bear all local costs, chiefly for general services and local construction work.

b. Execution

Not surprisingly, erection of the extremely complex CIR was slowed by a series of technical problems. In all, these difficulties stretched the original building schedule from two and a half years to some four years —a delay which at least one major Canadian professional journal found distressing. Accusing Canadian engineers of "bungling," an editorial in the May 1960 issue of *Modern Power and Engineering* denounced what it called "a tragi-comedy of errors"; as a result, went on the writer in the journal's August 1960 number, Canada had been "debited (with her agreement) for scores of thousands of dollars. . ."

[40]Most of the factual material in this sketch is based on three papers written by Indian and Canadian scientists: R. D. Sage, D. D. Stewart, N. B. Prasad and H. N. Sethna, "The Canada-India Reactor," in *Proceedings of the Second United Nations International Conference on the Peaceful Uses of Atomic Energy* (Geneva, 1958), pp. 157–73; W. B. Lewis and H. J. Bhabha, "The Canada-India Reactor: An Exercise in International Co-operation," *ibid.*, pp. 355–8; and a more critical study by W. B. Lewis and H. J. Bhabha, "The Canada-India Reactor: A Case History," working paper no E/CONF.39/J/15 of the United Nations Conference on the Application of Science and Technology for the Benefit of the Less Developed Areas, Geneva, 1962.

While costs to both Canada and India did rise in the end to about $19,000,000, shared almost equally, an investigation by the House of Commons Special Committee on Research in 1961 showed that the alleged mistakes were not for the most part imputable to the scientific supervisors, Atomic Energy of Canada Limited (AECL).[41] This Crown agency was doubtless responsible for time-consuming changes in the ventilation system; for weaknesses in the design of the cooling circuit; and for delays in preparing shut-off rods. But the most costly and troublesome problems occurred in the civil construction work. Considerable losses resulted when Canadian manufacturers supplied defective materials for the reactor dome; inspection of heat exchangers in Canada failed to remove quantities of tallow, machine cuttings, and deposits of rubber; and the general contractor was seriously handicapped by a lack of suitable construction equipment. Further delays grew from circumstances beyond the engineers' control, such as a North American steel strike and sub-soil water in the ground at Trombay.

These technical difficulties were aggravated by problems of administration described by the leading Indian and Canadian scientists as "quite onerous."[42] The project organization included the atomic agencies of both governments, each in constant touch with numerous interested departments at home; a firm of Canadian consulting engineers; a Canadian general contractor; and ten major and twenty minor contractors in Canada and India. Although important matters were settled only by representatives of AECL, the Indian Department of Atomic Energy, the consultants and the prime contractor, "there was continual need for reference and approval between the various parties concerned."[43] Under these conditions, authority became somewhat diffuse and technical arguments tended to be magnified on lines of administrative loyalty. This lack of a strong centre of responsibility was probably a key factor in a disagreement over the safety of the reactor dome which led in 1960 to the resignation of the Canadian project manager.[44]

In spite of these obstacles, personal relations between Indians and

---

[41]See Canada, *House of Commons Special Committee on Research, Minutes of Proceedings and Evidence* (Ottawa, 1961), nos. 17, 24, 26 and 27. (Hereafter referred to as *Special Committee on Research*). On June 1, 1961, the President of AECL explained to the Committee the rise in the CIR's costs: ". . . the total Canadian cost, I think, was $9.2 million. This should not be related directly to the [original estimate of] $7.5 million because we added some parts to the project as we went along. . . . $7.5 million was a guess, it was arrived at in an afternoon of estimating." (p. 1115).

[42]Lewis and Bhabha, "The Canada-India Reactor: A Case History," p. 2.

[43]*Ibid.*, p. 2.

[44]Both sides of this controversy between the project manager and AECL are presented fully in the *Special Committee on Research*, 1961, no. 26, pp. 1074–98.

Canadians, particularly at the upper levels of scientists and engineers, were trusting, friendly and informal. Again, as on other projects, professional affinities eclipsed cultural differences in a shared enthusiasm for the task at hand. This very close collaboration was evident both at Trombay, where up to thirty Canadian and Indian engineers and staff directed a work force of 2,500, and at Chalk River, where a total of a hundred Indian scientists received specialized training in all phases of reactor operation. These trainees, stressed a joint Indo-Canadian report to the 1958 UN Geneva Conference on the Peaceful Uses of Atomic Energy, "quickly became integrated with their Canadian associates both on and off the job."[45] The CIR of course had its share of the individual psychological misfits to be found in any undertaking of this size; but given the extraordinary tensions imposed by the project's technical and administrative complexity, co-operation between Indians and Canadians left little to be desired.

c. A provisional assessment

In spite of published criticism of the CIR's construction and of the very concept of reactors fuelled by natural uranium and moderated by heavy water, the reactor early proved itself the central instrument of India's atomic programme.[46] It is true that technical setbacks, especially a slime-forming bacterial contamination in the flow passages, prevented the CIR from reaching full power until January 1962, almost two years after completion. But once these initial difficulties had been solved, the reactor "helped to accelerate the development of the Indian atomic energy programme in a decisive manner."[47] By mid-1964 all its planned technical objectives were being realized; and, supported by a trained Indian staff of over 1400 scientists and engineers and more than

[45]Sage, *et al.*, "The Canada-India Reactor," p. 164. See also Lewis and Bhabha, "The Canada-India Reactor: An Exercise in International Co-operation": "this . . . remarkable spirit of co-operation . . . was even more clearly brought out while the Indian staff were at Chalk River. As individuals they shared the work of their Canadian colleagues and played a real part in the community life of the towns in which they lived. Their presence led to many enduring personal friendships and we look forward to further close co-operation between the atomic energy establishments of our two countries." (p. 357). The training programme had to be extended several times because many of its graduates were drawn from Trombay into other Indian industries and departments. In June 1965 there remained at Chalk River some twenty Indian trainees, several of whom were preparing for the Rajasthan project.
[46]A detailed criticism of Canadian reactor principles is given by an independent Canadian scientist, Mr. Winnett Boyd, before the *Special Committee on Research*, 1961, nos. 20 and 21.
[47]Lewis and Bhabha, "The Canada-India Reactor: A Case History," p. 6.

2200 technicians, the CIR was being employed at its expected high efficiency.[48]

While generalizations about the CIR's economic benefits must be tentative, its first fruits are promising. On April 27, 1964, India signed a contract worth $37 million with Canada to purchase a 200-megawatt nuclear power station for Rajasthan. This was the first foreign application of a Canadian-designed nuclear power plant, and a vindication of Canadian research theories which by mid-1965 had led to Indian decisions to build with Canadian help three more units of the same type. These new units will bring to Canadian industry further contracts worth probably many tens of millions of dollars. India herself expected to benefit from the CIR by adapting Canada's nuclear power system to exploit large domestic reserves of thorium, thereby making her projected chain of power reactors an economic source of electricity.

Finally, the CIR reaped for Canada not negligible satisfactions of a political nature. Representing a popularly exciting symbol of scientific progress, the reactor helped to create an image of Canada as a highly advanced industrial nation; and for the same reason, it commanded, in both Indian and Colombo Plan publications, a remarkable outpouring of publicity—an advantage greatly amplified by the Indian Prime Minister's personal responsibility for his government's Department of Atomic Energy. "The first thing that I stress," said Nehru before the representatives of forty nations at the CIR's inauguration on January 16, 1961, "is that this is a project of intimate co-operation and goodwill between Canada and India."[49]

So close indeed did this co-operation become during construction that exchanges and friendships between Indian and Canadian scientists continued long after to link the Trombay and Chalk River establishments

[48]The Indian Department of Atomic Energy's *Brief Annual Report* for 1963–64 summarized the CIR's use as follows (p. 3): "The year under review witnessed a steady raising of the power of CIR till it attained the full rated capacity of 40 MW at 15.10 hours on October 16, 1963. The reactor has since operated at 40 MW with a fuel charge consisting of rods fabricated in India. . . . Since CIR attained first criticality on July 10, 1960, it has been operated for a total of 13,004 hours, with an output of 6,997.18 MW days. . . . During 1963 over 760 samples were put in the reactor for irradiation. In addition, 14 rods containing some 8,496 slugs of cobalt are being irradiated. The thorium oxide and thorium metal produced in the Establishment, originally put in the reactor during its first criticality, are still undergoing irradiation. 16 experimental holes are being used for experimental purposes."

[49]*Daily Indiagram*, Information Service of India, Ottawa, Jan. 17, 1961, p. 2. A colour photograph of the CIR was chosen as the cover for the Colombo Plan Bureau's widely distributed anniversary booklet, *The Colombo Plan Story: Ten Years of Progress* (Colombo, 1962).

in relations of exceptional confidence. "I see Dr. Bhabha (Director of the Indian Department of Atomic Energy) four or five times a year," the AECL President told the Special Committee on Research on May 31, 1961; "we have excellent relations with the people in India. Dr. Bhabha has said publicly that this is the best and largest international co-operative program in atomic energy in the world. They are more than satisfied with the final result."[50] "We had some difficulty with this project some years ago," conceded Dr. Bhabha himself in a letter to the President of AECL on April 5, 1960, "but these are now matters of the past and it would be a pity if they were raked up again. As things stand, the Canada-India Reactor has certainly contributed to better relations between our two countries, and we greatly appreciate the assistance which Canada has given."[51] This trust and gratitude, in a branch of science with such strategic potential, necessarily have more than personal meaning; they show that the CIR, whatever its birth pains, may have been a wise and timely investment in diplomacy.

5. INDUSTRY: THE MAPLE LEAF CEMENT PLANT

Industrial projects devoted directly to production are not in strict theory a proper activity for development aid. They form in fact the second stage of development, building on the infrastructure of institutions and services which external aid normally seeks to strengthen. Nevertheless, industries producing primary materials for local manufactures or basic construction can be fairly considered as accessory to infrastructure, and thereby make a reasonable secondary claim on aid funds. At least unconsciously, Canada has probably followed such arguments in assigning industrial projects a very low priority: by June 1965, Ottawa had approved only four projects, and of these only two had gone beyond the stage of a pilot study.

Significantly, the largest of Canada's industrial projects, the Maple

[50]*Special Committee on Research*, no. 26, p. 1098.
[51]*Ibid.*, no. 27, pp. 1114–15. On November 14, 1963, Canada and India signed an eight-year agreement to "freely exchange scientific and technical information regarding the development of heavy-water-moderated reactor systems." (*External Affairs*, March 1964, p. 115). This exchange, covering "detailed design data, including plans and working drawings," appeared certain to engage the co-operation of Indian and Canadian nuclear establishments at nearly every level. The new programme began with a gift to India of Canadian information valued at $5 million, offered in addition to Colombo Plan and World Bank consortium commitments.

TABLE 6.6
Canadian Capital Projects in Industry (1950–March 31, 1965)

Country	Project	Allocation (Canadian dollars)	Year
ASIA			
Burma	Hardboard Test Project	50,000	1962
India	"Non-project, non-commodity assistance"*	1,500,000	1964–65
Malaysia	Pulp and paper industry survey	10,232	1963
Pakistan	Maple Leaf Cement Plant, (Daudkhel)	6,439,502	1953–57
	Khulna Hardboard Mill	1,850,000	1961–63
Total		$9,849,734	

*In the vernacular, spare parts, or extra equipment to enlarge a completed project. Such aid is meant to help recipients exploit without waste or interruption project aid already given.

Leaf Cement Plant, was also her first capital project of any kind. In 1953, when the plant was approved, the theory of development aid was still primitive; neither Canadian nor Pakistani planners had found time to formulate working definitions of infrastructure or even to imagine priorities.

At a time when much of the Pakistan government's energies were absorbed by reconstruction and by settlement of refugees, greatly increased supplies of primary building materials were in any event needed urgently. Traditional local materials being cement and processed clay—even for many public works projects normally built in Canada with brick or steel—a strong case could be made for help with cement, in whose manufacture, at least, Canadian experience was relevant. Consequently, the two governments agreed to build jointly a major cement plant near an area of refugee settlement in West Pakistan. The plant, to be located in the remote village of Daudkhel in the Sind Desert, would sustain an annual capacity of 100,000 tons of first-grade cement, enough to bolster radically West Pakistan's inadequate production.

A single important technical difficulty arose, and it was overcome by changes in design. The problem appeared early, when engineers made preliminary borings revealing that beneath the clay topsoil was a layer of quicksand which threatened to sink under the weight of the planned foundation. To surmount this obstacle, engineers designed a foundation shaped as a cellular raft of the same weight as the excavated earth.

More troublesome was the confusion in administration. Much of the uncertainty attending construction resulted from the two governments' failure to conclude a project agreement even before the job was completed, after five years, in 1958.[52] With no precedents to guide even an enlightened pragmatism, many decisions at the site were left to improvisation. But most of the project's administrative disputes stemmed from awkwardness of the administrative arrangements governing the separate participation of each government. Pakistan, without consulting the Canadian supervisors, hired a contracting firm organized locally by Europeans described by a close Canadian observer as "incompetent." These contractors, handicapped financially by their low bid, did work unacceptable to the Canadian engineers[53]; and subsequent debate between the contractors and Karachi over fees retarded completion. Canada, for her part, gave the whole contract for design, supervision, construction and supply to a consortium of Canadian firms, while the process design and equipment were subcontracted to a specialized Danish company. The Canadian firms, working under the ill-defined leadership of one of their number, found relations with each other uneasy and susceptible to more than usual disagreement. This "little bit of friction," as a participant put it, grew from the difficulty of independent and loosely co-ordinated firms "sleeping in the same bed." Although the first project manager did a "very good job," his attempts to push work forward disturbed both his Canadian and Pakistani colleagues; and the resulting impasse led to his resignation.

In spite of such tensions, which one might expect to be intensified by the loneliness and heat of life in a desert village, the Canadian engineers carved out for themselves a surprisingly pleasant existence. After initially camping in rest houses, then in mud-brick huts that washed away in heavy rains, they lived in comfortable clay-brick houses built specially for them by the Pakistan government. By the time they left in 1958, they had planted gardens and organized a community life that several were reluctant to abandon. Nurtured by these congenial amenities of North American suburbia, the Canadians' early good relations with their Pakistani hosts blossomed into friendship.

By mid-1964 the technical and economic success of the plant was abundantly proved. Every year since its completion, the factory had substantially surpassed its rated annual capacity of 100,000 tons, usually

[52]On September 10, 1951, however, Pakistan and Canada signed a "Statement of Principles . . . for the Co-operative Economic Development of Pakistan" a document originally thought sufficiently detailed to guide the intergovernmental administration of individual projects. Experience at Daudkhel and elsewhere soon pointed to the need for more specific agreements adapted to each undertaking.

[53]Some foundations and even whole buildings found by Canadian inspectors to be unsafe had to be abandoned or destroyed.

as early as October. Several dozen refugees were being employed full time; the living standard of the whole town of Daudkhel had risen visibly; tens of thousands of new houses had been built for displaced persons; and production had speeded many public infrastructure works, included Warsak and Shadiwal.

The political value of Daudkhel to Canada was quickly affirmed. When finished, the factory gathered much publicity as the first major Canadian project to reach fruition; and, in a friendly and then uncontroversial gesture, Pakistan asked that the factory be named the Maple Leaf Cement Plant—the crowning characteristic of the classical monument-type project, a title forever honouring the donor. Some of this fame may have faded when Ottawa failed to seize a chance in 1958 to carry out an expansion of the plant which had been prepared for, at considerable cost to Canada, since the beginning. As a result, the project's second stage was financed by Czechoslovakia which, building on Canadian slurry tanks and grinding mills, was able to triple the plant's capacity at a cost that naturally made Canada's work appear expensive by comparison. Still, the Maple Leaf title remains; and while some may fear that Canada diluted her prestige by allowing foreigners to share it, perhaps, after all, it is the Czechs who obscured their prestige by letting it be overgrown with maple leaves.

VII. Commodities

Between 1950 and 1965, industrial and agricultural commodities accounted for slightly more than half of all Canada's bilateral grants of capital aid. After 1958, this proportion rose still higher, explained the Director General in December 1963, "due to coinciding pressures . . . from the producers in Canada to find a larger place for their products in our aid programmes . . . and from the receiving countries who have been requesting from Canada larger amounts of non-project aid."[1] It is pertinent to ask how such gifts of raw materials and staples—obviously for short-term consumption—can be included in an aid programme devoted to basic economic development. For they are "not designed," as the 1963 DAC *Review* emphasized, "to finance new capital projects, but rather to cover the needs for general maintenance imports. . . ."[2]

The immediate uses of industrial commodities and foodstuffs vary so widely that the relation of each to development is best studied separately. Yet there are two common techniques for establishing this relation. On one hand, gifts of commodities are converted into so-called "counterpart funds" in local currency, which are in principle allocated by agreement with the donor to genuine development schemes; and on the other, such shipments "may contribute indirectly to economic development when . . . related to sensible management of its total resources by the recipient country."[3] Before reviewing these, and other distinctive, ways in which commodities may be justified, it will be helpful to summarize the composition and distribution of this aid (see Table 7.1).

[1]H. O. Moran, untitled manuscript of speech delivered to the British Columbia Association of Professional Engineers, p. 8.
[2]*Development Assistance Efforts and Policies, 1963 Review*, p. 60.
[3]*Ibid.*, p. 60.

TABLE 7.1
Primary Allocations of Canadian Commodities under Bilateral Programmes
(1950–March 31, 1965)

Country	Commodity	Allocation	Country total (Canadian dollars)	Date
Burma	Wheat & flour	2,300,000	2,300,000	1959–64
Cambodia	Flour	100,000	100,000	1960
Ceylon	Flour	14,425,000	14,425,000	1953–65
India	Wheat	85,000,000		1951–65
	Metals	80,965,000		1953–65
	Fertilizer	5,050,000		1958–60
	Asbestos	5,079,000		1959–65
	Newsprint	3,466,000		1960–65
			179,560,000	
Indonesia	Flour	2,200,000	2,200,000	1958–64
Nepal	Wheat	60,000	60,000	1958–59
Pakistan	Wheat	40,100,000		1952–65
	Metals	24,851,000		1954–65
	Wood-pulp	6,850,000		1958–64
	Fertilizer	11,735,000		1959–63
	Sulphur	1,000,000		1963–65
	Rapeseed	1,000,000		1964–65
			85,536,000	
South Vietnam	Butter	60,000		1959
	Flour	790,000	850,000	1959–65
Total			285,031,000	

1. INDUSTRIAL RAW MATERIALS

These goods naturally go to countries having a relatively advanced industrial base; up to and including the programme for 1964–65, Canada had delivered them to only two such recipients, India and Pakistan. Industrial commodities aim to speed development essentially through feeding industries which, from a temporary lack of supplies payable in foreign exchange, are threatened with idleness. More precisely, they seek to help the recipient's economy in four distinct ways. First, in supplying materials available only from abroad and vital to the full use of capital equipment, they help to avoid foreign exchange crises; next, by keeping this equipment in production, they sustain employment and eventually the workers' purchasing power; further, by making it unnecessary for recipients to divert funds from approved new projects to rescue threatened existing industries, they allow development plans to proceed undiminished; and finally, by absorbing the increased expenditure and higher incomes caused by development itself, they tend to fight inflation. In countries faced with these problems industrial commodity aid can

be of high development priority, even though it may not lead immediately to lasting increases in productivity. The scope of potential benefits is easily realized from the list given in Table 7.2.

TABLE 7.2

Primary Allocations of Canadian Industrial Raw Materials
(1950–March 31, 1965)

Commodity	Canadian dollars
Metals (in order of importance: aluminum, copper, nickel, steel sheets, zinc)	105,816,000
Fertilizers	16,785,000
Wood-pulp	6,850,000
Asbestos	5,079,000
Newsprint	3,466,000
Sulphur	1,000,000
Total	138,996,000

The special problems of administering these transactions have often
led to delays in delivery, particularly before 1960. In 1951, when the
first allocations were made, private importers were not always available
in recipient countries to deal with Canadian suppliers, and recipient
governments sometimes had to set up new machinery with inexperienced
agents. But more awkward by far was the difficulty of synchronizing
recipients' needs with Canada's supplies of commodities whose availability and price were often subject to rapid fluctuation. Such uncertainty at times disrupted shipments of materials open to the shifting
demands of domestic and foreign military technologies—aluminum, for
example, during the late 1950's. For these reasons, some shipments of
urgently needed metals, before 1957, were delayed after original allocation for periods of between two and five years.

As both Canadians and recipients gained several years of experience,
however, these delays were gradually reduced; and after the general
reform of Canada's administration in 1960, the EAO agreed with recipients on new procedures that were more stable and rapid. Although
the procedures adopted varied slightly with each commodity, the administration of copper ingot shipments may be taken as a representative
model of methods followed for the whole 1964–65 programme.

After Canada confirmed allocation of funds for this commodity, the
recipient government authorized consumers having a priority claim on
copper imports to negotiate purchases from the local agents of Canadian
suppliers at the current prices of the London metal market. If individual
orders were small, the agent waited some months to accumulate others
before placing a collective order with its Canadian supplier. When first

notice of an order was sent to Canada, the consumer issued a letter of credit to the supplier to prepay ocean freight, and forwarded copies of its contract to the External Aid Office through the recipient's High Commissioner in Ottawa. The EAO, on the authority of the contract thus certified by the recipient government, placed a confirming order with the supplier for shipment FAS to a Canadian seaport. The supplier, after delivering to dockside in Canada, was paid for the order by the EAO, and for ocean freight by the consumer on surrender of the negotiable ocean bills-of-lading to a local bank against the consumer's letter of credit. This system, leaving most of the detailed administration to private agents of both governments, worked well; the only significant delays resulted from the occasional slowness of recipients to take up allocations by releasing foreign exchange, when needed, for ocean freight.[4]

The economic value of industrial commodity aid was frequently affirmed in exhortations of the World Bank in the early 1960's urging donors to offer up to half their assistance in this form. Canada, as one of the few donors having reached this goal, has witnessed in her commodity programme impressive and varied proof of the Bank's wisdom. Canadian non-ferrous metals have been made into conductors and wiring essential for power grids, and supported specialized manufactures ranging from bicycles to fuel rods for the CIR; "unless this [deficiency in zinc] can be made up," warned a Canadian Trade Commissioner in a typical letter to the EAO in October 1963, "there is a serious prospect of industrial activity being curtailed. This would mean a reduction in electrical transmission equipment, steel pipes and tubes, sheets, dry batteries, electrical components, and die-casting—all of which are significant in the industry to-day." Canadian fertilizers have saved and doubled crops, thereby educating sceptical peasants to the need for local fertilizer production and for widespread adoption of modern agricultural techniques; wood-pulp has kept a large paper mill in East Pakistan functioning for five years until suitable local bamboo matured; asbestos has been made into boards, sheets and pipes for fire-proof construction of factories; newsprint, while helping to keep Indian presses running, has blunted a temporary crisis in foreign exchange that could have slowed imports of capital equipment; and sulphur has allowed Pakistan to vulcanize rubber, make safety matches and produce sulphuric acid for industry. Almost always these shipments have cleared bottlenecks,

---

[4]Even though Canadian suppliers usually co-operated well with the EAO in delivering commodities, delays of several months still occurred, as with wood-pulp in 1964, when commercial demand in Canada was heavy.

released paralysed productive equipment, mobilized idle skills, or relieved constrictive pressures on development budgets.

As a result, industrial commodity aid usually brings to Canada powerful, if narrow, political benefits in appreciation. For even though such shipments are the most "anonymous" of any aid in their ability to attract popular gratitude, they deeply impress high-level politicians and industrialists charged with directing national development. This is so first because commodities, which are not necessarily tied to precise uses, permit planners great flexibility in adjusting budgets to changing priorities; and second, because final consumers pay for them no more than current world prices—while for some Canadian projects, equipment and services are charged to buyers at local currency equivalents of often high Canadian dollar prices. For these reasons, planners of recipient countries have described Canada's industrial commodities as "valuable aid of the first magnitude," "very significant in easing our foreign exchange position," and "the most welcome of any aid."[5]

This satisfaction does not mean that such materials should be given to more countries or even offered in greater quantities to the two present recipients. Industrial commodities are useful only to countries with industry— and only when these countries have built productive capacity so quickly that resources in foreign exchange are temporarily unavailable to exploit it. India and Pakistan were at this stage from about 1958 to 1965, and may remain there for a few years more; but they, and recipients elsewhere, should not be encouraged to rely permanently on gifts of aid funds for such a significant part of their imports of current maintenance. The primary function of development aid is to build infrastructure in harmony with recipients' ability to absorb it; and its failure to do so is measured by recipients' demands for consumer imports—which are usually an admission of poor planning. To acquiesce in standing requests for commodities may not only weaken recipients' incentive to plan with discipline; it may nibble away the broad basis of popular support for aid in Canada which, in the end, requires that the economic benefits of giving aid be widely shared by many Canadians in a balanced and diversified programme.

2. FOODSTUFFS

The role of foodstuffs in economic development is more than doubtful; it is fiercely controversial. Even the language of debate invites argument:

[5]Comments by members of the Indian and Pakistani Planning Commissions during interviews in February and March 1960.

is grain for the hungry masses really "food aid," as the euphemism of its supporters would have it, or is it merely what sceptics persist in discounting as "surplus disposal"? Canada, though the world's second largest donor of foodstuffs (albeit very far behind the United States), has never been perfectly sure. And in practice, this uncertainty has led her to feed the starving with a good conscience in the short run, but— by thereby neglecting development—a bad one for the long run.

TABLE 7.3

Primary Allocations of Canadian Foodstuffs under
Bilateral Programmes (1950–March 31, 1965)

Commodity	Canadian dollars
Wheat	126,435,000
Flour	18,540,000
Rapeseed	1,000,000
Butter	60,000
Total	146,035,000

It is true that in the early years of her programme Canada tried with a clear purpose to restrict her aid funds to legitimate development projects, dismissing proposed gifts of food as wasteful and irrelevant welfare assistance. "The Colombo Plan was not designed for that kind of relief," insisted the IETCD Administrator in October 1951; "the intentions . . . were to provide capital equipment of a permanent nature which could raise the standards of living."[6] "We are most anxious," he declared in 1955, ". . . not to dissipate our funds in relief measures. It is most unfortunate that many of these people should not have enough to eat, but they will always be in that condition unless we use our funds to put them in a better condition."[7] "We are trying," he confirmed a year later, ". . . to give these people . . . facilities to grow their own food and to help themselves. . . . They will never become self-supporting if we send them food."[8]

These statements of rigorous development orthodoxy were soon drowned out, however, by the famine cries of impoverished Asians. In 1951–52, her very first year of giving capital aid, Canada was pressed

[6]*Statements and Speeches*, no. 51/38, p. 4.
[7]*Standing Committee on External Affairs*, 1955, p. 704.
[8]*Ibid.*, 1956, p. 143. This view of food aid is broadly shared by the World Bank, whose consortia do not allow donors to count foodstuffs as part of development aid commitments. It has been argued by the Administrator and others, moreover, that Canadian wheat aid is of limited value because many recipient peoples are "rice-eaters who would not know what to do with wheat if we sent it." *Ibid.*

by India to supply in wheat more than three quarters of the total $19,800,000 Indian allocation to help overcome a threat of mass starvation from crop failure. The Administrator's explanation for Canada's agreement to this gift—and those that followed it every year—reveals succinctly the conscientious donor's dilemma. "It is extremely difficult to turn . . . down [requests for grain]," he conceded in his 1951 speech, ". . . but as our Oriental friends point out to us, and their argument is unanswerable, 'it is useless to give us beautiful equipment for use in two or three years time if in the meantime we have all died of famine.' "[9] ". . . The wheat gift was not really in accordance with Colombo Plan principles, or so we felt," he added in 1955, ". . . and we did not particularly want to give this food, but at that time . . . there was famine and if a Commonwealth partner comes and says 'We are in a famine condition', what can you do?"[10]

Such scruples haunted the new Conservative régime in 1957 less painfully. Boosted to power in part by a wave of Prairie resentment at Ottawa's alleged neglect of western farmers, Prime Minister Diefenbaker not surprisingly reasoned that Asian hunger and Canadian grain surpluses were logical antidotes for each other. In 1957–58, the first Conservative aid budget—whose total in bilateral grants was unchanged from the $34,400,000 of the previous year—raised the allocation for foodstuffs from $645,000 the year before to $5,000,000. And when the total in bilateral grants was raised in 1959–60 to $50,300,000, the portion earmarked for foodstuffs rose to $12,500,000. While the proportion of foodstuffs within the bilateral grant total had fallen in the last year of the St-Laurent administration to 1.9 per cent, in 1958–59 it reached a peak of 29.6 per cent, then levelled off in subsequent years at 25 per cent.

The government justified its new emphasis on foodstuffs by pressing into service arguments used to buttress a deceptively similar, yet more valid, case for industrial commodities. ETAB, in its March 1960 *Report on Canada's Economic Aid Programmes* suggested three ways in which Canada's food aid had brought recipients "direct benefit":

First, in times of emergencies, such as droughts and floods, it has helped these countries to carry forward their development programme without having to call upon and use resources which are urgently required for basic economic development. Second, it has helped to alleviate pressure on scarce

[9]*Statements and Speeches*, no. 51/38, p. 4.
[10]*Standing Committee on External Affairs*, 1955, p. 701. See also *Statements and Speeches*, no. 52/52, p. 6: "It was never contemplated that the Colombo Plan should be a food relief measure, but nevertheless, how could we refuse our Commonwealth partners, suffering from a severe famine?"

foreign exchange resources, and third, it has served to moderate the inflationary impact of the growth in domestic consumer demand that is being generated by increasing development expenditures and rising incomes.[11]

To these supposed benefits the EAO's May 1961 *Report on Canadian External Aid Programmes* added the standard justification that foodstuffs, like industrial commodities, generated counterpart funds which, it maintained, "are used for economic development purposes as agreed between Canada and the recipient country."[12]

But the government's prime motive for increasing food allocations appeared to have little to do with the development of recipient countries. During his Asian Commonwealth tour in the autumn of 1958, Mr. Diefenbaker expounded a quite different—and, if nothing else, commendably frank—doctrine, by insisting that one of the aims of the Colombo Plan as a co-operative aid programme of mutual advantage should be to help donors surmount their own economic difficulties. On December 9, 1958, the *Civil and Military Gazette* of Lahore prominently quoted the Prime Minister as saying in New Zealand:

"In view of the fact that we have in Canada a tremendous surplus of wheat, we would naturally hope, if not expect, that these countries would take a large share of wheat and flour under the Colombo Plan. It is our hope that in the next few years a substantial portion of our contribution will be made up of wheat."

Such wheat shipments would help to cut Canada's vast surplus as well as play their part in the Asian Governments' battle against their ever-present food shortage, the Prime Minister reportedly argued. He also took the view that the Asian countries, as fellow Commonwealth members, should be willing to help Canada's problems as well as their own, the sources said.[18]

Yet at least the two largest recipients, India and Pakistan, were increasingly unwilling "to help Canada's problems." Even though both countries continued to need substantial imports of foodstuffs, relatively good crops after the mid-1950's greatly diminished the threat of famine and therefore the demand for food imports on a really massive scale. But more decisive still in making wheat and flour less welcome as part

[11]*Standing Committee on External Affairs*, 1960, p. 35.
[12] P. 3.
[18]The *Ceylon Daily News* of November 27, 1958, also reported Mr. Diefenbaker as stating that Canada "was hoping, if not expecting, that a suitable proportion" of Canadian aid would be accepted in surplus wheat. Canada's carry-over of wheat at the end of the 1960–61 crop year was 608 million bushels; at the end of 1961–62 it had fallen to 391 million bushels, a drop that may partly explain the government's readiness to make the 1962 austerity cut from the aid budget entirely in wheat. Some Canadian administrators say privately that food aid is needed to ensure that Canada will keep a fair share of Asian markets when recipients are rich enough to buy all their foreign wheat.

of Canada's development aid was the passage in 1954 of the United States Public Law 480, offering these and other foods on terms less burdensome to recipients than Canada's. Under Title I of PL 480 (providing for sales in local currencies) and especially under Title II as amended in 1960 (permitting outright grants), the United States paid either part or all of the ocean freight charges; and since the merchant navies of even India and Pakistan were small, this concession offered a valuable saving for each in foreign exchange. Canada's wheat aid, on the other hand, was delivered only FAS at Montreal or Vancouver, leaving recipients to pay all ocean charges including eventual demurrage at dockside in Canada. Consequently, Canadian wheat given even as a grant proved more costly to recipients, in terms of foreign exchange, than American wheat sold for the receiver's currency. Largely because of this discrepancy, the United States was able to conclude four-year Title I agreements with both countries: with India in May 1960 for $1,081,000,000, and with Pakistan in October 1961 for $927,000,000. These supplies, which were wanted less for immediate consumption than to form stocks against famine and speculation, met nearly all the recipients' needs of outside food.

In these circumstances, Canada's insistence between 1958 and 1962 on allocating development aid funds to food shipments caused the Indian and Pakistani governments to react privately with dismay and resentment. By clearly announcing her intention to use foreign aid to relieve her own domestic economic troubles, Canada not only cast doubt on her frequently proclaimed altruism; she allowed the good of her legitimate development aid to be interred, in recipients' minds, under tons of unwelcome wheat.

Certainly not all recipients of Canadian foodstuffs during these years were dissatisfied. Several countries making less rapid progress towards industrialization, such as Ceylon, Burma, Indonesia, Nepal, Cambodia and Vietnam, greeted shipments of foreign food with varying degrees of enthusiasm. This attitude occasionally reflected a positive desire to generate counterpart funds for development; but more often than not, it seemed to coincide with a failure to formulate coherent plans requiring foreign capital equipment—or merely with a habit of taking any aid, however useless, as long as it was free. It is hard to imagine, for instance, that Canada's $60,000 shipment of surplus butter to South Vietnam in 1959 was a contribution of high priority in either the economic development or popular diet of that country—especially since the United States International Co-operation Administration (ICA) "had repeatedly declined to approve the importing of surplus cheese and butter into Vietnam.''[14] And gifts of wheat or flour to Indonesia, Ceylon, Cambodia and Burma inevitably reached only a small Westernized middle-class population in capital cities, for the great, really hungry mass of these peoples ate, and wished to eat, only rice. It is true that Burma and Ceylon normally imported commercially small amounts of flour, so that gifts of it did in theory release foreign exchange for purchasing capital equipment; and these same countries made fruitful investments of Canadian-created counterpart funds: notably for the Thaketa Bridge at Rangoon, and the Katubedde Institute and a widely appreciated rural roads programme in Ceylon.[15] But the arguments justifying counterpart funds, when applied to countries like Cambodia and Nepal whose development planning was at best primitive, were inept rationalizations; and applied to Indonesia, where endemic corruption and inter-island tensions deprived planning of all meaning, they approached mockery. To all of these countries, foodstuffs were welcome not so much because they fostered development as because, being accepted mainly to please the donor, they provided a convenient disguise for bungling development.

Recognition of these evils probably influenced Ottawa's decision to make all of the $8,500,000 cut in aid funds under the May 1962 emergency austerity measures from the allocation for foodstuffs. This move, leaving most of the remaining $41,500,000 of the Colombo Plan allocation for true development aid, was sustained by the returning Liberal régime in the programme for 1963–64. Then on July 24, 1963, the government took a positive, if still somewhat ambiguous, step toward an orthodox redefinition of food aid as welfare assistance when the Minister of Trade and Commerce, Mr. Sharp, announced that beginning with the 1964–65 aid budget, Canada would give foodstuffs under a new special programme distinct from development aid. The new programme would consolidate all Canadian food assistance, including contributions to the UN-FAO World Food Programme and the UN Relief and Works Agency (UNRWA), as well as bilateral grants. The total fund for food would rise "over . . . the next few years" to reach an annual expenditure of about $40,000,000, starting with an allocation in the first year of $15,000,000. Since the programme would give away almost nothing but wheat and wheat flour, the Minister hoped that it would "prove of both short-run and long-run advantage to western wheat producers"; then he added, in contradiction with the government's

[14]John D. Montgomery, *The Politics of Foreign Aid* (New York, 1962), p. 221.
[15]So widely appreciated in fact that a former Ceylonese Finance Minister reported in an interview in May 1960 that engineers building roads at Ceylon government expense were often asked to "thank Canada for her continued help."

apparent intention to separate foodstuffs from development aid, that "food aid . . . should be a continuing and important part of our external development assistance as long as the need for food exists."[16] This seeming retreat from the just-implied principle that wheat was not development aid elicited from the Leader of the Opposition, Mr. Diefenbaker, a recollection of Liberal criticism of his own earlier food aid policy and the remark that he and his colleagues were "very happy at the conversion of those in the Liberal party who previously held the very reverse of the opinion inherent in the announcement today."[17]

The new programme's potential value will not be clear for several years, but the circumstances of its launching suggest it was conceived essentially to stabilize surplus disposal. This impression emerges not only from the Minister's initial defence of the programme as "the right approach to the problems that confront western wheat producers,"[18] but from its quickly demonstrated subordination to commercial pressures: scarcely ten weeks after announcing the new programme, the Minister was forced by unexpectedly large wheat sales to the Soviet Union to admit that "it might take a little longer to build up to the $40 million which was mentioned. . . ."[19] The food programme, it appears, will not respond primarily to actual needs of recipients, but will dispense surpluses left from time to time by the fluctuating success of Canada's commercial sales. Such a conception is not immoral; yet it does place the food aid programme on an unreliable footing likely to undermine singularly recipients' year-to-year planning.

Nevertheless, if administered more closely than foodstuff grants in the past, the new food programme might be significantly related to development. Serious administration should question each request for

[16]Canada, *House of Commons Debates*, July 24, 1963, pp. 2559–60.
[17]*Ibid.*, p. 2560.
[18]*Ibid.*
[19]*Ibid.*, Oct. 4, 1963, p. 3206. Although the Minister said the delay occurred "in view not of the shortage of grain but of the limitation on transportation" (p. 3207), the priority given commercial sales still had the result of postponing grain shipments as aid. In a speech in Washington on March 5, 1964, Mr. Sharp stressed that the new food programme "is not surplus disposal. We do not look upon food aid as a means of getting rid of embarrassing surpluses." But his following sentence indicated that he defined "surplus disposal" to include only cut-rate sales likely to harm established markets of competitors: "Every bushel of wheat donated by the Government of Canada as food aid is bought from the Canadian Wheat Board at going market prices and we try to ensure that food aid does not inhibit or endanger normal patterns of commercial trade." (*Canada, Department of Trade and Commerce*, Trade Publicity Branch text no. 22/64, pp. 7–8).

food specifically according to its probable contribution to development in a given time and country. Will the food be used, for instance, to finance the mounting salaries of productive workers? Is it needed to support hungry peasants while modern farming methods and agrarian reform effect lasting improvements in agricultural productivity? Or is it required to surmount a temporary crisis in the recipient's crops which could otherwise be met only by diverting foreign exchange from the development budget? In sum, Canadian planners would have to remember, as the OECD Ministers of Agriculture agreed on November 20, 1962, that food aid can hasten development only "during a relatively limited transitional period . . . in circumstances where food shortages constitute a factor limiting the rate of development, and where a country has inadequate foreign exchange to import additional food on a commercial basis."[20]

The techniques for fruitfully investing food aid approved against such criteria have been carefully studied by FAO, DAC and, under PL 480, by the United States government. The most direct method uses food to employ idle workers on development projects—paying salaries either with counterpart funds created through local sale of foreign food or by offering the food as salary-in-kind. This technique is well known to Canada, but has not been applied often enough under dependable supervision to ensure that the great bulk of Canadian food aid has indeed served development. A second way is to use food aid to build reserves against sudden shortages, thereby allowing local planners to be more bold and flexible in charting development; this was one of the functions of the four-year Patil-Eisenhower agreement in 1960 under PL 480. Were Canada to give food on such terms, her contribution, to be effective in any single large country, would doubtless have to be pooled with those of other substantial donors. A third method, also indirect, uses food aid to soften hardship caused by experiments in long-term agricultural reform. Extra grain supplies can build up livestock production either by serving as feed or by permitting farmers to return cultivated land to pasture; the resulting greater supply of protein enriches the workers' diet and must sooner or later raise their productivity. Likewise,

[20]*Food Aid: Its Role in Economic Development* (Paris: 1963), p. 6. Professor Nathan Keyfitz suggests that in evaluating the potential contribution of foodstuffs, or indeed of any aid, to development, "the essential criterion is the accounting notion of capital as against income. Nearly any of the commodities which are ordinarily donated is likely to be capital in a developing country, income in a static one." "Foreign Aid Can Be Rational," *International Journal*, vol. 17, no. 3 (Summer, 1962), p. 241.

temporary outside food shipments can encourage recipients to undertake fundamental land reforms by offsetting possible short-term reductions in crops caused by disrupting the old agrarian order.

Plainly, these techniques demand intensive study of recipients' development plans so that food aid can be efficiently co-ordinated with foreign aid in capital equipment and with each recipient's own development resources. "There is a close relationship," stressed the OECD brochure *Food Aid* in 1963, "between the volume of investment in the receiving country and the amount of food aid that can usefully be absorbed. The aim in all cases is to ensure that extra supplies of food correspond in amount to the additional demand for food resulting from increased incomes, above that which can be supplied from an expansion in domestic agricultural production."[21] Too much food aid may displace sales by domestic farmers and commercial importers; while too little, by leaving demand unsatisfied, may lead to inflation. It donors are to walk this tightrope successfully, they cannot content themselves with the arbitrary disposal of surpluses left over from normal marketing; they must seek individually and together to relate their giving of food to recipients' changing absorptive capacity, trying constantly to measure the usefulness of food aid against that of alternative forms of aid.

This does not prevent foodstuffs from being given as freely as surpluses allow for what FAO calls "social development"—school meals, famine relief, and welfare. This essentially charitable purpose should continue to be supported both bilaterally and through such agencies as UNRWA. But if donors, for whatever motive, pretend that foodstuffs speed *economic* development, they must take steps to translate their sometimes careless propaganda into fact. For Canada, this means first equipping herself with a staff of economists competent to apply objective standards for judging recipients' real capacity to use food for development. But in the long run, Canada's best hope of serving development with food is through multilateral channels, notably through the UN-FAO World Food Programme. This plan, established in 1963 following President Eisenhower's earlier "Food-for-Peace" proposals, could become a reliable central agency for matching food surpluses and shortages on a world scale. Many of the problems it raises—sharing costs between food donors and simple cash contributors, possible disruption of commercial channels, co-ordination of donors' planting policies, new techniques of international administration, choice of recipients—are intricate

---

[21]P. 19. A succinct and authoritative survey of the problems of world hunger and food aid is found under the title "La Faim dans le monde," *Le Monde diplomatique*, Paris, May 1963, pp. 9–12.

and thorny. But some of them already face bilateral donors, most of whom are impotent to solve them alone. Only the UN and FAO offer the technical experience and facilities for co-ordination that could distribute surpluses equitably and constructively to the areas of greatest need. While there are good reasons, at least in the present world political climate, for continuing to give most capital aid bilaterally, the World Food Programme provides a rare opportunity for concrete experiment in pooling aid. And, as an imaginative symbol of human solidarity relatively untainted by the quarrels of Cold War politics, it is also one of the most promising avenues open for strengthening the authority and practical usefulness of the United Nations itself.

3. COUNTERPART FUNDS

Long presented as a valuable supplement to project aid, counterpart funds have been shown by experience to support development less than decisively. Indeed, the discrepancies between an attractively simple theory and far more complex practice reveal that the notion and use of counterpart funds need considerable fresh research.

These funds were conceived to reconcile commodity aid, always given for current or later consumption, with the legal requirement of Canadian legislation that assistance should further long-term development. "Since . . . commodity assistance . . . is sometimes not regarded as development aid in the strict sense," explained the EAO Deputy Director General on August 20, 1963, ". . . Canada asks recipient governments to set up counterpart funds in local currency equivalent to the value of the commodities. These counterpart funds belong to the recipient country but they can be used only with Canadian agreement for economic development purposes, frequently in connection with Canadian capital projects."[22]

[22]P. M. Towe, "Outline of Canadian External Aid," manuscript of speech distributed by EAO, pp. 19–20. In 1961 the Canadian Auditor General gave the following official definition of counterpart funds: "By agreement with the recipient countries, when goods that are not directly related to economic development are financed by grants from the Government of Canada under the Colombo Plan and sold or otherwise distributed by the [recipient] governments concerned, 'counterpart funds' are to be set aside for subsequent use in connection with agreed economic development projects in their countries. These funds are to be paid into special local currency accounts, and the government of a recipient country is to report from time to time to the Government of Canada the position of its counterpart fund account and supply a covering certificate from its Auditor General." *Report of the Auditor General to the House of Commons for the Fiscal Year Ended March 31, 1960* (Ottawa, 1961), p. 17.

In theory, this arrangement means that any single shipment of commodity aid confers on recipients a double advantage: immediate consumption of the commodity, and a net financial contribution to the local costs of development. At times, it has even been suggested that it was this contribution, rather than the enjoyment of the goods themselves, that primarily justified commodity aid. "For every project which is inaugurated," said the IETCD Administrator in 1955,

... there is a certain amount of rupee expenditure which the people of the country concerned must necessarily carry out themselves—the building of concrete structures, and so forth, which of course we cannot send out to them. All this costs money and the more aid they accept the more these poor countries find themselves in need of rupee funds in order to carry out their share. Therefore we have had to help them out in the creation of rupee funds by sending out commodities which they can use to provide monies upon which they can draw to meet their rupee expenditure.[23]

Probably this device is helpful to countries unable to raise development funds from taxes and reluctant to create credit artificially. No doubt some Canadian counterpart funds have surmounted these fiscal and monetary obstacles and aided worthwhile development projects. Warsak drew some $36,000,000 in counterpart funds for local costs; the Canada Dam at Mayurakshi about $15,000,000; the Canada-India Reactor about $8,000,000; and Katubedde, Shadiwal, the Thaketa Bridge, the Ceylon rural roads scheme and the Indian engineering colleges smaller, but substantial, sums. Without the credit in local currency generated by Canadian commodities, argue the system's apologists, these sums would have placed a heavy extra strain on recipients' budgets. Even though the costs supported are restricted to goods and services produced domestically, local budgets must somehow provide the funds demanded or fail to exploit valuable opportunities to absorb foreign aid.

Sceptics reply that the only increase in recipients' real resources comes not from counterpart funds, a mere bookkeeper's illusion, but from the commodities themselves. Recipients cannot benefit fully from commodities, moreover, unless they seize the occasion to invest in development at a faster rate. "How this increased investment is financed," held the OECD experts on food aid in 1963, "is a secondary matter: counterpart funds may be used, or created money."[24] Counterpart funds, in fact, are more apt than printed money to cause inflation because they are usually released long after the sale of the commodities has temporarily reduced domestic purchasing power.

[23]Standing Committee on External Affairs, 1955, p. 697.
[24]Food Aid, p. 42.

Beside these uncertainties must be placed administrative anomalies that make the theory of counterpart funds seem still less cogent. To begin, the widespread notion that funds "set aside" by governments receiving commodities are "generated" from domestic sales is not always correct. Penniless peasants struck by famine cannot pay for foodstuffs, but must enjoy them at government expense; and industrial commodities sent to factories owned by the recipient's central government cannot be sold by one ministry to another with any net addition to consolidated revenue. Nevertheless, Canadian accounting procedures oblige recipients even in such cases to "create" on paper counterpart funds equivalent in local currency to the dollar value of the goods as determined by Canada.

This insistence early moved both donor and recipients, especially before 1961, to view the system with reservations. Recipients often regarded it as unrealistic and burdensome, for sometimes the funds realized from local sale of commodities were less than the sum set aside on the basis of official exchange rates, and at other times nothing at all was realized. In such cases, the recipient government could bridge the difference between the real sale price (if any) and the Canadian dollar value of commodities only by transferring funds from some other government department, by postponing a locally financed development activity, or by printing money. If creating new money seemed the least painful method when the goods were received, when counterpart funds were allocated it meant that the project ostensibly aided by the donor was being financed in reality from a deficit by the recipient.

Some recipients also tended to resent or ridicule the system because of its elaborate pretension to win for donors "double credit" from a single gift. While welcomed by countries like Burma and Ceylon which could easily sell Canadian wheat or flour to support local building costs, the arrangement failed to impress larger recipients whose wide public ownership of industry and occasional famines made the "additional benefit" of "generated" counterpart funds seem ironic. In these countries, the system could be seen only as a disruption of normal planning, a promotion of what one Canadian official in Asia called "twice-cooked meat" that had to be accepted "to keep the Canadians happy."[25]

Most of the time before 1961, happy meant indifferent. For years the fictions and imperfections of the system led Canadian administrators to supervise the funds with at best sporadic attention. Not surprisingly,

[25]The metaphor was pursued by a chief official of an Asian Planning Commission who, during an interview in March 1960, described the system as "baloney, a mere publicity device designed to humour the donor."

the hostility or apathy of each side to the whole idea of counterpart funds resulted during the first decade in an extremely slow rate of certification and of allocation to development activities. The full decline was revealed only in March 1961, when the Canadian Auditor General criticized the failure of the IETCD and ETAB to extract from recipients accounting certificates showing the true amounts of counterpart funds on account and allocated. In his report for the fiscal year ended March 31, 1960, the Auditor General announced receipt of certificates for no more than $29,000,000 in counterpart funds, while $85,600,000 were unaccounted for. "We have not seen any evidence that we regard as satisfactory," he complained further to the Standing Committee on Public Accounts on March 8, 1961, "that these funds are actually on deposit in these countries. . . . I do not believe there has been any audit of these funds and I do not think we can be assured about them."[26] Called to reply for the policies of his predecessors, the newly appointed Director General of the EAO disagreed: "I think they [the funds] have been accounted for. . . . there is no difference of view between myself and the authorities of these three countries as to how much is in the counterpart fund account of each country. Now, an accounting technicality apparently requires the Auditor General in the receiving country to issue a certificate. . . . I am not worried that he has not produced that certificate."[27] Later the same day, assuring that he proposed in future to verify the accounting of the funds "continuously," the Director General suggested that earlier delays had occurred simply because recipients "are all still weak in the statistical field. There is an Asian country that could not give you a population figure."[28]

Out of this testimony came the still more distressing information that

[26]Canada, *House of Commons, Minutes of Proceedings and Evidence of the Standing Committee on Public Accounts*, March 8, 1961, p. 76. Hereafter cited as *Standing Committee on Public Accounts*. Detailed statistics on Canadian counterpart funds were published for the first and only time in the *Standing Committee on External Affairs*, 1960, p. 142. Even these figures were incomplete, listing funds for only India, Pakistan and Ceylon.

[27]*Standing Committee on Public Accounts*, 1961, p. 75.

[28]*Ibid.*, p. 79. He emphasized this weakness of recipient governments again before the same committee in November 1963, adding: "These countries do not have the degree of administrative efficiency we know in Canada. It is all part of their underdevelopment." (*Ibid.*, 1963, p. 142). After avowing that "we have written continuously and persistently to the governments of these countries . . . pointing out that they are in default in respect of the certificates," he concluded (pp. 144 and 145) that "on the whole . . . the counterpart procedure is causing a lot of work. . . . It will always be a continuing problem. We will be diverting time and effort to getting these certificates."

of some $168,800,000 in Canadian counterpart funds presumably set aside since 1952, hardly more than $61,100,000 had been allocated to "agreed economic development projects." This meant that almost two-thirds of the funds so vigorously defended as supporting development were lying idle in real or imaginary Asian accounts; or that nearly one third of Canada's total bilateral aid, including projects, commodities and technical assistance, had not yet been used for development at all. Even though the counterpart funds might be invested later in development, this rate of utilization was unacceptably lower than that of major donors, which was usually estimated at no less than 80 per cent.

There were plausible, if not persuasive, reasons for this delay. Often recipients could not offer, for counterpart assistance, projects to which Canada was also supplying the foreign exchange content—and Ottawa strongly preferred Canadian participation to remain exclusive. Fearing a similar reaction, recipients sometimes hesitated to ask that counterpart funds be applied to projects financed by local authorities alone. Another cause of delay was the Canadian Finance Department's insistence that accumulated funds be spent only on current or future projects; applying them to completed projects, it was argued, was tantamount to covering a budget deficit. As a result of Canada's refusal to apply funds retroactively to Indian work on the first stage of Kundah, the United States agreed to pay these earlier costs from its counterpart fund account; and now Canada's most expensive project, which by 1965 had absorbed nearly $44,000,000 in Canadian equipment and services, is legitimately presented by Washington as an "American-aided" undertaking. Some recipients were reluctant, moreover, to apply funds which had never really been "generated"—to allocate these funds would have meant diverting them from some other activity or, by inflationary means, creating them. Finally, Canada's normal and wise demand that all projects meet high standards of economic priority and local support diminished drastically the number of allocation proposals that recipients dared advance.

Following the Auditor General's exchange with the EAO Director General in the Public Accounts Committee, some of these obstacles were overcome. Soon after its establishment, the EAO tightened its surveillance of dormant counterpart funds and within a few months reduced the unallocated balances to reasonable levels. Since EAO reports did not subsequently publish statistics on allocation of the funds, however, the Standing Committee on External Affairs was unable to control their use any more closely than before. Even by June 1965, there was no public evidence to prove that the record of allocation had radically improved over the $107,676,000 in unallocated balances condemned by the Auditor General three years earlier.

TABLE 7.4

Canadian Counterpart Fund Accounts as at December 31, 1960* (Canadian dollars)

Country	Counterpart funds set aside	Allocated to projects	Unallocated balance
India	108,935,000	45,000,000	63,935,000
Pakistan	46,931,000	11,700,000	35,231,000
Ceylon	10,421,500	4,421,500	6,000,000
Nepal	60,000	nil	60,000
Burma	1,200,000	nil	1,200,000
South Vietnam	300,000	nil	300,000
Cambodia	100,000	nil	100,000
Indonesia	850,000	nil	850,000
Totals	168,797,500	61,121,500	107,676,000

*SOURCE: Canada, *House of Commons, Minutes of Proceedings and Evidence of the Standing Committee on Public Accounts*, March 8, 1961, p. 78. These figures, which are approximate, include $35,000,000 in "Special Grants" of wheat and flour to India, Pakistan and Ceylon outside the Colombo plan.

In reality, the EAO and recipient governments manage at present to agree more promptly than before on new allocations, frequently within a year of original shipments. But in spite of great progress between 1961 and 1963, the certifying of precise sums on account remains sluggish. Even though Canada sends recipients a quarterly statement estimating in dollars and local currency the amounts of counterpart funds generated by all shipments during each quarter, more often than not recipients submit different estimates. Lengthy, rather hair-splitting correspondence then follows; and by the time common figures are at last accepted, recipients send Canada audit certificates usually two or three years late.

The EAO's procedures are undoubtedly more efficient than previous ones; yet the whole system of creating and spending counterpart funds remains of questionable value. Perhaps its poor performance in countries with feeble planning machinery, corruption or civil disorder could be bettered by placing the funds, after the American fashion, in the hands of the donor. Certainly this added responsibility would require more Canadian staff in the field; but such postings would be well worth their cost in terms of effectively allocated funds, and could, with proper authorization, be paid for partly out of the funds themselves. Yet such a small reform would not make the system itself realistic, or even necessarily more useful than unconditional commodity grants. Probably the arrangement's most important function is to satisfy public opinion in donor countries that surplus disposal is somehow more constructive than it really is. But this purpose, however clever politically, should not hide the system's intrinsic defects which, on economic grounds alone, clearly recommend its abolition.

4. SPECIAL EMERGENCY RELIEF

Commodities given explicitly for immediate relief deserve, in strict theory, no place in a discussion of development aid. Yet more often than not, they reach peoples of developing nations, thereby briefly making the inevitable human sacrifices of economic progress less acute; and in the initial stages at least, such goods are administered through the same machinery as development aid.[29]

Like development assistance, Canadian relief aid is dispensed through two channels, multilateral and bilateral. Canada's multilateral contributions in kind up to December 31, 1965, totalled roughly $13,000,000. Eight and one-half million dollars of this represented wheat flour sent to Palestine refugees under UNRWA; the rest was in various surplus foodstuffs, like dried milk and canned pork, distributed under the World Food Programme partly for relief, partly for development. All such gifts are administered jointly by the Department of External Affairs and the External Aid Office. After other interested departments are consulted, the EAO orders the relief goods from the supplier (most often the Wheat Board or the Department of Agriculture); then shipments are taken in hand by the receiving agency, which is responsible for both transport and distribution.

Bilateral relief assistance is designed mainly to aid victims of natural disasters. Unlike multilateral relief aid, which is given annually to permanent programmes, it is therefore granted only from time to time in response to urgent temporary needs.

Appropriation of bilateral relief monies from 1945 to 1964 alternated between two methods, the *ad hoc* request and the standing contingency fund. Until 1953 no special fund existed for such purposes, each emergency being met, as were those from Greece and Yugoslavia between 1951 and 1953, by a separate Parliamentary vote. When the great floods of 1953 struck the European Lowlands, the government gave

---

[29]This section does not discuss $271,070,000 in post-war relief and reconstruction grants made from 1945 to 1948 or $1,767,150,000 in post-war reconstruction loans made in 1945–46. (See Appendix B.)

$1,000,000 to a fund also supported by private citizens, and out of this was supplied assistance-in-kind like blankets, outboard motors and cattle. In 1956, the cabinet asked Parliament to transform the unexpended balance of this account totalling $648,461, into a new International Relief Fund from which any overseas disaster aid might be drawn over a period of years. This fund was exhausted, after helping distressed areas throughout the world, by a donation in 1963 to the UN Congo Medical Programme. From then until 1964, the cabinet again had recourse to special votes in the supplementary estimates to meet each disaster. Finally, after finding this arrangement unwieldy and time-consuming, the cabinet established in the 1964–65 estimates a new annually lapsing fund, known as International Emergency Relief, with a regular yearly vote set initially at $100,000. This sum corresponded roughly to the average amounts spent for such crises during each of the two preceding years.

Procedures for aiding disaster areas are extremely flexible. A request for help may come directly from the recipient to Ottawa or, if one is present, to the local Canadian mission; it may come indirectly through an international relief agency; or even as a general appeal through the press, in which case Canada may decide to offer help spontaneously. Although the aid given can demand more work of Canadian administrators than do multilateral grants, most of the detailed planning and distribution is again handled outside the government, this time by the Canadian Red Cross. Acting always in close consultation with the EAO, the Red Cross administers official relief grants in two basic ways. Most often, once the EAO has advised the cabinet to allocate a given sum, the amount approved is paid to the Red Cross, which then places orders within or outside of Canada for goods urgently needed. The Red Cross can use part of the funds allocated to pay shipment by commercial means to its sister society in the country afflicted. The second technique leaves purchasing to the EAO itself which, again with the advice of the Canadian Red Cross, buys the appropriate goods directly. These are then forwarded commercially, or by the Department of National Defence in an RCAF transport whose use is charged to training costs. The aid is finally distributed by the recipient's national Red Cross Society, whose competence and reliability are usually known to its Canadian affiliate. In both cases, assistance-in-kind may be partly or wholly replaced by an outright grant in Canadian dollars to the Canadian Red Cross for transmission to the League of Red Cross Societies, which often co-ordinates international aid from all sources for major disasters.

The criteria fixing the amount of each Canadian relief contribution are somewhat obscure. But among the factors which appear influential are the channel by which the request for help reaches Canada; the type of aid needed; the recipient's ability to absorb aid; the size of other foreign contributions; the depth of press coverage in Canada; and, partly as a result of this coverage, the popularity of each cause among Canadian voters. As with other Canadian aid, Commonwealth and NATO friends seem to enjoy some preference—though not to the exclusion of worthy requests from elsewhere. Obviously allocations are based on no careful calculus of humanitarian merit; each decision emerges from a process to some degree capricious. Yet however subjective and inconstant this procedure, one cannot deny it a certain realism in trying to reconcile rapidly the interests of donor and recipients. And even though personal philanthropy may find in relief aid its most authentic expression, for governments this reconciliation of interests is probably the only proper and constitutional purpose.

VIII. Financial Aid

Development aid encompasses more than goods and services; in the broad definitions given it by DAC and the World Bank it includes any transfer of long-term financial resources.[1] Government grants, official lending, contributions to multilateral agencies, guaranteed export credits, private investment—even war reparations—can thereby claim to be useful parts of the total flow of development capital. Obviously, these disparate elements cannot validly be listed together in a single summary purporting to compare each donor's volume of "aid"; but they can be studied with a view to judging the relative quality of contributions, for each form of capital confers peculiar benefits upon recipients and demands peculiar sacrifices from donors.

Financial aid—meaning the supply of cash or credit—has always formed the core of Canada's multilateral assistance. Yet until 1961, when Ottawa established new long-term export financing, Canada's bilateral aid consisted almost entirely of gifts of goods and services. Since then, Canadian financial aid through both multilateral and bilateral channels has expanded substantially, and assumed several new forms. In addition to traditional cash grants and subscriptions to programmes

[1]*Development Assistance Efforts and Policies, 1963 Review*, while admitting that "no fully satisfactory definition has ever been given to this term ['aid']," goes on to say the word's "normal" usage covers "only" the flow of government grants and official lending exceeding 5 years and contributions to multilateral agencies from official sources." (See footnote 76 of Chap. I for a fuller explanation). The *Review* immediately enlarges this restrictive meaning, however, by adding that private capital exports "also may have an element of aid to the extent that they are officially guaranteed against some element of risk or are the outcome of a policy of special incentives. A policy . . . even of permitting the free outflow of private capital can . . . also involve certain costs to the donor country . . . [and] presumably . . . could to that extent be called 'aid'." (p. 21).

associated with the United Nations, the financial resources extended by Canada up to 1965–66 included bilateral concessionary loans, export credits, private investment, and special grants to Canadian voluntary agencies.

Before reviewing Canada's assistance to UN programmes, it should be noted that these contributions represent no more than about one-fifth of all official Canadian development aid since 1950. The reasons for and against keeping multilateral aid at this relatively low level are worth recalling.

Multilateral aid is most often defended on political grounds. Aid from the UN, it is argued, is more acceptable to recipients because it comes from an international body which they partly control; this arrangement diminishes both "imperialist" or "neo-colonialist" threats to the recipient's sovereignty and the humiliation of accepting help direct from national donors. Multilateral aid, being allocated by international secretariats, also escapes many of the wasteful Cold War (and even inter-allied) competitions that infect allocation by single states. It allows donors to insist on rigorous selection standards, and even (for sound technical reasons) to cancel programmes, with little risk of diplomatic tension. "It is awfully hard," said the Director General of the EAO in 1961, "to withdraw from a country bilaterally . . . [without a] strain in relationships with one particular country."[2] But most important of all, aid entrusted to the United Nations or its agencies strengthens international co-operation in general and the peaceful authority of the UN in particular.

Buttressing these arguments are alleged administrative and financial advantages. Multilateral programmes enable national donors with no field representation to give aid knowing it will be carefully (though sometimes expensively) supervised; and it simplifies administration for recipients as well, by leaving them to deal with one donor agency. Finally, since multilateral aid is untied to national procurement, it can purchase goods and services, to the benefit of donor and recipient alike, almost anywhere in the world on the most favourable terms.

To these points the partisans of bilateral aid reply with both political and technical arguments. Bilateral aid, almost always tied to procurement in the donor country, is believed to bring the donor's taxpayers and politicians to accept a higher global level of assistance: to workers, tied aid means employment; and to governments, it means a safeguarded balance-of-payments position. Popular support for aid in donor countries

[2]*Standing Committee on External Affairs*, 1961, p. 180.

is sustained also by the satisfaction bilateral aid offers to national pride: Canadian advisers and teachers, for instance, have shown a clear preference to work abroad for Canada instead of for the UN. Likewise, the gratitude that aid is supposed to earn may heighten, some suggest, the donor's influence on the recipient's diplomacy. And as a matter of simple efficiency, say many others, most bilateral programmes are administered more cheaply, quickly and effectively, because they are free from cumbersome international machinery and inter-agency rivalries. Decrying the UN's "excess of formal parliamentarism," its "intolerably time-consuming and tedious" debates, and the tendency of specialized agencies to act as "sovereign states," Andrew Shonfield insisted in 1960 that, at least when large sums are at stake, the UN, "as it stands, is not an executive organ which is capable of exercising discriminating and purposeful control over a development programme."[8] This objection does not apply to the World Bank and its affiliates, it is true, for these are in fact controlled by a relatively small group of donors and escape the worst defects of a heavy international bureaucracy obsessed with carefully balanced representation. Nevertheless, multilateral administration of any kind is nearly always slower than bilateral co-operation for the simple reason that it places an intercessor between donors and recipients. Beside the ideal of increased multilateral aid, then, bilateral aid appears a necessary and perhaps more realistic expedient; yet each channel, bilateral or multilateral, offers distinctive advantages, and each deserves to play a role in the aid effort of every donor desiring to combine administrative efficiency with political flexibility.

1. GRANTS

Since grants demand no repayment, unlike loans they impose no extra burden on the recipient's future balance of payments. Developing countries therefore welcome grants—in particular politically unexceptionable multilateral ones—perhaps more than any other form of aid. All of Canada's development grants in cash have been directed to programmes associated with the United Nations. Most of these donations have been made voluntarily through programmes under the aegis of the General Assembly or the World Bank; but smaller amounts have also been given as obligatory assessments to the regular budgets of the UN and its specialized agencies.

[8]*The Attack on World Poverty* (London, 1960), pp. 94–5.

a. Voluntary contributions
Canada is on the whole the third largest donor to the UN General
Assembly's seven voluntary programmes, three of which are devoted
to economic development in the strict sense, and four to social development.

The first major UN economic development activity to receive Canadian aid was the Expanded Programme of Technical Assistance
(EPTA), founded in 1949 to co-ordinate previously disjointed UN
technical assistance. Between 1950 and December 31, 1965, Canada's
contributions to EPTA totalled US $31.4 million, a sum surpassed by
only five other donors. The annual budget of EPTA in 1965 reached a
new high level of US $54 million which, less administrative costs, was
used to finance missions by technical experts (who absorbed about three-
quarters of the funds), training tours in advanced countries, and equipment and materials of every kind needed to transmit technical knowledge.

The sharing of EPTA's resources rests on a rather complicated system
of formal co-operation and informal consultation between nine participating—and often intensely competitive—organizations.[4] Always among
the foremost recipients is the Secretary General's own operating agency
within the New York Secretariat, the Bureau of Technical Assistance
Operations (BTAO). This body provides assistance in a wide variety of
fields which have fallen to it less by logic than by default: mainly public
administration, industrialization, resources planning, transport, social
welfare and the OPEX programme (supplying operational and executive personnel for routine, rather than advisory, functions). BTAO's
rivals for portions of the EPTA account are with one exception specialized agencies, and each has a more precise vocation defined clearly
enough by its name. The four agencies receiving the largest allocations
from EPTA are the Food and Agriculture Organization (FAO), World
Health Organization (WHO), United Nations Educational, Scientific
and Cultural Organization (UNESCO), and International Labour
Organization (ILO); the lesser recipients are the International Civil
Aviation Organization (ICAO), International Telecommunication
Union (ITU), World Meteorological Organization (WMO), and International Atomic Energy Agency (IAEA)—the latter not officially a
UN specialized agency. Unlike the four major recipients, these smaller
agencies do not exist primarily to dispense aid, but each makes a modest

[4]See Walter R. Sharp, *Field Administration in the United Nations System*
(New York, 1961), pp. 379–87.

provision for technical assistance in a budget otherwise devoted to activities of regulation and co-operation.

The General Assembly's other principal aid programme is the Special Fund. This was created in 1958 following the refusal of major donors, including Canada, to accept the developing countries' proposal for a more ambitious Special United Nations Fund for Economic Development (SUNFED). As a compromise between the donors' wish merely to enlarge EPTA and the developing countries' desire for a capital development fund like SUNFED to dispense financial grants and long-term, low-interest loans, the Special Fund was designed to offer so-called "pre-investment" technical assistance. This aid includes resources surveys, pilot projects, feasibility studies and other planning tasks too costly for EPTA, and it is meant to encourage "new capital investment of all types by creating conditions which will make such investments either feasible or more effective."[5] Although the Fund's activities can offer no more than a serious hope that capital financing will follow, they are clearly development aid of the highest priority.

The Fund operates through more simple machinery than EPTA, relying only on a Managing Director with a small staff, guided by a Governing Council of which Canada has always been a member. Much of the Fund's technical assistance, and thus part of its current administration, are performed on contract through BTAO or the specialized agencies. Regrettably, the Fund was unable to reach its announced annual goal of $100 million even after six years: in 1965 the total achieved was still only US $91.6 million, of which Canada's share, the same as in 1964 though almost doubled from 1963, was US $4.6 million —the fifth largest donation. Since the United States has for some years held its contributions to all UN activities to no more than 40 per cent of each programme total, Canada's 1964 increase, it was hoped, would tend to raise the Fund's general level by still more than the increase itself.

In addition to these two central programmes, the General Assembly maintains five smaller voluntary aid accounts. The Office of the UN High Commissioner for Refugees (UNHCR) received from Canada between 1951 and 1965 US $2.8 million (the fourth largest contribution), after its predecessor, the International Refugee Organization (IRO) had received Canadian grants of some US $18.8 million. Canada is the third largest donor to the United Nations Relief and Works

---

[5]Cited in ibid., p. 32. Pressure continued in 1965, nevertheless, for creating a UN capital development fund similar to SUNFED, probably by first amalgamating EPTA and the Special Fund.

Agency for Palestine Refugees (UNRWA), having given between 1949 and 1965 some US $17.9 million, about two-third of which were in cash, and the rest in wheat flour. And she is the second largest donor to the United Nations Children's Fund (UNICEF), having given between 1946 and 1965 about US $16.4 million; although roughly half of this contribution was in milk powder, official donations were significantly increased by regular cash gifts from private sources in Canada. To these long-established programmes, finally, can be added two more recent aid schemes. The International Atomic Energy Agency (IAEA) has had since 1959 a small separate operational budget for technical assistance, to which Canada, giving US $57,400 in 1965, is the third largest donor. And beginning in January 1963 Canada started fulfilling a pledge to give a total of US $5 million over three years to the new UN-FAO World Food Programme (WFP), one-third being in cash, and the rest in acceptable commodities. In the WFP Canada is the second largest donor.

Canadian government participation in all these programmes is the responsibility of the Economic Division and United Nations Division of the Department of External Affairs, acting in close consultation with the Finance Department's International Programmes Division. Although members of the External Aid Board may be sounded informally on multilateral allocations, the level of these donations is fixed officially by the Department of External Affairs, in whose budget they are included.

The factors guiding the Department in recommending each year the size of contributions appear to reflect a variety of domestic and foreign pressures. Most basic is certainly the Canadian people's willingness to support both the United Nations and external aid as key instruments of Canada's diplomacy. Without such a consensus, which Ottawa both nurtures and exploits, contributions on the comparatively generous scale of the past would be inconceivable. This readiness to pay for multilateral grants is doubtless sharply tempered by the reluctance of the Canadian government and people to spend more than a small fraction of aid funds on programmes untied to procurement in Canada. But on the other hand, it tends to be strengthened by the hope of encouraging other donors to give more—an expectation that partly motivated both Canada's virtual doubling of her Special Fund contribution in 1964 and, before 1962, her so-called "contingent" grants to the operational budget of the IAEA. In addition to these underlying and conflicting tendencies are weighed three factors which may move the level of Canadian contributions either up or down. These factors aim to measure not the usefulness of the grant but its proportion; they seek to preserve (as one Canadian official put it in July 1964) a "reasonable relationship" between Canada's contributions on one hand, and those of other major donors, the total of all contributions, and Canada's assessment to each agency's regular administrative budget on the other. The whole process of applying these principles is necessarily pragmatic and in some ways intuitive. It shows plainly that the size of multilateral, like bilateral, contributions cannot be decided purely in the light of ideological preference or technical merit; in the end, the crucial influences are political, and it is only in political terms that debate on such allocations can be realistic.

Most of these influences also help to determine the level of Canadian pledges of cash grants to the World Bank's Indus Basin Development Fund. This account, designed to co-ordinate contributions of Indus Basin Club donors to the great scheme for apportioning power and irrigation benefits of the Indus river system between India and Pakistan, is the only programme of untied or multilateral aid administered by the External Aid Office. Canadian cash contributions to the Fund—whose expenditure is administered by the Bank itself—by December 31, 1965, reached approximately $20.6 million of the total Can. $38.9 million Canada has pledged to provide by 1970.

b. Assessments

The second type of grants includes obligatory assessments for the regular budgets of the United Nations and its twelve specialized agencies, as well as the IAEA. The part of these assessments used directly for aid operations varies greatly in each budget; and for this reason, and because developing countries themselves pay assessments, such payments are not normally counted in official summaries of aid. Yet assessments finance the administrations dispensing aid, and in this sense they are an indispensable accessory of aid programmes. Further, since the richer countries must pay, through a complex accounting formula, an exceptionally high proportion of total assessments, their indirect contribution to aid activities is considerable. Canada's assessment for the UN regular budget in 1965 was 3.17 per cent (estimated at US $3.3 million) of the total, and in the specialized agencies it ranged from 1.54 per cent for the Intergovernmental Maritime Consultative Organization (IMCO) to 4.51 per cent for ICAO. Although the relatively modest sums devoted to each of the fourteen UN budgets may rise to meet increased future needs, the proportion of each national contribution, including Canada's, may of course decrease slightly as new members are added.

2. LOANS

Canada extends general-purpose development loans through both multi-lateral and bilateral channels. The conditions of making each kind of loan differ widely.

Multilateral loans are all directed through the three closely affiliated and complementary lending institutions located in Washington and known as the World Bank Group. The Group's central agency is the International Bank for Reconstruction and Development (IBRD), whose popular designation as the World Bank gives the whole complex its name. The IBRD grew out of the 1944 Bretton Woods Conference which also led to creation of the International Monetary Fund (IMF). While the IMF is not usually considered a development agency—it specializes in fairly short-term, general balance-of-payments aid, and its facilities for currency stabilization have often been used by advanced countries (including Canada in 1962)—the Bank itself has come since about 1951 to concentrate almost exclusively on development, primarily the financing of projects. Indeed, with its subscribed capital of US $21.6 billion, the Bank is now by far the world's largest single source of long-term development funds.

Perhaps as important as its financial strength is the Bank's recognized skill in reviewing development plans, screening projects and offering expert advice. The essential function of the Bank is to finance productive, economically justified enterprises for which private capital cannot be found on reasonable terms. In achieving this aim it submits each proposed project to rigorous economic standards, especially to "assure that the most useful and urgent projects are dealt with first."[6] In addition to investigating the project's feasibility and probable economic value, the Bank pays "due regard to the prospects that the borrower . . . will be in a position to meet its obligations under the loan."[7] A part of this early investigation and of continuing supervision, finally, is the provision of economic and technical advice, including "help in the determination of priorities among different projects, suggestions on the technical plans for projects, . . . recommendations on administrative and organizational arrangements and on means of financing the local costs of projects . . . and . . . recommendations to form the basis of

[6]*The World Bank, IFC and IDA: Policies and Operations* (Washington: IBRD, 1962), p. 4.
[7]*Ibid.*, pp. 4–5.

204 A SAMARITAN STATE?

long-term development programs."[8] In one well-known case, moreover, the Bank lent its good offices to settle a major international economic dispute, bringing India and Pakistan to develop together the waters of the Indus under a Bank umbrella. For all these reasons, the Bank's authority as a superbly effective, non-political development agency is unparalleled.

The financial role of the Bank rests on a flexible combination of public and private enterprise. Officially the IBRD is an intergovern- mental organization, and in the first instance its funds come from government subscriptions. Subscriptions, and subsequently voting power, are related to each member government's economic strength; and Canada's subscription, after being more than doubled in 1959, stood in 1965 at US $750 million or 3.47 per cent of the Bank's total. Of this subscription only 10 per cent was actually paid into the Bank (1 per cent in US funds, 9 per cent in Canadian), the rest being on call in case of a default on outstanding Bank loans. This "callable" portion has never yet been required, and it places no real strain on Canada's budget.

While the Bank draws its initial resources from paid-up government subscriptions, however, some two-thirds of its lending derives from private financing guaranteed by the "callable" part of subscriptions through the sale of IBRD bonds in the world's capital markets. As of March 31, 1965, for example, the Bank held effective loans equivalent to US $110.2 million in Canadian currency, part of which must obviously have come from bond issues in Toronto or Montreal. Canada is the Bank's sixth most important member in terms of subscriptions; she is also, therefore, the sixth most powerful in voting strength. And it is this weighted system of voting, as much as the IBRD's intrinsic useful- ness, that explains why Canada and other major subscribers consider the Bank an aid institution that is uniquely responsible.[9]

The second member of the Bank Group is the International Finance Corporation (IFC). While the IBRD lends either to governments or to private entrepreneurs with government guarantees, the IFC is designed exclusively to foster private enterprise. This it tries to do by co-operating with private investors, without government guarantee of repayment, to provide financing "in cases where sufficient private capital is not avail-

[8]*Ibid.*, p. 7.
[9]It is sometimes argued also that Canada should "increase her support" for the Bank because, judging from the past (notably the early 1950's), up to twice the Canadian subscription would return to Canada in the expenditure of IBRD loans. This argument is fallacious, for the Bank, whose aid is untied, cannot promise to spend its funds in any particular subscribing country.

able on reasonable terms"; by creating new investment opportunities through "bringing together domestic and foreign investors and experienced management"; and by generally stimulating the "flow of private capital into productive investment."[10] The IFC was created in 1956 to supplement the public or government-guaranteed lending of the IBRD; and to ensure the closest co-ordination of the two bodies, the IFC, while using its own operational staff, adopted most of the Bank's key officers.

But this small affiliate of the Bank, whose subscribed capital does not reach US $100 million, has proven proportionately much less effective than the IBRD because its policies are less flexible. On one hand, it has sought to realize higher profits than the Bank, with the result that some borrowers have found its terms of lending unacceptably harsh. And on the other hand, until 1960 it was prevented by its charter from investing in capital stock or shares, a restriction which discouraged potential investors: "IFC found that it had been sent into the world as an international investment institution deprived of the power to make the most familiar, most established, and most saleable form of investment, equity investment."[11] Charter reforms in 1961 and creation of a Development Bank Services Department have broadened the scope of IFC activities considerably; and every dollar of IFC loans has generated three or four more dollars in private investment. In August 1965, moreover, members of the IBRD authorized the Bank to lend IFC up to four times the latter's subscribed capital, thereby further notably enhancing IFC's financial resources. But the scale of IFC operations remains as yet extremely modest, the total of its effective loans and equity investments at March 31, 1965, being no more than US $61.2 million. In view of this failure of IFC to fashion for itself the role of a really large-scale catalyst to private investment in developing countries, Canada's fully paid-up subscription of US $3.6 million appears, at the very least, adequate.

Of vastly greater significance is the Group's third member, the International Development Association (IDA). This body was established as an IBRD affiliate in 1960 with an authorized capital, soon almost fully subscribed, of one billion US dollars. IDA was intended to be, with the UN Special Fund, a kind of consolation prize for the developing nations after the major donors had torpedoed their proposal for SUNFED. The Special Fund took up, with a goal of US $100 million, SUNFED's idea of pre-investment grants; and IDA, having exchanged domination by a mathematically democratic UN majority for control by

[10]*The World Bank, IFC and IDA*, p. 95.
[11]*Ibid.*, p. 97.

a handful of wealthy donors, assumed on a scale ten times greater than the Special Fund SUNFED's planned programme of long-term, low-interest loans. As a sop, IDA was not niggardly; the recipients' only complaint against it (and the only reason donors support it so powerfully) is that IDA's policy tunes are picked by those who pay the piper.

IDA's special function is to provide on extremely easy terms substantial amounts of development capital to countries "whose need for, and ability to make use of, outside capital is greater than their ability to service conventional loans."[12] Since IBRD personnel also staff IDA, project proposals must satisfy equally sound criteria of selection. But while IBRD interest rates vary from 4 to 6 per cent, IDA waives all interest on its loans, charging only a nominal fee of ¾ of one per cent for administrative costs; and while IBRD maturities only occasionally exceed 20 years, IDA's reach 50 years, always with ten-year grace periods. Under these conditions, IDA has quickly come to fill a broad gap in lending that neither the Bank nor IFC can fill.

Subscribers to IDA are divided into two categories, advanced and developing countries. Canada, counted among the advanced members, has paid a subscription of US $37.8 million. Although now paid in full, this subscription, like those for the IBRD and IFC, may be enlarged whenever subscribers generally agree an increase is needed—a probably frequent eventuality, for the very slow repayment of its loans condemns IDA's resources to swift depletion. Canada made her first "supplementary contribution" of US $41.7 million for the three-year period 1965–67. Nevertheless, IDA's subscriptions are true loans in the sense that they can be fully recovered (though without interest) at any time a subscriber decides to withdraw from the Bank Group institutions. Since these payments are made to bodies whose interests are essentially financial and non-political, they are administered in Canada by the Department of Finance. This Department's International Programmes Division consults closely on subscriptions and other major policy questions concerning the Group with the Bank of Canada.

Canadian bilateral lending activities are less well developed. Until 1964 Canada's only bilateral loans on concessionary terms were made in 1957 and 1958 to India and Ceylon for purchases of Canadian wheat and flour. These loans were extended to relieve famine before the great expansion of United States PL 480 shipments, and were at 4.5 per cent with a three-year grace period and repayment over seven years.

Only in 1964–65 did Canada begin a permanent programme of

12World Bank, IDA: What They Are, What They Do, How They Work (Washington: IBRD, 1962).

development loans, in establishing a new "soft loan" fund. This fund, with an initial capital of $50 million (renewed in 1965–66), offers development loans on terms comparable in generosity to those of IDA. The sums lent are tied to Canadian procurement, and are given for "such economic, educational and technical projects as may be agreed upon by Canada and the developing countries or recognized international development institutions."[13] Being administered by the External Aid Office, these loans are often closely linked to Canadian grant aid; but they are also open to countries outside Canada's traditional areas of concentration, notably to Latin American countries.

It is premature to estimate the value these loans may have in the long run for either borrowers or lender; in the short run, no doubt, they are tantamount to grants—and are in fact classified by DAC as "grant-like contributions." Whether eventually repaid or consolidated, the soft loans offer to Canada a challenging new instrument of aid and to recipients new opportunities for development that are both politically and economically attractive. If sensibly invested, the loans should bring to Canadian policy a welcome flexibility at negligible cost in administration.

3. EXPORT CREDITS

Flexibility has for some years been achieved also through the specialized type of loans known as export credits. Although the Canadian government's Export Credits Insurance Corporation (ECIC) began to insure short- and medium-term export credits in 1945, it started direct long-term financing of exports only at the end of 1960. By expanding then the interpretation of Section 21A of the Export Credits Insurance Act, Ottawa gave developing countries a means to make in Canada substantial purchases of essential capital equipment. These arrangements, which allowed financing for periods beyond five years and up to twenty, quickly became a valued supplement to existing grant aid.

Yet even though counted by most aid agencies as a legitimate and useful form of development assistance, export credits are far from conceived primarily to help recipients. Nowhere in the Act or in subsequent official statements can one find reference to any aim other than the promotion of Canadian commercial exports. "Through this . . . arrangement," the Minister of Trade and Commerce, Mr. George Hees,

[13]*Supplementary Estimates for the Fiscal Year Ending March 31, 1965 (A)* (Ottawa, 1964), p. 27.

told the Commons in explaining the new 21A credits in November 1960, "Canadian industry is being given full support to help increase Canadian exports and to stimulate employment. . . . Canadian exporters of capital goods will thus be enabled to meet credit competition from foreign suppliers."[14] The long title of the Act itself set out the single policy aim of promoting "the revival of trade by provision of Dominion Government guarantees to encourage exports from Canada."[15] Indeed, the boldest defence of the credits as aid was a somewhat apologetic comment by a later Minister of Trade and Commerce, Mr. Mitchell Sharp, on March 13, 1964, suggesting that "while this type of 'hard aid' was initially designed to place Canadian manufacturers in a competitive position with exporters in other aid-giving countries, these loans also represent a flow of financial resources which are greatly desired by the less-developed countries."[16]

The criteria applied by ECIC to requests for 21A financing accurately mirror the Act's commercial intention: "the transaction must involve the purchase of capital goods of a sophisticated nature and be of substantial value (at least $2 million); the project must be economically feasible; the foreign buyer and the country of purchase must have a satisfactory credit standing; the Canadian content must be not less than 80%; and the transaction must give rise to significant employment and industrial benefits in Canada as well as giving promise of continuing export trade."[17] Once the Canadian exporter has developed a potential contract, ECIC applies these principles, all of which tend to secure safe and profitable business for large Canadian secondary manufacturers; if the contract is approved, ECIC pays the exporter cash in full and extends its credits (so far always at 6 per cent) directly to the purchaser.

The gains by Canadian manufacturers from 21A financing are impressive. Of the total authorized maximum of $400 million for outstanding credits, ECIC had by May 31, 1965 committed $230.2 million. Several of the contracts financed resulted directly from Canadian grant aid projects, notably the sale to India in April 1964 of a CANDU nuclear reactor under a credit worth $37 million. This profit to Canada does not, of course, reduce the practical value of the credits to recipients. Most of the thirty-one contracts approved by the end of May 1965

[14]Canada, *House of Commons Debates*, Nov. 25, 1960, p. 189.
[15]*Export Credits Insurance Act: Office Consolidation, Part I* (Ottawa, 1963), p. 3.
[16]Department of Trade and Commerce, Trade Publicity Branch, text of the minister's speech, pp. 5–6.
[17]*Annual Report and Financial Statements: 1963*, ECIC (Ottawa, 1964), p. 8.

supported infrastructure or equipment projects of high priority. But, as the 1963 DAC *Review* pointed out, "The range of projects and countries concerned in . . . these credits will probably tend to be more a matter of the competitive potential and salesmanship of the donor country's exporting industries than of a deliberate attempt by anyone to determine priorities."[18] Moreover, went on the report, "The co-ordination of export credits with other forms of assistance raises special problems, since the credit is normally provided to the supplier and since the government of the recipient country may not have been involved in the negotiations."[19] All of this demonstrates that export credits are only "aid" in the sense that they speed the commercial flow of capital goods and services to the developing countries. In this role they can be highly profitable to both lender and borrower. But their contribution as aid must always be assessed remembering that they can benefit only countries demonstrating a relatively high degree of credit-worthiness and economic maturity. In other words, export credit is designed primarily not to assist countries that may need help most, but those that can use it best. As with all other kinds of aid, the measure of its virtue resides less in any abstract merit than in its appropriateness to the concrete needs and absorptive capacity of each recipient.

4. PRIVATE INVESTMENT

Although exported with the single aim of enriching the investor, private capital has been recognized by DAC as an indispensable part of the flow of resources loosely called aid. In some countries with capital surpluses, like the United States, Germany or Japan, governments insure exported development capital against risks of expropriation, inconvertibility and armed conflict, or otherwise stimulate its outflow by special incentives. But more often, as in Canada, capital is invested abroad on the unaided initiative of capitalists themselves. In neither case is it normally possible to produce accurate figures showing the net flow of private capital to developing countries.

The most recent official estimate of long-term Canadian private investment overseas was published in late 1964 by the OECD, and it set Canada's total net private effort in developing areas during 1956–63 at $320 million.[20] Three years earlier a similar report had observed, in

[18]*Development Assistance Efforts and Policies, 1963 Review*, p. 62.
[19]*Ibid.*, p. 62.
[20]*The Flow of Financial Resources to Less-developed Countries: 1956–1963* (Paris, 1964), p. 137.

discussing this investment, that "by far the greater part was in the Western Hemisphere. Rather more than half this total [then $200 million] is estimated to have been reinvestment of earnings."[21] Some large companies with Canadian head offices nominally control holdings in developing nations valued in the hundreds of millions of dollars: the Aluminum Company of Canada Ltd., Brazilian Light, Power and Traction Ltd., Jamaica Public Services Ltd., and International Power Corporation Ltd. are firms which have contributed remarkably to industry or infrastructure in developing countries.[22] But some of these corporations have a high proportion of non-Canadian stockholders, and may repatriate to these investors earnings that are not recorded against the original outflow from the Canadian head office. This and other technical problems leave assessments of total net private investment actually originating in Canada a matter for speculation. It is probably safe to assume, however, in view of Canada's own notorious need of foreign capital, that Canadian private investment in overseas development is now very small and is unlikely soon to become significant.

5. SUPPORT FOR VOLUNTARY AGENCIES

As private Canadian agencies for aiding developing countries have proliferated in recent years, many voluntary groups have made formal or informal requests to Ottawa for grants. Even though nearly all such agencies wish to preserve a fundamentally voluntary character, most feel the need for a stable source of funds to ensure continuity in administration and operations.

Until 1964, Ottawa resisted all these requests, though beginning in 1961 it gave useful, if limited, administrative support to Canadian graduate volunteers through existing diplomatic missions abroad. Appeals from voluntary groups for more concrete assistance failed partly because some agencies appeared unreliable, or their activities unsuited to official support; but the prime obstacles to such help were the government's reluctance to finance international activities it could not fully control and, above all, its fear of stirring fresh demands from a multitude of agencies, some of which, if disappointed, might accuse the government of favouritism.

Between 1960 and 1965, public and parliamentary pressure in favour

---

[21]*The Flow of Financial Resources to Countries in Course of Economic Development: 1956–1959* (Paris, 1961), p. 120.

[22]*Financial Post Survey of Industrials* (Toronto, 1963), pp. 108–9, 111, 196.

of "voluntary aid" abroad intensified steadily, roughly paralleling the proven success of various agencies. After blessing the voluntary agencies for several years with expressions of goodwill and admiration, the government gradually responded to this pressure by adding to its lofty faith the more convincing demonstration of works. The first substantial official aid came in the summer of 1964 when the government, appropriately converting swords into ploughshares, agreed to fly to fields of service some 150 Canadian University Service Overseas (CUSO) volunteers in RCAF transports; the returning aircraft carried 29 overseas students sponsored by the African Students Foundation (ASF). This help with otherwise expensive transportation was extended again in 1965, each time being charged to RCAF training costs. Then, on April 14, 1965, the Secretary of State for External Affairs announced the first financial grant to a voluntary agency: during the fiscal year 1965–66, he promised, CUSO would receive federal funds "in the order of half a million dollars."[23]

It is not yet clear whether the government intends to give cash grants to other deserving agencies; or whether, indeed, CUSO will continue to operate as an essentially voluntary organization: the government now provides roughly two-thirds of its income and is establishing a Company of Young Canadians with apparently similar aims. But assuming that CUSO and other agencies will retain their basic independence, Ottawa could recognize their fine human achievement most aptly through carefully measured assistance. The difficulty would be to encourage the agencies' voluntary spirit without dominating their budgets and policies. Applying the same principle of absorptive capacity used in aiding foreign countries, the government might follow some formula of matching grants related, within reasonable limits, to each agency's ability to raise funds and spend them usefully. This would tend to weed out irresponsible groups, and to strengthen those demonstrating technical competence and substantial popular financing.

Should Ottawa decide on this policy, it would still face thorny problems of administration. Many of these, including the most delicate one of apportioning funds among competing groups, might be surmounted by inducing potential recipients to join together in a single national body. Such an organization could co-ordinate policies, evaluate operations and, above all, distribute government grants *en famille* without abetting unseemly rivalries. While the government would need a full-time representative in this body's council to ensure liaison and sound management, the common agency would be an authentically

[23]Press Release no. 22, Department of External Affairs, Ottawa, 1965, p. 1.

democratic reflection of the operating groups themselves. Any attempt to co-ordinate voluntary agencies from above would probably prove unwelcome. An effective grouping would likely not be a central directing authority but a free association of active voluntary agencies. Formed and controlled by the working agencies themselves, such an association might offer the best hope of reconciling the agencies' sometimes conflicting needs of private inspiration and official subsidy. And at least as important, it could spare Ottawa the constant importunities of contending private demands, leaving the EAO to its original and proper task of helping governments.

IX. Technical Assistance

Simply stated, technical assistance spurs development by providing knowledge. It aims to furnish the human contribution to economic progress, galvanizing recipient peoples through the ideas, skills, information and optimism without which capital aid would be in great part futile. Equipment, commodities and money alone can never build a modern economy; always these must be transformed, organized and rationally invested by competent and resolute human beings.

Few developing countries form such persons quickly enough, if at all. Consequently, donors wishing their capital aid to bear lasting fruit are obliged to supply suitable instruction as a matter of first priority. This instruction may include gifts of equipment for research or demonstration; but essentially it is given by mingling the donor's and the recipient's professional élites. "Technical assistance," summarized the EAO Director General, ". . . means sending abroad Canadian professors, teachers and technical advisers, and bringing students and trainees to Canada for courses in both the academic and technical fields."[1]

This exchange of Canadians and recipient nationals began well before Canada's capital aid programmes, and it has always formed a vital, if financially small, part of the total Canadian effort. Since 1960, in response to heavy demands from new African and Commonwealth programmes, Canada's technical assistance has expanded faster than ever before, in five years the number of participants having multiplied almost by five. At the same time, an earlier emphasis on practical and technical instruction at postgraduate levels has given way to an impressive

[1]Speech to the Canadian Exporters' Association, Toronto, April 29, 1964, p. 3. Some authorities, notably the Colombo Plan Bureau, define technical assistance to include not only contractors' staffs on projects, but equipment used for teaching or research; as a result, the Bureau's comparative figures do not always give an accurate impression of Canada's full technical contribution.

growth of academic education at all levels, including the undergraduate and secondary. This evolution in both the size and quality of aid has already begun to mark the EAO's operations profoundly; and before reviewing the two main types of technical missions, it may be helpful to recall the intrinsic problems of technical assistance—economic, psychological, political, administrative—which these changes are likely to aggravate.

1. BASIC PROBLEMS

The primary objective of technical assistance is the efficient use of development resources, both domestic and foreign. To achieve this goal, technical assistance must be carefully co-ordinated with capital aid. Capital without technical and administrative skills to control it may lead to extravagance and corruption; technical and educational aid without capital to absorb its human products may spawn political tensions and socially harmful unemployment. Each request for technical assistance must be judged, therefore, against the recipient's ability to support the desired aid with adequate funds, equipment, institutions and managerial strength—the crucial ingredients of sound infrastructure.

The characteristic problems of technical assistance are psychological. Dealing in human beings of different cultures, technical assistance is not fully effective unless its participants have unusual ability to understand, and adapt to, strange peoples. Every teacher, adviser, scholar or trainee faces throughout his mission not only the normal personal conflicts that separate individuals, but a host of cultural strains imposed by his new environment—differences of national philosophy, psychology, customs, morals, even semantics.[2] Good technical assistance must find ways of choosing resilient subjects, and of preparing them to meet such difficulties calmly and intelligently.

The control and autonomy of participants pose a political problem. Advisers and teachers require a wide freedom of speech and action to contribute usefully, but recipient governments are reluctant to allow them a direct influence on policy. When foreigners try to command as well as advise, the result may be resentment on one side and frustration

[2]See Nathan Keyfitz, "Western Perspectives and Asian Problems," *Human Organization*, vol. 19, no. 1 (Spring, 1960), pp. 28–31; and Hugh Tinker, "The Human Factor in Foreign Aid," *Pacific Affairs*, vol. 32, no. 3 (Sept. 1959), pp. 288–97.

on the other.[3] Likewise, though less often, trainees may wish to change programmes and administrative procedures against the plans of donors. At every stage, donor and recipient must consult to ensure that technical demands in no way offend national sovereignties.

Perhaps the most complex difficulties in technical assistance confront the donor's administration. Since technical, unlike capital, aid is made up almost entirely of human imponderables, administrators must display extraordinary gifts of judgment, intuition and versatility. They must be able to improvise creatively, finding rapid, sensible answers to an endless series of major and minor crises: a trainee's homesickness, an adviser's quarrel with local colleagues, problems of allowances, curricula, housing or transport. This indispensable attention to detail demands an administrative staff far greater than that needed to spend equivalent funds on capital aid. While technical assistance in 1964–65 absorbed only 12.5 per cent of Canada's total bilateral grant funds, a study sponsored by the EAO showed that it used up 74 per cent of internal office services and executive salaries. "Translated into work load," reported the Director General to the Standing Committee on July 21, 1964, ". . . a shift of about $1.75 million of aid funds from capital assistance to technical assistance would relieve the administration of the former by one man-year of work and would increase technical assistance administration by some 30 man-years of work."[4] Partisans of immediate, large increases in technical assistance—if they also care for the quality of aid—ought to find these figures sobering.

2. CANADIANS ABROAD

Probably the most spectacular growth in aid operations wrought by the EAO has occurred in the number of Canadians sent on overseas assignments. In the five years following 1960 the total of Canadians serving abroad increased almost nine times, rising from 48 in June 1960 to 418 in May 1965. This increase resulted mainly from the change in emphasis from practical to academic assistance following the

[3]The adviser's delicate role is well illustrated by the story of the "Colombo Plan bull." A certain host country, it is said, invited a foreign bull to enrich local herds, but was disappointed when the visiting "expert" stayed for several months eating grass in the corner of a field stocked with friendly cows. When asked to explain his aloofness, the bull allegedly replied with the serene assurance of orthodoxy, "You realize, of course, that I am only a consultant."

[4]*Standing Committee on External Affairs*, 1964, p. 1615.

independence of new Commonwealth and French-speaking nations in Africa and the Caribbean. In the programme's first decade, Canadians sent overseas unattached to capital projects were nearly all senior specialists, called technical experts, in a rather narrow field of science, engineering, technology or medicine; but the backwardness of many of the countries emerging around 1960, especially in Africa, called for general education at every level.

Consequently, Canadian technical assistance personnel now divide themselves into two quite distinct types. On one hand are the traditional technical experts (in 1960 more aptly renamed "advisers"), who act as consultants in a highly specialized discipline; and on the other are teachers, who perform operational or routine duties either directly in the classroom or indirectly as teacher trainers. Many of the difficulties faced by both groups in the field are similar; but the functions of each differ so widely that the Canadian administrative methods governing their selection and preparation are best studied separately.

a. Recruitment

Recognizing these differences in function, the EAO in early 1961 created a separate Education Division, one of whose tasks was to hire teachers; recruitment of advisers, trades instructors and UN experts was left with the Technical Assistance Division. This apportionment of labour, while sometimes causing duplication of effort, seems reasonable because of the different ways in which requests for advisers and teachers are put forward.

Advisers are for the most part recruited singly, in response to a specific request. Such requests may arrive at any time, and recruiting goes on throughout the year. When a request is received, the EAO's Advisers Section (in June 1965 composed of five officers) first determines whether Canada can in principle supply the funds and expertise required and whether the recipient is likely to exploit the aid effectively. If the request is accepted on these grounds, the EAO next draws up a detailed "job description," frequently based on further enquiries to the host government or, under multilateral programmes, to the UN. Once this description is complete, recruitment may follow one or more of several paths.

To begin, the recruiting officer may consult the EAO's permanent roster of persons having already made known their willingness to serve abroad. Some of these names, which are cross-referenced by discipline, are former advisers wishing another mission; but the great majority of the thousands listed are volunteers who have written over the years to offer their services. Few advisers are in fact recruited through the roster, partly because it is incomplete, but mainly because it goes constantly out of date. Addresses change, enthusiasm flags, or timing or country of service is unsuited: "our experience [with the roster]," observed the Director General in 1961, "is that when you approach a man he will say: 'I cannot go this year because my wife is pregnant' or 'I have just signed a contract for an additional year's employment with my company.' Another will say 'When I volunteered, I had Asia in mind, and you are now asking me to go to Africa.' "[5]

Another method of limited value is advertising in technical or professional journals. At the outset, this technique is slowed by the need to await a publication date; most often the latter is quarterly, while the adviser may be needed abroad within two or three months. Furthermore, experience shows that advertised appeals attract few people with truly outstanding qualifications. Contented employees do not read "help wanted" columns; while many of those who do reply are inexperienced, and some may be misfits, failures or adventurers. Still, advertising produces results in underpaid professions such as nursing, and even, at times, in the rarer scientific and engineering fields where the EAO has no established contacts.

A far more fruitful device is the approach to a government department or private company for secondment. With frequent success, the EAO invites such institutions to release temporarily an employee whose competence and personal qualities they can guarantee. Many organizations welcome the chance to give staff the broadening experience of service overseas. A few employers, to be sure, appear not to resist strenuously the temptation to unload deadwood; but in general, whether moved by philanthropy, patriotism or pride of reputation, they offer excellent candidates. Such persons are usually encouraged to accept a foreign posting by an agreement to safeguard rights of seniority and pension, whose potential loss often deters candidates approached independently. The one drawback of this system is that it requires recruiting officers of a rank and maturity the EAO has found difficult to hire. "If you are going to . . . talk to the Chairman of the Ontario Hydro Commission," explained the Director General bluntly in 1961, "you do not send a boy."[6]

The channel used most profitably of all is the informal "old-boy network," cultivated over many years by the IETCD and ETAB and further refined by the EAO. Probably three-quarters of all advisers are

[5]*Ibid.*, 1961, p. 162.
[6]*Ibid.*, 1961, p. 177.

located in this way, through the good offices of a few dozen contact men in federal or provincial government departments, Crown corporations and professional associations. These contacts are frequently consulted about the job description itself, then are asked to suggest names of possible advisers or reliable sources for finding them; finally, the contacts may interview candidates for the EAO, assess references and make recommendations. The voluntary help of these unofficial "panels" was clearly essential in enabling the EAO's four recruiting officers in 1964, for instance, to recruit and administer a total of 89 new advisers.

Once a candidate is located, an EAO officer interviews him at home or in Ottawa. When possible, this interview includes the candidate's wife, for her ability to adapt to unfamiliar surroundings abroad weighs heavily on her husband's professional efficiency. If both the candidate and his wife appear fitted to the mission psychologically, they are checked for physical defects by a doctor from the Department of National Health and Welfare and for defects of character (involving security, morals and possible criminal record) by the RCMP. If these tests and further enquiries to friends, references and colleagues are favourable, the candidate's name and qualifications are forwarded to the host government for final approval, following which he is offered a firm contract.

Recruitment of teachers follows a different, though no less thorough, procedure. Since the demand for teachers is always great and the academic year in host countries normally starts in September, the Education Division begins recruitment on a large scale long before specific job requests arrive. Although recruiting methods in 1961 were makeshift, the EAO has now evolved a careful schedule of steps that start the recruitment process almost a year ahead of the teachers' departure.

Planning for the following academic year begins in September. Recruiting officers, after consulting the Planning and Policy Co-ordination Division, recommend to the Director General the numbers, disciplines and countries of service of the next year's teachers. These recommendations are based on the funds available, the numbers of teachers already abroad, the host countries' earlier demands, the likely total of Canadian teachers that can be spared, and the size of the EAO's own administrative staff. When this draft programme is approved, it is circulated to Canadian diplomatic missions for their comment and for the information of host countries. At the same time, the EAO advertises in teachers' professional journals, and invites provincial departments of education to re-establish annual interview panels. Before these panels screen local candidates, the EAO sifts through the roster for eligible candidates, sending to each a programme announcement and a questionnaire on his present position, salary and qualifications. All candidates who fill out Personal History Forms, whether reached by roster or publicity, are examined in November and December by the interview panel in their province. Meanwhile the EAO invites references to forward confidential assessments of candidates directly to Ottawa. These appraisals are matched against the recommendations of the interview panels, and by the end of December the EAO selects a pool of candidates suitable for nomination. Since details of the host countries' precise needs are by now catalogued (in a "Request Book"), successful candidates can be mated with appropriate posts normally by the end of January. Even before nomination, candidates in the pool of approved teachers undergo the standard EAO medical test and their names are sent to the RCMP for character clearance. A few fail the medical test, and very occasionally some the police check. Those remaining are immediately proposed to host governments; and, on the latter's acceptance, they are placed under formal contract usually no later than the end of March.

This system, which is used by both English and French sections of the Education Division, seems to suffer no major weaknesses. It works well because it plans long in advance, co-ordinates each phase in a fairly rigorous time-table and, above all, because it fully exploits the recruitment facilities of provincial governments. The Division's six administrative officers could obviously never have hired by themselves the 314 teachers under contract in May 1965. But by fully respecting and using the provinces' intimate control of education, this extremely small team can recruit great numbers of well-chosen candidates even while administering the hundreds of teachers already abroad. Another reason for the Division's increasing success in Quebec is the abundance and quality of the literature it now distributes in the French language. Most of the recruiting and publicity documents are translations; but for the first time, beginning in 1964, they are good translations, and they are backed by French-Canadian administrators who know their province well.

b. Preparation for service
The "orientation" or "briefing" of Canadians for service abroad is less satisfactory. Again techniques differ for advisers and teachers, even

though in each case the aim is identical: to supply information and counsel that will help the departing Canadian adapt to his new environment.

While the EAO has slightly improved briefing literature, the preparation of advisers remains much as it was before 1960, hasty and uneven. One reason for this is the lack of experienced staff: in June 1965, only one of the five recruiting officers in the Advisers Section had himself visited a developing country, and then for but a few weeks. Yet month after month these men must advise departing Canadians on every aspect of the life, culture, psychology and institutions of over sixty unfamiliar countries. During selection interviews, it is true, many advisers meet professional colleagues in the "old-boy network" who have served abroad; and for some missions there may exist recent detailed reports from Canadian advisers having filled a similar post. But the adviser's chief guide and confidant both before and during service is his recruiting officer, and not even the richest knowledge of service problems culled from files can give an officer's advice the authentic insights of personal experience in the field. This defect results directly, of course, from the EAO's early policy of posting no aid administrators abroad. Under pressure from host governments and overworked Canadian diplomatic missions this policy apparently changed in late 1963[7]; but no action has followed. And even if enough new staff were found, they could probably not complete their training in Ottawa and overseas in less than two or three years. Meanwhile, some departing advisers can stop over for extra briefing with UN officials in New York or Europe, an exercise which, however instructive, cannot often equal in understanding and intimacy a similar briefing by a Canadian officer.

During the short time the adviser spends with his recruiting officer (rarely more than five or six hours, including recruitment interviews), he receives a specially tailored, though invariably sketchy, set of briefing documents. These always include a pamphlet on the psychological phenomenon known as "culture shock," a brochure on health dangers in the tropics, a mimeographed paper on administrative arrangements, and an official public report or speech on Canadian aid. Often the EAO adds a "post report" on living conditions by the local Canadian government mission; but even though these reports are revised each year and specially amended for the EAO, many still describe mainly the peculiar *dolce vita* of the diplomatic compound in capital cities, and therefore

[7]See *ibid.*, 1963, p. 63, where the Director General said on December 12: "I think we badly need people stationed overseas. The other advanced countries have representatives right on the ground."

seem to mislead as much as they inform. If available, one or two reports from former advisers may be lent to convey a more earthy view of survival in the field. Occasionally the kit offers reference papers on the host country's political institutions, economy and geography, but for the most part each adviser is expected to search out such background materials for himself, through either public libraries or bookstores. In sum, documentation for advisers is of unequal merit, though never more than adequate. Like some modern couturiers, recruiting officers apparently strive to cover only the essential while revealing enough to quicken interest.

Critics of Canadian aid have urged that briefing of advisers be strengthened by formal group orientation courses lasting several days or weeks. While desirable in principle, this proposal is not practical. To begin, advisers leave singly at all times of the year, and could not be grouped for classroom courses without disrupting service schedules at great inconvenience. And even if a number of advisers did happen to depart in the same week, courses exceeding a few days would unreasonably cut short effective overseas service—which in some cases is not more than one or two months. "The difficulty in trying to arrange [briefing courses] of longer duration," suggested the Director General hyperbolically in 1963, "is . . . related to the release of the men by their employers. If an employer says: 'I will let you have this man for 12 months,' we have to make a choice. Shall he be kept six months in Canada for preparation and six months doing his job in the overseas country, or should it be a week in preparation in Canada and 50 weeks in the overseas country doing his job?" Besides, went on the Director General, "my personal experience has been that there is little to choose between three days and three months because you cannot accomplish enough in three months to make an important difference."[8] This second objection is at least arguable; but the case for giving orientation courses to advisers is not convincing, except perhaps when made on behalf of occasional groups assembled on contract by universities, companies or professional associations for a special team project.

Briefing of teachers is organized more fully, partly because the problem itself is simpler. On one hand, the concentration of large numbers of teachers in a relatively few countries of service—and indeed the similarity of all teachers' work—permit much greater uniformity of literature. And on the other, the mass departure of most teachers at the beginning of the academic year makes formal group courses not only possible, but inevitable.

[8]*Ibid.*, 1963, pp. 64–5.

Literature is first sent to each teacher in March or April, shortly after notice of his appointment. The briefing kit, most of which is loaned, is far more complete and balanced than that given advisers. Of course the kit includes the EAO's standard pamphlets on culture shock, tropical health problems, service abroad and administrative arrangements, as well as post reports. But it also offers official tourist brochures, maps and—most useful of all—reports by former teachers that cover the host country's background and living conditions in remarkable detail. Finally, the kit gives names of Canadian teachers having taught previously in the school assigned, and the name of the school's principal; the departing teacher is urged to write these persons for information still more precise and recent.

Naturally, these kits, whose quality varies with each country of service, fall short of perfection. There is clearly a need for some general publications, either books or articles, on the theory and practice of foreign aid. A brief bibliography of readily available writings would interest those wishing to deepen their understanding of aid problems or host countries further—even though many administrators doubt whether advisers and teachers read all they receive already. In particular, the EAO needs more of these materials in French—until the summer of 1964 a field almost ignored.

Perhaps, indeed, it would be worthwhile for the Technical Assistance Division and Education Division to establish jointly a combined briefing room and library. Such a room could stock not only publications, colour slides and films for departing Canadians, but materials on Canada for visitors from abroad. And perhaps as important, it could encourage EAO officers themselves to keep abreast of current thought on foreign aid, activities of other aid agencies, political events in developing nations, and new techniques of administration. At present, the EAO has no central place where employees can do serious research or evaluation; many of the best books and periodicals on aid are either unknown or not purchased. In fact, under the pressure of an expanding programme and chronic understaffing, time for developing a library and time merely for serene reflection on policy or methods have always been scarce. In meeting both the immediate purpose of better briefing and the underlying need constantly to review policy, an EAO documentation centre might quickly prove a vital and inexpensive instrument of reform. In mid-1965, some such facility seemed at last to be under preparation; but its purpose, scope and methods remain to be defined.

Group courses for teachers are of two types. Teacher trainers and teachers of English as a second language attend special courses in July on pedagogic methods. Then on the eve of departure, the entire annual group of teachers meet at Macdonald College, close to Montreal Airport, for a final four-day "briefing conference." This session brings the teachers together for the first time with the EAO staff, and their meeting is the occasion for settling all manner of administrative and psychological questions unresolved by earlier correspondence. Besides this personal attention, participants are exposed to seminars, talks and films, mostly on problems of adaptation and life abroad. In attendance are returned teachers and advisers from previous years, university specialists in area studies, and usually, for a last, uplifting speech of send-off, the Secretary of State for External Affairs. The knowledge gained by teachers in this short symposium cannot be great, and if the conference aims to transmit useful sums of information it should certainly last longer. Nevertheless, by quieting the teachers' fears and doubts in a common sense of mission, the meeting forges an *esprit de corps* likely to sustain the faltering dedication of many in the lonely days that lie ahead.

c. Service abroad

Once advisers and teachers leave Canada, their problems are broadly similar. Three kinds of difficulties may arise: administrative, psychological and professional—by all accounts the most troublesome being administrative. Not only do the latter cause dismay in themselves; they are often the source of personal and professional maladjustments.

In general, Canadian administrative support for expatriate Canadians has been helpful, though severely handicapped by a lack of representatives in the field. Since Canada's diplomatic missions do not always have enough staff to handle day-to-day complaints, advisers and teachers must rely for settlement of most problems on the EAO itself. The routine tasks of supporting Canadians abroad impose on Ottawa administrators burdens both complex and compelling. Every day Canadians overseas write for help with allowances, furloughs, health care, disagreements with local authorities, housing, transportation and a multitude of highly specialized requests. These appeals must be met promptly with advice or direct action which much of the time—in the absence of detailed information—can spring only from ingenuity or inspired common sense; for when subjects and administrators are thousands of miles apart, and official regulations constantly shackle initiative, no problem, however ordinary, is simple. Shipping excess baggage, clearing up misunderstandings on customs duties, fixing an airline route, or even reserving a hotel room can provide administrators with egregious frustrations.[9]

All recent research points to weakness of the host country's administration as the most discouraging of all problems met by Canadians abroad. This is no cause for outrage, for such weakness is of course a characteristic of the underdevelopment that aid is supposed to remedy. But the deficiency should be recognized frankly, so that its worst results can be softened.

Canadians serving overseas complain that host authorities fail them most frequently in supplying adequate housing. Three of every five returned advisers answering a questionnaire in 1961 said that no

[9]And occasionally with entertainment, as when ETAB in 1957 tried to have the Canadian mission in Rome hold hotel space for a fisheries adviser stopping off for talks with FAO. Informed that the Easter rush of pilgrims had already filled local hotels, ETAB sent the mission an answering memorandum in iambic pentameter of rare poignancy:

ANSER ROMANUS
(stuffed for Easter)

"Si scivissem te venire serpentem coxissem"
Your problems sprang, it seems, from failure to explore
The Eternal City's vast resource, its store
Of Monuments. In case you think this twaddle
Kindly observe the Sacred Geese that toddle
On the Palatine—they give an intimation
Of mingling rest with lofty education.
Their Augurs might have bid you stake out rooms
In the dim recesses of the grisly Catacombs
Or, creating a diversion with Discord's Golden Apple,
Ensconce our Expert comfily in the Sistine Chapel
Where, while the Chaste Huntress ran her nightly cycle
He could savour deeply of Angelic Michael.
Nay, more, you might have even flopped the fella
In the capacious Tomb of C. Metella
Out on the Appian Way—or even storum
At the Soldier's Tower by Trajan's Forum. . . .
Then there's the Pantheon, the work of M. Agrippa;
Here, in the cool of evening, he might sip a
Tuscan bumper, and musing on the Sack of Rome,
Watch pigeons defecate upon the mighty dome.
And what about the home of that consumptive
Keats, at the Scala Spagna? More presumptive,
You might attempt to seize an attic in
The Abyssinian College of the Vatican
And there, despite the fulminations of the Pope,
Deposit suitcase, Baedeker and soap
Braving, for this unique accommodation,
The thunderbolt of excommunication. . . .

From ETAB Memo no. 36:8C:E3 of May 7, 1957. Quoted by kind permission of the author, Mr. Euan Smith.

permanent accommodation was ready when they arrived; and subsequent reports and interviews confirm that housing is still the point of greatest tension with their hosts.[10] "Cette question est la plus importante de toutes," wrote a teacher to the EAO in January 1964, "elle revêt . . . un caractère spécial qu'on ne saurait imaginer. . . . Les appartements qu'on nous offre sont pour la plupart infectes dans un délai normal de deux semaines. . . . Le professeur qui arrive . . . a l'impression d'y être venu non pas pour enseigner, mais pour se chercher un logement. Effectivement, il met trois mois pour le trouver." "The roof leaks in the bedroom in ten places," went on another teacher, "the kitchen, pantry and store . . . are unscreened and have deteriorating windows permitting the free entrance of birds, lizards and insects which make dirt on provisions and dishes. P.S. If we don't get decent accommodation, my wife is returning to Canada as soon as the six months period arrives and I may have to do the same thing." While such grievances are not general, neither are they untypical. Even though sometimes excellent, even luxurious, housing is provided, many Canadians are hampered in their work by unprepared or primitive quarters. Ideally, departing Canadians should be held in Canada until a local Canadian mission inspects and approves housing; unfortunately, not all host countries have Canadian missions and those that do occupy the small Canadian staffs with political or commercial problems. But in areas like Africa and the Caribbean where teachers are concentrated in some numbers, it should be possible to send out itinerant inspectors from the EAO a few weeks before the teachers arrive; and in all cases, attempts should be made to locate and keep good housing from year to year.[11]

[10]See the writer's article entitled "Quelques problèmes des experts techniques canadiens à l'étranger," *Canadian Public Administration*, vol. 5, no. 2 (June, 1962), pp. 209–18. Anonymous quotations from advisers, teachers and trainees in the following pages are from questionnaires returned to the writer in 1961 and from the EAO's files in 1964.

[11]See *Standing Committee on External Affairs*, 1964, p. 1622, where the Director General said on July 21,

". . . an increasingly difficult problem is the lack of adequate accommodation overseas. The developing countries are obtaining the services of more and more teachers and advisers from many of the Western countries and the housing problem is perhaps the most restrictive factor at the moment in our effort to enlarge the program. It is not money but, as I say, accommodation, a place for them to live. Not only is it important for the individual's morale and comfort but if his experience has been an unhappy one and he comes back and makes known this fact to his colleagues it prejudices our recruitment program. . . . We have had people go out under a promise of accommodation which has never materialized. On occasions they have had to return their families to Canada. Others have had to live in substandard hotel rooms month after month, and sometimes they have finished their assignment and accommodation still has not been forthcoming."

Host governments often fail also to provide adequate local transportation—an oversight that can easily defeat the whole purpose of a foreign visitor's service. "I have repeatedly asked the people here to make arrangements for visits to plants and laboratories," complained one scientist, "and while the answer is always affirmative, the arrangements are never made." Even daily transport to work is sometimes uncertain: "une camionnette antédiluvienne vient me prendre de temps à autre pour me conduire au collège," wrote a distressed teacher in December 1963. Other Canadians denounce slowness in paying local allowances, the poverty of health services, and the lack of demonstrating equipment or office space. Again, none of these weaknesses should scandalize; but many could be overcome if Canadians were supported by full-time resident aid administrators in the field.

In spite of such vexations, Canadians as a national group, whether English- or French-speaking, seem to blend into host societies with surprisingly little tension. This adaptability probably owes something to the Canadian's habitual lack of ethnocentric bias, as well as to his instinctive sympathy for young countries forging a pioneer tradition similar to his own. But it also grows from the widespread kindliness with which Canadians appear to be received. Whether Canada enjoys a good name because foreign hosts know little about it or because they respect Canadians' innocence of a colonizing past really does not matter; the joy of being easily accepted encourages Canadians to reciprocate their hosts' goodwill and, in the end, to feel at home. "Dans l'ensemble," wrote a delighted teacher in January 1964, "nos collègues sont sympathiques et acceptent bien le Canadien. Il est heureux de constater que notre réputation ici est des plus enviables. . . . l'Africain en général nous porte une affection toute spéciale." In most cases, such affection leads beyond courteous collaboration with professional colleagues to at least a few warmly spontaneous friendships. "Relations with other staff," assured another teacher, "can only be described as very cordial . . . the feeling of racial difference is virtually nonexistent. . . . 'Visiting', that old-fashioned and enjoyable pastime, is very common." For many Canadians, indeed, such visits offer a chance to understand local customs that is eagerly seized and savoured:

Côté africain, nous avons été invités à des réceptions autochtones : inauguration de l'usine à café, visite de Madame la Présidente de la République. C'est à la fois pittoresque, agréable et très cinérama : nous y avons rencontré une élite très raffinée, des chefs hauts en couleur, des matrones à vêtements technicolor et à largeur cinémascopique. Ces réceptions et ces fêtes sont souvent animées de danses traditionnelles et toujours accompagnées de généreuses libations, de plantureux méchouis (moutons entiers rôtis à la broche, épousant des formes de sculptures hittites).

It would be wrong, of course, to conclude that Canadians, through some uncommon genius or cultural eclecticism, are supremely and uniformly tolerant. Like all donor countries, Canada has her share of misfits, malcontents and even paranoiacs. Some Canadians, perhaps one in twenty-five or thirty, return home before completing their mission because they are frustrated in their work or dissatisfied with living conditions. Others, though probably not more than one in a hundred, are ordered home because the strain of entering an alien society provokes either revolt or total emotional breakdown. For convenience, all these rejections of the host society have been grouped under the expressive label of "culture shock"—a disease doubtless known in less scientific days as severe homesickness. This affliction is known to favour housewives, whose daily routine, unlike their husband's professional work, may differ extravagantly from life in Canada; but it fully spares no one. Every Canadian staying abroad senses some discomfort from collisions of cultures; and not a few react openly and bitterly with symptoms long ago typed as classical:

... excessive washing of hands, excessive concern over drinking water, food, dishes, and beddings; fear of physical contact with attendants or servants; the absent-minded, far-away stare (sometimes called the tropical stare); a feeling of helplessness and a desire for dependence on long-term residents of one's own nationality; fits of anger over delays and other minor frustrations; delay and outright refusal to learn the language of the host country [*extremely few Canadians ever do learn a local language*]; excessive fear of being cheated, robbed, or injured; great concern over minor pains and irruptions of the skin; and finally, that terrible longing to be back home, to be able to have a good cup of coffee and a piece of apple pie, to walk into that corner drugstore, to visit one's relatives and, in general, to talk to people who really make sense.[12]

Expatriates who survive both administrative and cultural tensions may still find their contribution threatened by technical or professional obstacles. To begin with, if the original job description proves inaccurate, they may have to perform tasks they consider time-wasting or unfitting. Worse, if the description is poorly defined, they may be given no precise duties at all. "The assignment is so vague," complained one report, "that unless the government concerned is anxious to make the best use of the man he could conceivably do nothing for two years and be regarded as a good acquisition because he did not upset normal routine." Further, the Canadian's technical skills, if highly bookish or too narrowly

[12]Kalervo Oberg, "Culture Shock and the Problem of Adjustment to New Cultural Environments," p. 2. Mimeographed paper, US Government, dated Aug. 3, 1954.

related to conditions in Canada, may not be readily intelligible to students formed by another culture and working with different tools. The good adviser or teacher quickly learns to express his knowledge in terms meaningful within the local *milieu*—an atmosphere sometimes presenting, as one worried science teacher observed, a challenging inhospitality: "mais attention aux mathématiques, à la physique et à la chimie. Là vous faites face à un mur pratiquement infranchissable. . . . En troisième année, nous avons entendu la remarque suivante : 'Monsieur, tout ça, c'est de la magie des Blancs, ce n'est pas pour nous les Noirs.' "

Once these introductory problems are solved, the adviser or teacher trainer (though not the ordinary teacher) must try to instruct local specialists so that the fruit of his skills will not wither when he leaves. In these cases, the expatriate's role is not to fill temporarily a gap in administration or operations, but to stimulate his local colleagues in their continuing efforts of self-improvement. Ultimately, the expatriate's success must be measured by the performance of those he leaves behind: "l'expert ne doit pas se rendre indispensable. . . . son rôle est justement de se faire remplacer par les techniciens du pays. . . . S'il n'a pu laisser après son départ les techniciens qu'il aura formés et qui lui succéderont c'est que sa mission n'est pas réussie."[13]

More often than not, the foreign expert's skills are supposed to be perpetuated in the host country through a local colleague, called a "counterpart" or "understudy," who is attached to the expatriate during his mission. In strict theory, the expatriate only teaches or advises, while the local national executes—and of course absorbs the foreigner's knowledge. But in practice many Canadians are forced to carry out operational tasks, either because the counterpart is inadequate or, not infrequently, because no counterpart is even named. The results of such a failure are administrative confusion and a largely wasted foreign contribution. The expatriate may be burdened with responsibility not bolstered by authority; and the host country may pay the foreigner high living allowances for many months only to keep, when he is gone, no more than a pleasant memory of his visit. Not all host governments, moreover, take stringent care to place former counterparts where their newly learned skills can serve most effectively; many counterparts are moved or promoted from their planned post within a year or two of the expatriate's departure. Fortunately such cases are becoming rarer in Canada's programme, both because the EAO insists more closely on the appointment of suitable

[13]Michel Debeauvais, "L'Assistance technique des Nations Unies et son mécanisme," in *Les Nations Unies et les pays sous-développés*, Collection Tiers-Monde (Paris, 1961), p. 65.

counterparts and because the contribution of teacher trainers is virtually assured once they are given classes. But the usefulness of advisers is far from generally guaranteed; and for them Canada's demand that good counterparts be named—and later used—should be tireless and uncompromising.

d. Evaluation

As in most other sectors of the aid programme, Canadian administrators of advisers and teachers have been too busy sustaining current operations to review earlier work in depth. Judgments of general past performance are mainly impressionistic, based as they are on the haphazard sampling that each EAO officer can make in the course of his daily labours. Yet the almost total absence of systematic information on the contributions of advisers and teachers undermines all attempts at serious reform, and condemns even the planning of normal expansion to proceed by intuition.

Future assessment might profitably seek to use returned Canadians in three ways. First, the EAO could undertake or commission a survey by detailed written questionnaire of all such persons whose addresses are available, inviting frank appraisals of overseas assignments and of Canada's methods of recruitment, briefing and administration. Next, "de-briefing" or "terminal interviews" could be made obligatory for each returning Canadian (only about 20 per cent now have such an interview) and be expanded from a hurried, superficial chat into a two- or three-day session of talks and meetings organized rationally—perhaps, for general matters, recorded on tape. Finally, the reports of former aid personnel could be catalogued and studied with these recordings by one or two officers with the time and detachment to study them objectively, and the stature to propose indicated reforms. In this way, the EAO might for the first time form a coherent picture of Canada's human contribution; and departing Canadians could draw for their orientation on a store of precious experience that now, except for isolated scraps, escapes them in an unwieldy mass of files.

3. OVERSEAS TRAINEES

Almost as striking as the increase in Canadians serving abroad has been the growth of programmes for training overseas visitors in Canada. Excluding people trained in Canada under UN and other auspices, the number of persons studying under Canadian government programmes almost quadrupled in the EAO's first five years, rising from 323 in

March 1960 to 1242 in March 1965.[14] Although the EAO estimated in December 1963 that 15 per cent of academic visitors were enrolled in French-language institutions, by far the greater part of the increase came from new Commonwealth programmes.

Visitors brought from overseas by the EAO, collectively called "trainees," fall into two basic categories. The more numerous are training fellows receiving practical instruction on a resident or travelling fellowship; these persons are most often mature public servants, who visit Canada for periods of a few weeks to two or three years in order to observe the techniques of Canadian colleagues—usually, though not invariably, in some branch of science, technology, engineering or administration. In addition to these fellows, Canada has received since 1958 growing numbers of academic scholars, normally younger persons who study as graduates or undergraduates in a university or other institution of higher learning. Although this distinction between fellows and scholars is partly consecrated in the apportionment of administrative functions between the EAO's Technical Assistance and Education Divisions, it is plainly arbitrary. In some practical ways, indeed, it is illogical, for during the successive stages of selection, preparation, study in Canada, and evaluation, many problems met by all trainees are similar or identical.

a. Selection

One of the few times fellows and scholars present peculiar problems is during selection. No doubt general criteria for choosing both are the same: proven competence, aptness at learning, likelihood of useful employment—standards designed to produce "people who have a stake in their country, who have developed objectives in life. . . ."[15] But the nature of trainees' study and the timing of their arrival in Canada require that fellows and scholars be chosen by different methods.

Training fellows are proposed to Canada throughout the year as needs arise and as candidates are available for release. All such candidates must first be approved by a single designated authority in the recipient government; and since most are already government employees, approval can be given fairly quickly upon well-justified recommendation by department heads.[16] The recipient government then forwards a formal request to Canada, and the EAO Training Section tries to tailor a pro-

[14]The grand total of persons trained in Canada under all agencies between 1950 and March 1965 was 6203.
[15]Robert E. Byron, EAO Director of Technical Assistance, cited in Barbara Beckett, "For Foreign Students, a Problem: Culture Shock," *Globe and Mail*, Toronto, April 2, 1964, p. 13.
[16]Typical of the kind of criteria applied in selecting trainees are the following

gramme in Canada to suit the candidate proposed. Sometimes the EAO asks for more details on either the training desired or the candidate himself; and if proper instruction cannot be arranged in Canada, the request for training is refused. If, on the other hand, the EAO can find an appropriate government department or other public or private institution to act as a training agency, it invites the recipient government to release the candidate for study in Canada.

Since EAO training officers are few (there were only ten in June 1965), and bottlenecks in recipient governments are not infrequent, the time from the first departmental request until Canadian acceptance may vary between three and eighteen months. During this interval, it is not uncommon for requests to be withdrawn because candidates have been promoted, moved, or sent to another donor country. Much of this wasted effort is unavoidable. But some of it could certainly be saved by increasing EAO home staff and, above all, by appointing resident overseas aid attachés with the time and special skills to investigate each request in depth. These attachés might greatly expedite requests by interviewing candidates, giving language tests, and generally helping recipient governments to meet Canadian procedures.

Academic scholars are also chosen initially by the proposing government, but the EAO delegates the screening of candidates and the arrangement of study programmes to special committees of eminent Canadian academics. One committee handles all of Canada's bilateral development aid programmes; the other advises on Canadian participation in the Commonwealth Scholarship and Fellowship Plan—a programme concentrating on humanities and social sciences, and open to students of both developing and advanced countries. Yet while these committees

terms published some years ago by the government of India (*Lok Sabha Debates*, Dec. 2, 1955, starred question 409):

"1. The proposal should be related to a specific development project.

"2. The proposal should be in respect of a person in whose case it is considered that the acquisition of expert knowledge in his specialized field would help in the implementation and completion of a project.

"3. Only such training facilities should be sought as are not available in India.

"4. The proposal should be for 'practical training' as distinct from 'academic training'.

"5. If experts have already been obtained in a particular field, special justification would be required in support of a request for training abroad in that field.

"6. The person recommended for training should possess qualifications and experience sufficient to enable him to benefit from training abroad.

"7. He should already be in employment, should be kept on the pay rolls of the employing authority while under training and must be usefully employed on return.

"8. He should be below 45 years of age (Relaxable up to 48 years in exceptional cases if full justification is furnished)."

assist with academic aspects of educational programmes, including admission standards, terms of scholarships, and selection and placement of candidates, the EAO keeps full control of finances and administration. The EAO's share in policy-making is further assured by the presence in both committees of the Director of its Education Division.

After the two advisory committees have chosen worthy candidates, the Secretariat of the Canadian Universities Foundation (for Commonwealth Scholars) or the EAO (for all others) tries to place each scholar in the institution recommended for him. If the institution agrees to admit the candidate, the EAO notifies his government of his nomination by cable. The benefits of this decentralized system are evident. The use of independent specialists for all academic phases of scholarship programmes ensures that policies on numbers, standards, fields and distribution of students will be geared realistically to Canada's changing university resources; in selection and placement it provides the government with experts of a calibre the EAO itself could not easily employ full-time; and it frees the small, relatively junior EAO scholarship staff for routine administration—in itself an art demanding exceptional skills.

A technique used increasingly to recruit both technical fellows and scholars is the so-called "group training approach." This method consists of organizing a special course for a number of trainees in a field of fundamental importance to one or several countries. Whether administered partly by the training agency or entirely by the EAO, the group training system presents many advantages. It can make a concentrated impact in a few vital disciplines—"instead," as the Director General told the Standing Committee on July 21, 1964, "of . . . scattering [trainees] across the country in a whole miscellany of fields of instruction."[17] Courses can be adapted to suit the particular needs of developing countries; administration is both cheaper and simpler; and, in theory at least, briefing can be more thorough. Realizing these potential benefits, ETAB began two or three experiments in group training as early as 1959; then, after a partial eclipse of about two years, the system was revived by the EAO which, in June 1965, operated six such programmes: in social leadership and in co-operatives (both at the Coady Institute at St. Francis Xavier University), in labour leadership (Labour College of Canada at McGill University), in public administration (Carleton University), in steel plant operation (a private steel firm at Welland), and in primary school teacher training (University of Alberta). As a donor whose technical and educational resources are

[17]*Standing Committee on External Affairs*, 1964, p. 1622.

generally limited (though in a few fields impressive), Canada naturally finds the group training approach attractive. It is probably the only expedient that can allow Canada to expand training rapidly without a significant loss in either administrative efficiency or the quality of trainees.

b. Preparation

Briefing of trainees is no more thorough than that of departing Canadians, and the reasons for its weakness are the same: a lack of trained staff and of good literature. These deficiencies are apparent in both Canadian missions abroad and the EAO at Ottawa.

Enough has been said of the inability of most Canadian missions to perform any kind of technical assistance administration without expert aid staff. Lacking time and professional incentive, many diplomatic and trade officers instinctively regard briefing talks with departing trainees as a dreary and burdensome routine. Except in cases where an officer feels a personal enthusiasm for meeting trainees, the missions rarely offer as briefing more than a short and jovial conversation on generalities. Only as if by accident is an officer able to answer in detail questions on training programmes, reception facilities in Canada or problems of adaptation. Few overseas officers know intimately how aid is administered in Canada, and none is professionally trained in counselling foreigners on life in Canada. Any merit that oral briefing does sometimes have is due strictly to the intelligence and sensitiveness of inspired individuals. This whole difficulty of oral briefing is sharpened by the absence, in many recipient countries, of any resident Canadian representatives at all.

But even untrained officials could do much better if they were supplied with an abundant and thoughtful documentation. Regrettably, such materials are still scarce and their distribution is unequal. Among materials that are available can be distinguished three broad types. First, there are general publications about Canada and its institutions, including the well-known *Canada* annual and *Canada from Sea to Sea*; both appear in English and French, and both, for their purpose, are interesting and instructive. At least one of these is supposed to reach each trainee, though many students receive a copy only on arrival in Canada. Next come brochures giving useful information on the visitor's status as a trainee. Although in earlier years trainees sometimes received a few mimeographed sheets of loosely assembled information, it was only in August 1964—fourteen years after the aid programme began—that Ottawa published a full-scale *Handbook for Scholars and Fellows*. This convenient, pocket-sized text fits into 30 pages a surprising volume of facts of the greatest practical value: notably on administrative arrangements, travel preparations, accommodation and life in Canada, allowances and return home. Published in French as well, it should relieve both trainees and the EAO of much of the day-to-day correspondence that previously grew from misunderstandings on customs or procedures. A far less complete *Administrative Guide* is supplied to students arriving under the Commonwealth Scholarship and Fellowship Plan.

The third type of pamphlet, covering the immediate *milieu* the trainee is about to enter, is much less satisfactory. Most trainees reach Canada with only the slenderest knowledge of their host agency or, in the case of travelling fellows, of their itinerary. Not a few have come to Canada virtually ignorant of their host agency's technical or educational facilities; some have not known even the name of the city in which they were to live. Naturally, in the rush to meet the opening of academic terms or to secure urgently needed technical skills, hard-pressed administrators can easily suffer oversights. Yet a systematic effort to acquire information about host agencies seems to be lacking, apparently on the assumption that trainees will learn quickly enough upon arrival.

Obviously, because great numbers of students are concentrated in similar academic host agencies, briefing material on universities is more coherent and thorough than that for technical fellows, whose host agencies vary remarkably. In addition to a few handbooks for foreign students published by individual universities, there exists a general brochure called *University Study in Canada,* prepared by the Canadian Universities Foundation. Yet although these pamphlets are usually detailed enough on administrative and academic questions, their attempts at explaining Canadian customs and prejudices are often less than sensitive. One of the most widely distributed of these brochures ponderously advises foreign students to thank their hostess after a dinner engagement (and indeed to help wash the dishes . . .), suggests that men stand up for ladies entering a room, and explains that some Canadian barbers might refuse to cut the hair of Asians, Africans and West Indians—because of inexperience.

Since briefing should be expressed in terms intelligible to the subject, perhaps one way of making up for weaknesses in Canadian staff and documentation would be to use returned trainees. Carefully chosen for balance and maturity, such persons could be invited (at Canadian expense) to meet departing trainees in their homeland: many returned trainees settle in capital cities, and could be easily contacted by Canadian missions. Returned trainees could also be asked to write, or record on tape, both impressions of Canada for general use and specific advice for departing nationals of their own country. Having lived in Canada under the same conditions as their successors, and sharing their cultural heritage, returned trainees might give briefing an invaluable relevance and authenticity. Still, they could never be more than an adjunct to trained Canadians and sound Canadian publications; for it is on Canada's own resources that briefing policy, like all aid policy, must essentially depend.

When trainees reach Canada, their final briefing by the EAO is hardly more elaborate than in the mission abroad. No doubt training officers supply more details on the host agency, and try to answer specific questions about allowances, accommodation and courses. But again officers lack overseas experience permitting them to relate Canadian society to the trainee's background; and usually, their knowledge of the host agency is indirect and superficial. All the average trainee receives on arrival is a one- or two-hour interview with one officer—and until 1965 this normally took place in the middle of a large busy room in which a relaxed and frank exchange was difficult. If time allows, the officer may take the trainee to lunch at EAO expense, and introduce him to a voluntary welcoming committee at International House, situated in central Ottawa. Those trainees who enter Canada through Vancouver for study in Western Canada often do not come to Ottawa for briefing at all, though many of these are briefed later by an EAO officer who visits their institution for this purpose.

These deficiencies are no fault of the officers, who are overwhelmed by the volume of a burgeoning programme. The necessary reforms touch on administrative structures and techniques: perhaps regional technical assistance offices in four or five Canadian cities, and collective briefing of academic trainees in formal courses at the start of each school year. Once again returning or already resident trainees could help in briefing, as they now sometimes help in local reception; but the leadership and basic facilities can be provided only by the EAO.

c. Study in Canada

When the trainee enters his host agency, he may encounter problems of three kinds: technical or academic ones related to the content of his work; administrative arrangements; and problems of cultural or psychological adaptation.

Technical or academic difficulties are perhaps the most susceptible to solution. Though many problems vary with the field of study, others are common. One of these is inadequacy in the language of study, whether

English or French—a problem some universities overcome by demand-ing success in an established test of language proficiency before a student is accepted; at other universities trainees may waste several months of study—even losing a year—bringing their English or French up to the required competence. A second obstacle is the high standards of some Canadian universities; in the early part of studies, numerous overseas students find that academic demands tax both health and morale. In the long run, however, the great majority succeed in their studies, and often, through their serious approach and maturity, finish brilliantly. Finally, not a few discover on arrival that the content of their training course does not coincide with their needs and expectation. Especially on technical fellowships where programmes are nearly always *ad hoc*, trainees may find it necessary to ask for modifications in the course of study, including changes even in the host agency or itinerary. Although the EAO rightly resists frivolous or capricious changes, it is usually ready to agree to minor improvements that are shown to be in the trainee's interest and of reasonable cost. Meanwhile, the trainee may spend some time in work that is professionally unrewarding.

Apart from the trouble of settling even trivial matters by writing to Ottawa, official administrative problems do not seem to worry trainees excessively. Long-range correspondence with the EAO on routine dif-ficulties appears in most cases to proceed fairly quickly—especially, as many trainees point out, when compared with the delays they have known in their home government. Health care is also handled adequately; all EAO trainees receive free medical, dental and hospital care, including drugs and eyeglasses. When convenient, such care is given by agencies of the Department of Veterans' Affairs; in isolated areas care may be given by private doctors, whose bills are then paid by the EAO.

Not surprisingly, the main administrative question that does invite trainees' complaints concerns financial allowances. Naturally, these vary appreciably with each trainee's type of study and status, basic living allowances ranging from $150 a month for undergraduate students to $20 a day for short-term senior travelling fellows. Added to the living allowance, which is meant to cover only "reasonable expenses in Canada for board and lodging, urban transportation, and miscellaneous ex-penses," are several special allowances suited to each kind of trainee. All trainees, of course, enjoy free transportation, at specified times, between Ottawa and their place of study; students receive allowances for books and laboratory equipment, and most have clothing allowances. All allowances may change from year to year, but they are constantly based on the average needs of Canadians in a similar environment.

It is difficult to judge the general adequacy of allowances beyond recording the widespread desire of trainees, like all human beings, to have more money—a standard at best rather uninformative. No doubt, as in any personal budget, the actual value of an allowance rests on each individual's prudence, the pressure of family obligations, and the availability of other resources. Some trainees are known to send a portion of their allowance home to support dependents, and still live comfortably; one generous student from a French-speaking country even suggested in July 1964 that his allowance be cut in half in order to bring another of his countrymen to Canada. But others, for reasons of their own, find allowances distinctly unrealistic. "It appears that your Office," wrote one disgruntled trainee to the EAO at about the same time, "is quite ignorant of the cost of living in this area. . . . it is scandalous for you to expect anyone to exist on $8 a day here. It is totally inadequate." A common grievance of students is an EAO rule that discourages them from earning money in odd jobs, like their Canadian colleagues, during summer holidays: any such wages are deducted from allowances, for the EAO wishes students to spend their whole Canadian visit in study or active training related to their mission. Others insist that long-term trainees, like Commonwealth Scholars, should be paid extra allowances for supporting spouses—a view endorsed by a private Canadian study group which in 1963 held earnestly, if ambiguously, that "if we really want overseas visitors to have a productive experience in Canada they should be permitted to bring their wives."[18]

Certainly the trainees' most unsettling problems, however, grow from the tensions of adapting to a strange society and culture. The great majority of visitors confess that the indifference of most Canadians, and the hostility of some, lead to frequent crises of loneliness. At least half, in different surveys, have told of meeting racial discrimination. Such barriers are most common in housing, but they also occur occasionally in public places; still more painful, at least for male trainees, are real or imagined rebuffs in relations with the opposite sex—though here most problems seem due less to differences of race than of customs and timing. Finally, foreign visitors, like Canadians abroad, suffer the well-known agonies of "culture shock," a malady that strikes trainees more sharply,

[18]Joint Planning Commission, *The Reception of Short-Term Overseas Visitors in Canada*, Canadian Association for Adult Education, Toronto, 1963, p. 3 (mimeographed). For information on trainees' financial problems, see C. S. Juvet, "Public Service Training in Canada under the Colombo Plan," M.A. thesis, Carleton University, Ottawa, 1959, p. 10; and Dominion Bureau of Statistics, *University Student Expenditure and Income in Canada, 1961–62, Part I—Non-Canadian Students* (Ottawa, 1963).

perhaps, because they find as consolations in Canada neither a community of permanently resident compatriots nor their own national equivalent of apple pie.

Until about 1962, the government showed little interest in actively encouraging Canadians to receive trainees more cordially, and even now the EAO's function in improving the atmosphere of reception is limited to discreet exhortations and modest subsidies. The main financial burden and human effort of welcoming trainees have always fallen to spontaneous private initiative. It is hard to assess the quality of the average Canadian's welcome to trainees because the experience of each visitor is so personal. "The warmth of heart of your people and . . . especially the hospitality which I received everywhere I visited have been most touching," wrote happily a returning trainee in early 1964. "I was treated everywhere as a Canadian, and I had a strong feeling of belonging wherever I went." Yet another, writing three years earlier in a letter no less typical, if less common, complained, "what irritates me is the lack of frankness of the [Canadian] people . . . and [their] arrogance . . . they feel that they are better . . . most of the people are indoctrinated that everything oriental is bad." Between these extremes are reports that only serve to remind that Canada is in more ways than one a pluralistic society.

A more coherent reaction emerges in response to the welcome extended by voluntary organizations. It is these that have given many trainees, through practical services and advice, their deepest acquaintance with Canadian life, a kindness visitors acknowledge gratefully. Much of this welcome comes from ordinary service clubs and church groups; but the central effort, especially in universities, has been provided for many years by a national organization called Friendly Relations with Overseas Students (FROS). Working with more general service agencies such as the World University Service (WUS), FROS built a network of facilities to greet, brief and assist foreign students in all major centres of study. Following several meetings of private and government representatives during 1963, a new expanded agency was formed in 1964 under the rather unwieldy title of Canadian Service for Overseas Students and Trainees (CSOST). This body's functions are still not fully developed, but its announced intention is to co-ordinate all other reception groups in a single agency handling both university and non-academic visitors.

d. Evaluation

The Canadian government knows still less about the effectiveness of its training programme than about the work of Canadian advisers and teachers. While returned Canadians can at least in theory be questioned on their usefulness abroad, repatriated trainees are with few exceptions lost from sight. Nearly all trainees, before leaving Canada, visit Ottawa for a final "de-briefing"; but this is invariably hurried and shallow. Once he is back home, the former trainee may send the EAO a cheerful "bread-and-butter" note and even, for a few years, a Christmas card. Yet almost never does he send a detailed and meaningful report on the use he makes of his training, for the good reason he is not asked to. And Canadian diplomatic and commercial officers, of course, have no time to visit returned trainees in person.

Some of the solutions proposed to evaluate the missions of advisers and teachers could doubtless be adapted to assess training as well: more searching "de-briefing" sessions, careful cataloguing and summarizing of final reports, and a full-scale written questionnaire that would be sent to former trainees one or two years after their return home. But another way of testing the influence of Canadian programmes, while preserving whatever good feeling trainees may have for Canada, might be the cultivation of some kind of permanent "follow-up" contact with returned trainees. By striving systematically to keep alive returned trainees' interest in Canada, the EAO might indirectly encourage them to write of their experience in applying Canadian training. This might be achieved by circulating to all returned trainees a quarterly or semi-annual bulletin of news about Canadian universities, trainees currently in Canada, and, by country, trainees who have returned home. Perhaps former visitors could be given a subscription to either a popular Canadian magazine or a Canadian professional journal in their discipline—items often inaccessible, even when desired, because of foreign currency shortages. Further, Canadian diplomatic missions could be granted a small budget to sustain local friendship societies of returned trainees; now, when a group of ex-trainees forms to promote good relations with Canada, the local Canadian mission, if there is one, has no funds to organize meetings, lectures, film showings, dinners or other activities in any but the most informal and sporadic fashion. At present, Canada seems content to dismiss and forget her guests with unseemly haste as soon as they finish their training; and so, after spending two to ten thousand dollars partly, as the public is constantly told, to win "ambassadors for Canada," Ottawa affords her unofficial envoys neither letters of credence, encouragement nor means of communication.

PART FOUR / Conclusion

X. Toward a Rational Statecraft

A meaningful global judgment on the numerous activities of Canada's aid programme seems objectively impossible. It is easy enough to assess each kind of aid separately on its own merits. But there exists no universally accepted standard for evaluating a total programme; criteria purporting to serve this function are invariably tainted with the narrow prejudices of single disciplines: economics, politics or sociology.

Until adequate methods of measurement are found, general judgments cannot really reach beyond the subjective and impressionistic. Has Canadian aid been "successful" or "effective"? The question is no more manageable than one asking whether a person "likes" a certain country. One can scarcely do more, in a few words, than reply vaguely that Canada's aid, compared with that of other large donors, appears to have been consistently high in quality, and free of spectacular waste or scandal; its administration has grown from makeshift to mediocre, then, since about 1960, to a steady competence tarnished only by a cramping weakness in the field and by understaffing at home; finally, its operations have enabled Canada to forge with several developing countries relations of intimacy, trust and fairly stable understanding. Any more precise opinions must be sought in detailed criticism of each type of aid taken by itself.

1. THE CASE FOR POLICY REVIEW

What is needed more than summary judgments of past performance is a sound method for keeping future aid policy—and its administrative and operational consequences—sensitively attuned to Canada's shifting interests. Such a method should recognize that Canada's interests are expressed in different, and sometimes conflicting, ways. And it should formulate aid policy within a continuing reappraisal of the role played by each of the instruments of Canadian foreign policy.

At present, this notion of co-ordinating the various aspects of foreign policy in a single coherent view of Canada's interest commands from Canadian leaders of all parties little more than the perfunctory homage of lip-service. They, like most of their compatriots, seem content to consider aid, trade, defence, cultural relations, immigration and classical diplomacy as problems somehow alien to each other, each to be studied *en vase clos* without reference to a common context. Deprived of this context, each area of action tends to assume an absolute importance. Individual ministers, instinctively seeking to strengthen the means of their personal initiative, come to believe their department's activities should go on expanding merely because of some historic momentum or supposed intrinsic virtue; consequently, the allocation of resources from a national viewpoint, comparing different means of reaching universal aims, is virtually abandoned.

This compartmentalization of policy machinery has left the popular Canadian conception of aid dangerously distorted. Rather than considering aid as simply one of several sometimes useful techniques of pursuing national goals abroad, many Canadians now see in aid a unique panacea for world tensions, a simple and sure remedy whose effectiveness grows mathematically with the size of the dose administered. Feeding on a deep-seated terror of communism, the aid mystique first gained plausibility by portraying aid as a radical weapon in the Cold War; then it clothed itself in Christian idealism, carrying on a charitable, proselytizing missionary tradition fathered by clergymen that most emerging countries were making unwelcome. Combining these motives of fear and hope, foreign aid quickly outgrew its initial status as a mere instrument of policy; it soon became a cause in itself, a self-justifying crusade, a powerful Messianic magnet for a generation of liberals hungry for a purpose to fit a uniting world. Supported by a plethora of writings, conferences, speeches and organizations both public and private, the foreign aid mystique is now for much of Western society a dogma attacked only by the cynical, the ungenerous, or the economically depressed.

Foreign aid has no innate right to this exalted role. It is neither sacred nor even, in some cases, sensible: giving a recipient millions in aid while depriving it of tens of millions in potential exports, many argue, displays an *a priori* absence of both altruism and logic. Given for its own sake, or merely through force of habit, aid is condemned to increasing misapplication; for planners, no longer challenged to rethink first truths, inevitably find their imaginations dulled by smugness and routine.

What Canada's aid programme needs more than any structural reforms or increase in funds, therefore, is constant, informed and critical review of its policies. This review should be guided by techniques and machinery that closely co-ordinate aid with all other instruments of Canadian intervention abroad.

2. TECHNIQUES OF POLICY REVIEW

Coherent policy-making should follow two steps: first, it should identify those interests deserving highest priority; then choose instruments of action best suited to protecting these interests.

Although a nation's underlying interests such as security and power tend to be permanent, its current interests change frequently. Governments must alter policies to meet new economic, social and political forces at home; and they must grapple with problems abroad which are both unpredictable and infinitely varied. One day the chief preoccupations of Canadian policy-makers may be European security, United States economic domination, the urgings of a domestic cultural group, disarmament, a distant brushfire war, or unemployment; later, they may be pacifist lobbies, tensions within NATO, Latin American revolution, tariff barriers, or racial conflict in the Commonwealth. Sometimes a single problem seems to sweep all others into the background; more often the conjuncture mingles several distinct problems. The first task of policy-makers is to recognize at every moment which challenges deserve their concentrated attention and eventually Canada's concentrated resources. Obviously this process demands alertness and flexibility; for while some policies may remain valid for years, others may prove outdated within months or weeks.

Once key problems are identified in some rough priority, policy-makers ought normally to ask which of the several instruments at their disposal should be used to solve them. Always a government's goal should be to meet each situation with the most efficient balance or "mix" of instruments possible. Taking as an example the long-range challenge of underdevelopment, Ottawa might react to each major "aid" problem by comparing the probable effectiveness of aid with that of three or four alternative means of action.

The most natural, though not the easiest, alternative to aid—if the donor wishes primarily to speed the recipient's economic growth—requires concessions in trade. No doubt the Canadian government is beginning to acknowledge verbally this option, by echoing the increasingly fashionable argument that emerging countries can achieve economic maturity only through freer access to the wealthy nations' markets. "For several years," avowed the Minister of Trade and Commerce, Mr. Mitchell Sharp, on May 21, 1964, "economists have been demonstrating that aid without trade is incongruous and self-defeating. There is no logic in giving aid to create modern factories, farms and mines if donors refuse to open their markets to the goods these enterprises produce."[1] No logic, but much expediency; for Canada, like most other aid donors, shows no serious intention of greatly opening its markets to the goods of developing countries within the visible future. The reason is well known: aid is the "soft option" (as the British economists P. T. Bauer and J. B. Wood put it); it allows politicians to spend aid funds at home and thereby increase domestic employment, instead of enduring foreign competition certain to threaten employment.

Still, the option of more liberal trade should not be rejected outright; on economic grounds, Canada's commercial disarmament theoretically offers developing countries a sounder basis for self-help than does aid; and politically it is far more acceptable to them. To the extent that Canadian public opinion can be convinced to bear the short-term sacrifices it may impose, freer trade should accordingly be considered a substitute (at least for certain kinds of capital aid) that gives Canadian policy a highly useful versatility.

A second alternative to aid—again if the donor's chief goal is to alleviate the recipient's economic distress—might consist of offering nationals of certain developing countries more generous terms of emigration to Canada. For a small overpopulated country like Jamaica, the opportunity of sending 20,000 or 30,000 persons to Canada could, by reducing unemployment, be worth several million dollars in development projects and welfare payments no longer needed. Such an initiative could easily trouble Canada with new inter-racial tensions; but it would also, for a time, dissipate incidentally the unhappy impression left by Canada's present restrictions on non-white immigration.

If the donor aims essentially not to stimulate the recipient's economy but to strengthen its own political influence, effective alternatives to aid

[1]Department of Trade and Commerce, Trade Publicity Branch, speech no. 46/64, p. 12. See also the statement by the Hon. Paul Martin, Secretary of State for External Affairs, on Canada's position at the UN Conference on Trade and Development held at Geneva in June 1964: Canada, *House of Commons Debates*, June 17, 1964, p. 4429.

might be military, diplomatic or cultural action. Planners might ask, for instance, whether in preventing some local tension from threatening world peace Canada should not curtail aid in order to concentrate her small resources on supplying peace-keeping forces for service with the United Nations. Similarly, one might easily imagine circumstances in which Canada could best serve peace by devoting most of her foreign policy resources to making atomic weapons or to participation in some NATO multilateral nuclear force. In both UN and NATO alternatives, Canada's immediate potential for preserving peace might at some time be so great as to make her possible long-term contribution to peace through aid seem futile.

Likewise, Canada might find it profitable to reduce her aid in order to expand greatly her diplomatic representation abroad. If aid is viewed as a means of ensuring a Canadian "presence" in developing countries, could Canada not extend her influence more cheaply by opening twenty or thirty new diplomatic missions? Aid would probably remain the principal source of routine contact with governments in developing countries; but the total aid budget might be cut, or distributed more widely, allowing each recipient just enough aid to interest it in sustaining a working dialogue with Canada.

Finally, if Canada wished to influence foreign governments more subtly over a much longer period, she might replace some of her economic aid with an impressive cultural and information programme. Following the example of countries like France, Great Britain and the United States, Canada might develop enormously her overseas broadcasting facilities, open Canadian libraries and schools abroad, foster Canadian-foreign friendship societies, finance many more scholarships and tours for overseas students and delegations, and pay for more frequent visits abroad by reputable Canadian artists, writers and musicians. Such a programme might make Canada better known—and better understood—than an impersonal capital aid programme costing far more.

These arguments do not imply that aid should be stopped altogether or necessarily even reduced. They suggest only, in a tentative and rudimentary way, that aid is perhaps overrated as an instrument for pursuing Canadian policy. They show that important changes in aid policy, whether affecting levels, types or recipients of aid, should always be made after considering alternative means of action in the broader context of Canadian foreign policy as a whole. For many developing countries, aid is likely to remain the only meaningful activity justifying a Canadian interest and presence. But no country presents a problem simple and stable enough for Ottawa to continue giving aid, year after year, in the unquestioning belief that aid is realizing Canada's aims in the most efficient way possible.

3. MACHINERY OF POLICY REVIEW

All of this is highly theoretical; much of it is stating the obvious. To pass beyond the genial truism into reality, the process of co-ordinating aid policy with Canada's general foreign policy needs new policy-making machinery. At present, no formal committee co-ordinates all foreign policy within the cabinet; harmonization of aid with other instruments of action can be attempted only hastily during plenary meetings, or informally and sporadically between two ministers whose interests happen to mesh. Below the cabinet the External Aid Board approaches aid interdepartmentally; but grouping only the EAO, the Departments of External Affairs, Finance, and Trade and Commerce, and the Bank of Canada, the Board lacks the scope to relate aid to the various means of foreign policy in the broad sense. And the House of Commons Standing Committee on External Affairs, whose function is merely supervisory, has traditionally interpreted its mandate to include no more than the policies and activities of the East Block.

Clearly neither the executive nor the legislative branch can envisage a rational foreign policy without creating machinery to study all the country's instruments of action in a single perspective of the national interest. The most practical way to achieve this would seem for both the cabinet and the House of Commons to establish new permanent committees broadly representing every major option open to Canadian initiative abroad.

The crucial arena of policy co-ordination is, of course, the cabinet. A cabinet committee reflecting the whole range of foreign policy instruments would have to include the Prime Minister as Chairman, the Secretary of State for External Affairs, the Ministers of National Defence, Manpower, Trade and Commerce, Finance, and (for cultural diplomacy) the Secretary of State. Attached to this group of ministers would be a permanent interdepartmental committee of high civil servants, sometimes including, for the Secretary of State, representatives of the CBC, the National Film Board and the Canada Council. Both these committees would operate in the customary fashion, civil servants advising, ministers deciding.

The House of Commons' decision in June 1965 to establish new standing committees to cover virtually all government departments tends, if anything, to compartmentalize parliamentary review of foreign policy still more rigidly. Yet perhaps several of the new committees could agree to delegate, at least a few times a year, three or four members each to a joint meeting. Such meetings would seek to fashion a common national perspective of Canada's external relations, including aid, diplomatic questions, defence, immigration, trade, and international cultural matters. At the same time, the traditional Standing Committee on External Affairs, in approaching aid, might make this common perspective more profound by diversifying its methods of gathering information. In particular, it might consider two techniques: study trips abroad by members, and commissioned research by independent authorities.

At present this Standing Committee could not contribute much to a Combined Committee on External Relations because its channels of information are too narrow. Members rely almost exclusively on the testimony of high civil servants who, whatever their competence and integrity, cannot fairly be expected to regard their own administration with detachment. As a result, members' questions rarely display the understanding and perception that could make the committee a force for vital reform. Overseas inspections and commissioned research, by raising the quality of investigations, might make the committee equal to this role. The obvious danger that trips abroad would become pleasure junkets for paying off political debts cannot be ignored; but even if some trips were wasted, others would provide the committee with a core of members well armed to lead probes in depth. Similarly, if committee researchers attained the high standards of their United States counterparts, the research programme could infuse debates with an authority (and, for civil servants, a sobering inspiration) now inconceivable.

4. A MOOD OF REAPPRAISAL

Policy cannot live on myths alone. Constantly, new facts must be faced; alternatives re-assessed; practical conclusions drawn; and prices paid. To demand that aid policies meet these standards is neither perverse nor cynical: in the true sense of the word, it is idealistic, for authentic idealism seeks above all the workable—the realistic. In the practice of foreign policy, idealism consists of choosing the most effective means of advancing the nation's interest, broadly and imaginatively understood.

Not enough Canadians have asked whether aid is always one of these means. Certainly aid has enabled Canada to appreciate better the aspirations of the Third World's renascent peoples; and it has engaged Ottawa in regular dialogue with their governments. But many Canadians appear to assign aid the visionary goal of saving the world from a multitude of dangers it is ill-fitted to allay; and in so doing, they thrust to the background a rich and varied arsenal of resources that could assure our country's policy a new dimension of flexibility. Worse still, they tend to present aid as a simple enterprise requiring for its success only unlimited funds and unlimited enthusiasm.

Nothing threatens the vitality and relevance of Canada's aid programme more than this, the peremptory urgings of its most eager partisans. By promoting aid as a unique cure for tensions of class warfare on a world scale, some of these champions dismiss informed criticism of aid as not only inopportune, but immoral. And by refusing to foresee the concrete implications of their demands, they renounce the intelligent calculation of options for infatuation with an ideal: how many advocates of multiplying Canadian aid two-fold or ten-fold even *want* to know whether Canada could administer, and recipients absorb, such sums without intolerable waste?

This is not to reject all future increases in Canada's aid or even to denounce conviction as a political posture. It is merely an appeal for responsibility. If Canadians decide, as they doubtless will, that they must continue to give aid, they should be mature enough to face the real cost and results of their commitment. Lacking this maturity, they are condemned to follow policies suited to a world of exhilarating illusion— policies for a society too afraid, or too lazy, to think.

Appendices

Canadian Bilateral Development Assistance
by Country or Area
1950–51 to 1965–66

Country or area	Population (millions)	Period covered	Total allocations (millions of Canadian dollars)
India	475.1	1950–66	332.0
Pakistan	110.9	1950–66	202.0
Ceylon	10.9	1950–66	33.5
Malaysia	11.0	1956–66	18.0
Burma, Indonesia, Philippines, Thailand	189.1	1950–66	14.0
Francophone countries	118.2	1961–66*	19.3
Nigeria	43.0	1961–66*	13.5
East Africa	26.8	1961–66*	8.5
Other Commonwealth African countries	21.8	1961–66*	8.6
Latin America	220.1	1964–66	20.0
Caribbean	3.5	1958–66	31.1
Miscellaneous (including Indus Basin Fund)			26.2
Total			726.7

*The Francophone African Program began in 1961 but some technical assistance was extended to Francophone Asia prior to this under the Colombo Plan.
SOURCE: External Aid Office, Ottawa, January 1966.

APPENDIX B

Canadian External Aid Commitments by Programmes
Fiscal Years, 1945–46 to 1965–66
millions of Canadian dollars

	1945–46 to 1949–50
I: POST-WAR RELIEF AND RECONSTRUCTION	
A. Grants:	**271.07**
Civilian Relief	105.22
UNRRA and post-UNRRA	168.85
B. Loans:	**1,767.15**
United Kingdom	1,185.00
Other	582.15
II: BILATERAL ASSISTANCE PROGRAMMES	
A. Grants:	**.06**
1. International Development Assistance	
2. International Emergency Relief	.06
3. International Food Aid	
B. Loans:	
1. Colombo Plan Wheat Loans	
2. Special Development Loans	
3. ECI Act, Section 21-A Credits	
III: MULTILATERAL ASSISTANCE PROGRAMMES	
A. Grants:	**19.44**
1. UNICEF	1.08
2. UNREF, IRO	17.05
3. UNHCR	
4. Palestine Refugees*	1.31
5. Other Refugee Programmes	
6. Korean Reconstruction	
7. UN Congo Fund	
8. EPTA	
9. Special Fund	
10. Indus Basin	
11. World Food Programme*	
12. IAEA Technical Assistance Programme	
B. Loans and Advances:	**70.70**
1. IBRD	70.70
2. IFC	
3. IDA	
4. UN for Suez Canal Clearance	
TOTAL	**2,128.42**
Addendum NATO Mutual Aid	

SOURCE: *Report on Canadian External Aid Programmes*, External Aid Office (Ottawa, May 1961), *Public Accounts* of subsequent years, and *Estimates for the Fiscal Year ending March 31, 1966.*
   *Cash contribution only. Food Aid contribution included in International Food Aid total.
   †Commitment of Section 21-A funds is not available for 1965–66.

1950–51 to 1954–55	1955–56 to 1959–60	1960–61 to 1964–65	Total	1965–66 Estimates
			271.07	
			1,767.15	
109.54	**219.48**	**286.09**	**615.17**	**68.10**
101.48	180.60	246.00		48.00
3.06	5.92	7.64		.10
5.00	32.96	32.45		20.00
	34.97	**272.30**	**307.27**	†
	34.97			
		50.00		50.00
		222.30		†
19.63	**33.68**	**56.26**	**129.01**	**17.14**
2.60	3.10	3.70		1.00
2.21				
	.95	1.45		.29
3.10	2.25	2.50		.50
.10	16.47	.70		.06
7.75				
		1.49		.50
3.87	8.85	11.15		2.33
	1.92	16.46		5.00
		16.58		7.00
		1.80		.40
	.14	.43		.06
.17	**4.52**	**57.27**	**132.66**	**15.03**
.17		16.60		
	3.52			
		40.67		15.03
	1.00			
129.34	**292.65**	**671.92**	**3,222.33**	—
1,068.18	473.57	117.26	1,659.01	11.63

APPENDIX C

Commitments of Bilateral Official Grants and Loans
by DAC Member Countries to Less Developed Countries, 1962–64
(million US dollars)

	Year	Austria	Belgium*	Canada	Denmark	France*
Total official bilateral commitments	1962	0.6	65.6	61.3	0.8	893.1
(A + B + C + D)	1963	0.9	77.1	125.2	6.8	843.1
	1964	14.4	79.2	152.7	6.3	874.1
A. Grants	1962	0.6	65.6	47.3	0.8	756.7
	1963	—	75.8	43.6	4.6	678.5
	1964	1.3	76.8	68.5	2.8	667.7
B. Loans repayable in recipients' currencies	1962	—	—	—	—	—
	1963	—	—	—	2.2	—
	1964	—	—	—	—	..
C. Net transfers of resources through sales for recipients' currencies	1962	—	—	—	—	—
	1963	—	—	—	—	—
	1964	—	—	—	—	..
D. Loans for more than 5 years' maturity	1962	—	—	14.0	—	136.4
	1963	0.9	1.3	81.6	—	164.6†
	1964	13.1	2.4	84.2	3.5	206.4‡
1. More than 20 years	1962	—	—	—	—	37.1
	1963	—	—	—	—	20.1
	1964	—	—	21.3	—	19.0
2. More than 10, up to less than 20 years	1962	—	—	13.1	—	79.2
	1963	0.9	1.3	55.7	—	116.2
	1964	4.8	2.4	57.3	3.5	136.0
3. More than 5, up to 10 years	1962	—	—	0.9	—	20.1
	1963	—	—	25.9	—	27.3
	1964	8.3	—	5.5	—	50.3
Memo item (not included in above): Loans for more than 1 up to and including 5 years' maturity	1962	5.8	—	—	—	4.3
	1963	—	1.8	—	—	7.7
	1964	3.0	—	—	—	4.4

SOURCE: *Development Assistance Efforts and Policies: 1965 Review* (Paris: OECD, 1965), p. 12
*For Belgium and France gross disbursement data have been used.
†Includes $1.0 million equity investment.
‡Includes $1.1 million equity investment.
§Includes $1.7 million the breakdown of which is not available.
||Includes $8.0 million the breakdown of which is not available.
#Negative figure results from recording new commitments less larger offsetting consolidatio
credit entries.

Germany	Italy	Japan	Nether-lands	Norway	Portugal	United Kingdom	United States	Total DAC countries
432.3	59.9	264.9	28.7	4.4	37.3	578.2	4,724	7,050.1
671.2	128.0	268.1	29.1	3.7	53.5	471.7	3,961	6,639.4
467.4	111.4	259.2	41.6	0.5	41.8	483.9	5,407	7,939.4
155.3	18.8	103.9	11.4	4.4	3.1	221.2	1,659	3,048.1
160.5	14.0	80.1	8.5	3.2	8.8	234.6	1,457	2,769.2
185.7	23.6	76.0	25.2	0.5	7.5	185.3	1,503	2,823.9
—	—	—	—	—	—	—	220	220.0
—	—	—	—	—	—	—	78	80.2
—	—	—	—	—	—	—	91	91.0
3.0	—	—	—	—	—	—	1,209	1,212.0
2.7	—	—	—	—	—	—	827	829.7
3.3	—	—	—	—	—	—	1,416	1,419.3
274.0	41.1	161.0	17.3	—	34.2	356.0	1,636	2,670.0
508.0	114.0	188.0	20.6	0.5	44.7§	237.1	1,599	2,960.3
278.4	87.8	183.2	16.4	—	34.3§	298.6‖	2,397	3,605.2
101.0	—	—	17.3	—	31.3	340.0	1,144	1,670.7
110.0	—	—	18.3	—	2.0	176.7	1,194	1,521.1
106.1	—	—	13.9	—	0.5	251.6	1,914	2,326.4
164.5	16.0	12.5	—	—	1.6	3.0	386	675.9
394.0	40.0	135.9	1.4	0.5	42.7	31.2	228	1,047.8
135.9	33.7	106.7	2.5	—	24.4	28.1	327	862.3
8.5	25.1	148.5	—	—	1.3	13.0	106	323.4
4.0	74.0	52.1	0.9	—	—	29.2	177	390.4
36.4	54.1	76.5	—	—	7.7	10.9	155	404.7
41.0	71.3	21.9	—	—	5.2	1.0	640	214.5
15.5	26.3	30.1	—	—	—	3.6	−84.0#	1.0
0.9	43.7	69.0	—	—	1.2	0.3	−24.0#	98.5

APPENDIX D

Net Official Flow from DAC Member Countries
to Multilateral Organizations in 1964
(million US dollars)

	IBRD and affiliated institutions				IDB		
	IBRD		IDA				
	Capital subscrip-tions	Bond pur-chases	Capital subscrip-tions	Total	Capital subscrip-tions	Bond pur-chases	Total
Austria	—	3.9	1.0	4.9	—	—	—
Belgium	—	—	—	—	—	—	—
Canada	—	—	7.3	7.3	—	—	—
Denmark	1.2	0.5	1.7	3.4	—	—	—
France	—	3.0	10.3	13.2	—	—	—
Germany	—	−15.0	10.2	−4.8	—	—	—
Italy	—	−10.0	3.5	−6.5	—	—	—
Japan	—	−0.1	6.4	6.3	—	—	—
Netherlands	—	—	5.4	5.4	—	—	—
Norway	—	7.5	1.3	8.8	—	—	—
Portugal	—	—	—	—	—	—	—
United Kingdom	—	—	25.2	25.2	—	—	—
United States	—	—	61.7	61.7	50.0	—	50.0
Total DAC Countries	1.2	−10.2	133.9	124.9	50.0	—	50.0

SOURCE: *Development Assistance Efforts and Policies: 1965 Review* (Paris: OECD 1965), p. 13*
*From Country Memoranda.

UN technical assistance and relief agencies	EEC capital subscriptions	Total net official contributions	Of which: grants and capital subscriptions
0.9	—	5.8	1.9
1.9	—	1.9	1.9
10.2	—	17.5	17.5
4.9	—	8.3	7.8
6.4	—	19.6	16.6
13.7	—	8.9	23.9
1.3	—	−5.2	4.8
3.2	—	9.5	9.6
10.7	—	16.1	16.1
5.4	—	14.2	6.7
0.1	—	0.1	0.1
19.1	—	44.3	44.3
114.0	—	225.7	225.7
191.8	—	366.7	376.9

APPENDIX E: ABBREVIATIONS

AECL	Atomic Energy of Canada Limited
AID	Agency for International Development (United States)
ASF	African Students Foundation
AUPELF	Association des universités partiellement ou entièrement de langue française
BTAO	Bureau of Technical Assistance Operations (UN)
CANDU	Canadian Deuterium-Uranium (reactor)
CCC	Canadian Commercial Corporation
CIR	Canada-India Reactor
CPRI	Canadian Peace Research Institute
CSOST	Canadian Service for Overseas Students and Trainees
CUF	Canadian Universities Foundation
CUSO	Canadian University Service Overseas
DAC	Development Assistance Committee (OECD)
DCL	Defence Construction (1951) Limited
DEA	Department of External Affairs
EAO	External Aid Office
ECIC	Export Credits Insurance Corporation
EPTA	Expanded Programme of Technical Assistance (UN)
ETAB	Economic and Technical Assistance Branch (Department of Trade and Commerce, 1958–60)
FAO	Food and Agriculture Organization
FROS	Friendly Relations with Overseas Students
GATT	General Agreement on Tariffs and Trade
IAEA	International Atomic Energy Agency
IBRD	International Bank for Reconstruction and Development
ICA	International Co-operation Administration (United States)
ICAO	International Civil Aviation Organization
IDA	International Development Association
IDB	Inter-American Development Bank
IETCD	International Economic and Technical Co-operation Division (Department of Trade and Commerce, 1951–58)
IFC	International Finance Corporation
IGCA	Interdepartmental Group on Capital Assistance
IGTA	Interdepartmental Group on Technical Assistance
ILO	International Labour Organization
IMCO	Inter-Governmental Maritime Consultative Organization
IMF	International Monetary Fund
IRO	International Refugee Organization
ITU	International Telecommunication Union
NORAD	North American Air Defence Command
OAS	Organization of American States
OECD	Organization for Economic Co-operation and Development
OEEC	Organization for European Economic Co-operation (replaced in 1961 by OECD)

OPEX	Division of Operational, Executive and Administrative Personnel (UN)
SCAAP	Special Commonwealth Africa Aid Programme
SEATO	Southeast Asia Treaty Organization
SF	Special Fund (UN)
SUNFED	Special United Nations Fund for Economic Development
TAA	Technical Assistance Administration (UN, replaced in 1958 by BTAO)
TAB	Technical Assistance Board (UN)
TCS	Technical Co-operation Service (Department of Trade and Commerce, 1950–55)
UN	United Nations
UNESCO	United Nations Educational, Scientific and Cultural Organization
UNCTAD	United Nations Conference on Trade and Development
UNICEF	United Nations Children's Fund
UNHCR	United Nations High Commissioner for Refugees
UNREF	United Nations Refugee Fund
UNRRA	United Nations Relief and Rehabilitation Administration
UNRWA	United Nations Relief and Works Agency for Palestine Refugees
WAPDA	Water and Power Development Authority (Pakistan)
WDPO	Warsak Dam Project Organization
WFP	World Food Programme
WHO	World Health Organization
WMO	World Meteorological Organization
WUS	World University Service

Index

absorptive capacity, 60–1, 115, 186; as factor in donor selection of aid activities, 82–5

administration of aid, 243; and counterpart funds, 189–93; early history of, 93–106; and industrial commodities, 176–7; in field, 83, 85, 98, 98n–9n, 115–18, 129, 130–5, 146–8, 152, 157–9, 167, 171–2, 192, 197, 223–6, 231, 233; and recruitment before EAO, 104. *See also* career service

Administrative Guide for Commonwealth scholars, 234

advisers, 112, 153, 215–29; briefing of, 219–21; counterparts or understudies for, 228–9; definition of, 216; evaluation of missions, 229; job descriptions for, 216; "old-boy network," 217–18; problems of service abroad, 223–9; recruitment of, 216–18; roster of, 216–17; secondment of, 217

aerial surveys, 131n, 152–62

Afghanistan, 17, 127, 160

Africa, 21, 59, 117, 225; absorptive capacity of, 82, 88; Canada's lack of colonial experience in, 153; cultural adaptation to, 148, 226; education needs of, 112; equatorial, 36; governments' administrative weakness in, 158; and intergovernmental project agreements, 131; navigational and meteorological equipment for, 151; road-building equipment for, 151; technical assistance demands of, 213, 216. *See also* French Africa

African Students Foundation, 211

Agriculture, Department of, 94, 97, 193

aid: alternatives to, 245–8; definition of, 40n–1n, 41–2, 196; stability resulting from, 15–22, 24; as long-term commitment, 104–5; irrational advocacy of increase in, 250. *See also* administration of aid, evaluation of aid

aims of Canadian aid policy: "classical trilogy," 4–5; economic: aid as short-term stimulus to Canada's economy, 42–5, aid's long-term effects on Canada's exports, 45–50; humanitarianism, 5–12; policy and propaganda need to be separate, 50–2; political: anti-communism, 3, 14, 22–39; raising allies' giving, 39–42; relevance of, 12–14; strengthening peace, 14–22

Alliance for Progress, 84

allocation of aid, 63–5; framework of, 53–75; projects and commodities, by fields, 125

Aluminum Company of Canada Ltd., 210

Antigua, 144

Asia, 88, 103, 124, 145; counterpart funds for unallocated, 191; cultural adaptation to, 148; field administration in, 130–1, 133; navigational and meteorological equipment for, 151; South, 117; Southeast, 117

Assam, 85–6, 139

Assessments for UN budgets, 202

Association canadienne-française pour l'avancement des sciences (ACFAS), 60

Ibadan, 156
idealism in practice of foreign policy,
249–50
immigration as alternative to aid, 246
India, 4, 19, 21, 28, 33, 34, 36, 55, 65,
67, 85–6, 117, 134n, 141, 160;
Department of Atomic Energy,
167, 170; Bombay State Transport
project, 78; commodities for, 175;
consortium (IBRD) for, 72; and
counterpart funds, 190n, 191, 192;
development budget of, 30; engineering colleges in, 188; export
credits and financing of CANDU
reactor, 208; field administration
in, 101; Five Year Plans, 79–80;
food aid to, 179–82, 192; industrial commodities, 66, 101, 175–8;
Indus Waters settlement, 202, 204;
military aid to, 36, 142; projects
in communications and transport,
143, in health, welfare and education, 163–4, in industry, 171, in
natural resources, 154, in power
and irrigation, 126; railway aid to,
151; aid-generated sales to, 46;
criteria for selecting trainees, 230n–
1n; wheat loans to, 206. *See also*
Canada-India Reactor
Indian Civil Service, 133
Indian Express (Madurai), 140
Indochina, 18, 28, 36, 57, 59, 61, 95,
103
Indonesia, 17–8, 21, 32, 36, 55n; misuse by of Canadian aircraft, 19;
commodities for, 175; counterpart
funds in, 183, 192; foodstuffs for,
182, 183; projects in communications and transport, 143, in health,
welfare and education, 164
Indus Basin: Canada's contributions to
Development Fund, 126, 202; settlement of dispute over, 18, 85,
204; World Bank Club, 72
industrial raw materials, 82, 88, 175–8;
alleged benefits of to recipients,
180–1
infrastructure, 124, 142, 151, 162, 170,
178
initiative in aid negotiation, 67–9
Inter-American Development Bank
(IDB), 62, 63; machinery for
international co-ordination, 74–5
Interdepartmental Group on Capital

Assistance (IGCA), 96, 99, 100,
101, 102, 105, 108, 128
Interdepartmental Group on Technical
Assistance (IGTA), 94, 96, 99
Inter-Governmental Maritime Consultative Organization (IMCO), 202
intergovernmental project agreements,
128–9, 130–1, 145–6, 157–8, 171–2
International Atomic Energy Agency
(IAEA), 19, 199–202
International Bank for Reconstruction
and Development (IBRD), 96,
108, 170n, 198, 204–6; its definition of aid, 196; view of food aid,
179n; Indus Basin Development
Fund, 202; on value of industrial
commodity aid, 177; machinery for
international co-ordination, 72–3;
and Pakistan aerial surveys, 160;
policies and methods of, 203–4;
policy control of, 198
International Civil Aviation Organization (ICAO), 94, 199, 202
international co-ordination of aid, 70–5
International Development Association
(IDA), 205–6, 207
International Economic and Technical
Co-operation Division (IETCD),
100–1, 104, 112; history of, 95–
100; and "old-boy network," 217–
8. *See also* Colombo Plan Adminis-
strator
International Finance Corporation
(IFC), 204–5, 206
International House, Ottawa, 235
International Labour Organization
(ILO), 199
International Monetary Fund (IMF),
203
International Power Corporation Ltd.,
210
International Refugee Organization
(IRO), 200
International Relief Fund, 194
International Telecommunication Union
(ITU), 199
Iraq, 38

Jakarta, 36
Jamaica, 117; emigration from as alternative to aid to, 246; projects in
health, welfare and education, 164,
in natural resources, 154
Jamaica Public Services Ltd., 210

www.ingramcontent.com/pod-product-compliance
Lightning Source LLC
Chambersburg PA
CBHW070614030426
42337CB00020B/3797